The Great War in History

Since the Armistice, a vast literature has been produced on the First World War and its repercussions. For the first time, two leading historians from the United States and France have produced a fully comparative analysis of the ways in which this history has been written and interpreted. The book identifies three generations of historians, literary scholars, film directors and writers who have commented upon the war. Through a thematic structure, it assesses not only diplomatic and military studies but also the social and cultural interpretations of the Great War as seen primarily through the eyes of French, German, and British writers. It provides a fascinating case study of the practice of history in the twentieth century and of the enduring importance of the national lens in shaping historical narrative. This groundbreaking study will prove invaluable reading to scholars and students in history, war studies, European studies, and international relations.

JAY WINTER is Charles J. Stille Professor of History at Yale University. He is a specialist of the First World War and its impact on the twentieth century. His numerous publications include *Sites of memory, sites of mourning: the Great War in European cultural history* (1995), and *1914–1918: the Great War and the shaping of the twentieth century* (1998).

ANTOINE PROST is Emeritus Professor of History at the Université de Paris-I. He is the author and editor of many books, including *Republican identities in war and peace, representations of France in the nineteenth and twentieth centuries* (2002) and *The emergence of European trade unionism* (with Jean-Louis Robert and Chris Wrigley, 2004).

Studies in the Social and Cultural History of Modern Warfare

In recent years the field of modern history has been enriched by the exploration of two parallel histories. These are the social and cultural history of armed conflict, and the impact of military events on social and cultural history.

Studies in the Social and Cultural History of Modern Warfare presents the fruits of this growing area of research, reflecting both the colonization of military history by cultural historians and the reciprocal interest of military historians in social and cultural history, to the benefit of both. The series offers the latest scholarship in European and non-European events from the 1850s to the present day.

For a list of titles in the series, please see end of book.

The Great War in History

Debates and Controversies, 1914 to the Present

Jay Winter

and

Antoine Prost

 CAMBRIDGE
UNIVERSITY PRESS

CAMBRIDGE UNIVERSITY PRESS
Cambridge, New York, Melbourne, Madrid, Cape Town, Singapore, São Paulo

Cambridge University Press
The Edinburgh Building, Cambridge CB2 2RU, UK

Published in the United States of America by Cambridge University Press, New York

www.cambridge.org
Information on this title: www.cambridge.org/9780521616331

Originally published in French as *Penser la grande guerre* by Le Seuil 2004
and © Editions du Seuil 2004. First published in English as *The Great War in History:
Debates and Controversies, 1914 to the Present* by Cambridge University Press 2005
and © Jay Winter and Antoine Prost 2005

English translation © Jay Winter and Antoine Prost 2005

Printed in the United Kingdom at the University Press, Cambridge

A catalogue record for this book is available from the British Library

Library of Congress Cataloguing in Publication data

ISBN-13 978-0-521-85083-4 hardback
ISBN-10 0-521-85083-5 hardback
ISBN-13 978-0-521-61633-1 paperback
ISBN-10 0-521-61633-6 paperback

Contents

Preface to the English edition   *page* vii

Introduction   1

1 Three historiographical configurations   6

2 Politicians and diplomats: why war and for what aims?   34

3 Generals and ministers: who commanded and how?   59

4 Soldiers: how did they wage war?   82

5 Businessmen, industrialists, and bankers: how was
   the economic war waged?   109

6 Workers: did war prevent or provoke revolution?   126

7 Civilians: how did they make war and survive it?   152

8 Agents of memory: how did people live between
   remembrance and forgetting?   173

9 The Great War in history   192

   Bibliography   214
   Index   241

Preface to the English edition

At the beginning of his book *French war aims in the First World War*, the British historian David Stevenson writes, 'For later generations, the First World War has seemed before all else to exemplify futility' (Stevenson, 1982, p. 5). What is evident for a British historian is not evident in any respect for either French historians or others. This difference in basic assumptions is in part the subject of this book. Its origins were French, and have come out of an active and growing literature produced by French historians about the Great War. It is obvious, as even a glance at the bibliography of this book suggests, that this field is entirely multinational and multilingual, and yet scholars remain separated from each other not only by linguistic barriers but also by more general frames of reference and basic assumptions. This book approaches the history of the writing of history in different national frameworks as a subject essential for an understanding of the vast literature produced on the 1914–18 war and its repercussions.

This version of the book has been changed in significant ways. We have extended the statistical material presented in chapter 1, and filled in gaps in our treatment of many particular issues. Nevertheless, as the book was originally written and published in French, there will be certain references and emphases that may strike an English-language reader as unusual, in the same way as Stevenson's assumption appears astonishing to French scholars, who tend to configure the war as a monumental struggle for the life of the nation. Futility there was, to be sure, but there was much more than that. It may be refreshing for English readers to recognize how unusual their own thinking is on the Great War, when placed alongside that of readers who bring to the subject entirely different assumptions.

One of the purposes of this book is to begin to transcend the national boundaries of historiographical enquiry, while affirming their continuing vitality over time, and by examining their different contours. But another is to view this mountain of writing on the Great War longitudinally. Once we approach the development of writing about the subject over time, we can see that certain themes and patterns of understanding preoccupied different generations in different ways. In addition we can examine the exponential growth in publications about the Great War through an examination of scholarly journals. Here we see a common upward inflection of historical interest in this subject from the mid-1970s to the present. Indeed this book is part of this rapidly growing field of interest.

A word or two is necessary about the problems of rendering into English a book originally written for a French audience. The title in French, *Penser la grande guerre*, is untranslatable. So are many terms and concepts we will address in the course of this book; we have tried our best to find a common language which does justice to the wealth of scholarship we here survey. If we have succeeded in showing the excitement as well as the obstacles in the way of creating a fully European history of the Great War, then we will have realized part of our aim.

Orléans, 17 July 2004

Introduction

The war of 1914–18 belongs to no one, not even to historians. Since its outbreak, there has been a veritable tide of publications destined for many different audiences throughout the world on the subject of the war. Certainly, interest has fluctuated; indeed, during some periods the First World War has been marginalized by the Second World War, but at no time has there been a consensus that the history of the Great War has been written once and for all. Even today, the subject remains an open one, and inspires passionate debate; although receding over the horizon of living memory, the subject remains vivid, and this fascination is evident in new books produced by well-known historians who are not particular specialists in this period. The eminent scholar Jean-Baptiste Duroselle completed his career by writing a new synthesis on the French people and the Great War (Duroselle, 1994).[1]

The volume of work in this field is dizzying in its magnitude. It would take several working lives just to read the existing literature on the Great War: more than 50,000 titles are listed in the library of the Bibliothèque de documentation internationale contemporaine in Paris. The French journal *Revue historique* published 757 reviews or bibliographical notices between 1919 and 2002; in the same period, there were 420 articles and reviews in a cluster of Anglo-Saxon historical journals, whose holdings have been digitized and preserved by the on-line repository, JSTOR. In the French case, since the 1970s the *Revue historique* has ceased to serve as a place of publication in this field, even though it has grown dramatically in the 1980s and 1990s. From 1983 to 1998 there have appeared more than 1,100 new books on the Great War in French, and over 100 were published in the year 1998 alone.[2] Each week new books are published in France or elsewhere, some of which break new ground, some of which go over the old ground again. Many articles, at times more important in the development of the subject than books, are published by journals, the number of which is growing as well. We must add too films, television documentaries, exhibitions, museums, internet sites whose narratives both draw on and contribute to the work of professional historians.

It is surprising, therefore, that ninety years after the war we still lack a general analysis of the ways in which this history has been written. Histories of the war, of its battles, its machines, its many facets, fill entire libraries, but no one to our knowledge has put the question as to whether this literature is structured in particular ways, or if, at particular moments, particular topics or questions were dealt with, or how successive developments related to one another. Is it the case that these studies repeat each other or do they pose new questions and provide new answers for different audiences in different contexts? Here is the heart of this book's enquiry.

To begin to respond to these questions, we must limit our field of vision to the history of the war itself, its conduct and its immediate consequences. To study the middle-term and long-term consequences of the war for the major belligerents and for the world it overturned is beyond our reach. Above all, we privilege books, and not scholarly articles, which are less accessible, although many of these play an essential role in the making of historical knowledge.[3]

In this dense and multiform forest, we have tried to trace the most important pathways. We certainly do not intend to provide prizes for outstanding works, or to pretend to offer an exhaustive review of such a huge body of writing. Of course we are well aware that there are many important books we have not cited. We hope readers will forgive us, and not conclude that our objective, already daunting, is thereby unattainable. First and foremost we aim to describe the trends or patterns of historical enquiry and knowledge in one particular field. We aim to show how the historical category 'The First World War' has been constructed. We are interested in the way historians and non-historians have contributed to this task, and by the different themes adopted in different periods by writers in different national contexts. This task transcends professional, chronological, and national boundaries. Our aim is to explore what questions have been posed, what definitions used, what themes have been broached. In sum, how has the history of the Great War been written?

Such a project requires as broad an approach as possible in order not to prejudge our findings. We have rejected three simplifications of this subject which would have eased our task, but which would have barred us from our objective. First, we do not restrict our discussion solely to professional historians, who after all do not hold a monopoly in this field. We do privilege the work of our colleagues, past and present, but accept that the boundaries of our profession are porous in at least two respects. Not only within the English-speaking academy, historians have been joined in this field by other specialists, by literary scholars and sociologists in particular, whose similar and different points of view help to deepen historical enquiry. But the academy itself is not a closed environment. Many historians write for a general public, and many central figures in the war itself published their memoirs in the form of historical accounts. Some writers and journalists have tried to write history, at times with success. In the chorus of voices which have contributed to the history of the war, historians have not been alone.

This historiography bears the marks of two kinds of crossing vectors, one outside the historical profession, one inside it. Public expectations and preoccupations have changed; the questions posed about the First World War have been transformed by the Second World War, by the wars in Algeria and Vietnam. For our generation, attitudes to tolerable levels of violence, and to the body, patterns of consumption, and modes of living are radically different from those of a century ago. French or British children pass through Europe now much more fully than their grandfathers passed through Britain or France. National sentiments are no longer expressed about the same questions. The reading of history has changed under the impact of different or complementary narratives. Professional history is not immune from these changes, but it follows particular trends and has massively expanded. There are new research centres; new archives have been opened. The mode of writing history has changed, and each generation writes its own dictionary of what it terms the 'new history'. The history of the Great War never escapes from this broader context, and forces us to ask how different this body of writing is from other fields of specialization.

Secondly, we refuse to recognize thematic or narrow temporal boundaries. The majority of books which bear the title 'history of the war' generally deal only with its military, diplomatic, or political aspects. If we had limited our discussion solely to these books, we would be unable to understand how this kind of history intersects with others – social, cultural, and economic history in particular. In more general books, in which the war appears only in some chapters or which deal with a longer span of time, new interpretations of the war can emerge. We therefore do not ignore studies which begin before or continue after the Armistice, since many of these books account for the significance of the war through their very periodization. A broad and inclusive approach to the field we are studying is necessary in order to account for the relative significance of political, diplomatic, military, economic, social, and cultural histories at different times and the ways in which these approaches take on different configurations.

Thirdly and finally, since war is a multinational phenomenon, it would have been absurd to restrict this study to the historiography of one country. If we were to focus on French writing in this field alone, we would be unable to appreciate the upward inflection of Anglophone scholarship. As the audience for French publications wanes, that in English grows ever larger, reflecting the growth of the English-speaking academy. In addition, we have taken into account aspects of the German literature in this field, either in the original or translated into English, and some studies written by Italian scholars. On the other hand, for practical reasons, we have neither treated the complex historiography of nationalities inside the Austro-Hungarian Empire, nor have we included works in Soviet and Russian historiography. Another deliberate omission is the growing literature on the Great War from the vantage point of Asian, African, and Latin American history. We leave these subjects to further consideration by our colleagues professionally trained to do so.

This threefold framework provides us with a flexible mode of analysing change over time and over themes. This interest in the diachronic and thematic requires us from to time to return to similar subjects. We have tried to limit such overlaps, but eliminating them all would have diminished our treatment of particular subjects. Many publications are not restricted to a particular domain, and in light of recent scholarly work earlier sources take on new significance. For example, the series sponsored by the Carnegie Endowment for International Peace has to be seen first as the testimony of those who ran important facets of the war effort. Secondly, it is the earliest pillar of our understanding of the economic history of the war. Thirdly, no one can write the social and cultural history of the conflict without reference to many of its volumes. After all, when visiting a town, if one passes time and again a central square, it does not mean that the visit is ill-planned, but that the square is indeed a central one.

These assumptions which we share inform our collaboration, which has emerged from discussions and a friendship decades long. But this wish to write in two voices, for each of which we both take responsibility, has been enlightening. It has enabled us to emphasize the dialogue between different national histories, and to stress the national framework which still dominates historical writing about the war. Hence this book about the history of the disintegration of an older Europe may serve as a kind of introduction to a more European history of the First World War, which one day must be written if Europe is ever to forge its own identity.

NOTES

1. In order to lighten the weight of references in the text, we refer to works cited in the bibliography in this form, familiar to sociologists, in which author's name and date suffice to indicate first publication of the work in its original language, and page references are given for quotations from individual works.
2. Jean-Charles Jauffret, 'Quinze ans d'historiographie française sur la Grande Guerre 1983–1998: essai de bilan', in Maurin and Jauffret, 2002, pp. 39–67, followed by a research bibliography, pp. 68–143.
3. Key references to scholarly articles will be cited as endnotes to the text of each chapter.

1   Three historiographical configurations

For the soldiers, at least on the Western Front, there is no doubt: the war which began in 1914 ended on 11 November 1918, when they no longer had to fear for their lives. But for heads of state, the war ended later, either with the peace treaties or with their implementation. It had begun before mobilization, at the moment of the assassination of Franz-Ferdinand at Sarajevo, or even earlier, with the Balkan wars, or the Franco-German crisis over Agadir. Professional soldiers include the war plans which unfolded on both sides in August 1914. For the French administration, the end of hostilities was fixed by law as 24 October 1919, and emergency regulations lapsed on 15 November. Hence the boundaries of war are not fixed once and for all, because war is not a discrete entity, but something intricately lived, conceptualized, and imagined. It is an actual experience, to which contemporaries gave meaning by thinking about it. The vocabulary acutely discloses this diversity of experiences and meanings. Of course, the words 'the war of 1914–18', 'world war', or 'Great War' do not have precisely the same meaning.

Historical writings are part of this social construction of the historical object. The passage of time induces a kind of sedimentation, and close to a century after these events historians may persuade themselves that they hold a monopoly on this history. The multiple voices, which, in the turmoil of collective and individual emotions, conjured up these events, died out progressively, while the voices of historians were amplified, buoyed up by prior studies. If we wait long enough, the Great War will join the Thirty Years War or the Peloponnesian wars in the broad domain reserved exclusively to historians. But when passions and anxieties were still vivid, everyone spoke about the war, and many tried to share their understanding of it. Everyone had something to say about it. Here is a clear sign of great historical events, moments in history about which people continue to speak.

At the same time history, as a particular kind of narrative, defined by its own rules and procedures, progressively emerged from a set of discursive fields outside it, some of which have historical elements – like first-person accounts or comments – which are not yet history but will become part of it. It is all too easy to separate history from the materials out of which it is constructed; the opposition of the witness and the historian, of the document and the historical narrative, of the construction of evidence and of its interpretation, all provide the basis for a reassuring epistemology. This conception gives the historian a pre-eminent position, because it makes him the master of meaning who renders order out of the chaos of evidence and documents. Unfortunately, things are not so simple. To make this point, it is sufficient to analyse how the history of the First World War has been constructed.

The first configuration: military and diplomatic

When historical actors and professional historians were one

Very rapidly contemporaries understood that they were living through an exceptional event, of epic character, which formed part of history on the grand scale. They named it the Great War already in 1915.[1] Its history did not await the silencing of the guns. One is struck by this precocity. Just as it was won and lost, the Battle of the Marne became an historical subject. Here it is impossible to separate different narrative forms: generals telling the story of their battles speak as witnesses as well as historians. Their testimony rests on direct knowledge which professional historians later analyse and utilize. Of course generals write with a view to defending their reputation and their strategic choices, and these motives are not sufficient to discredit their narratives. This braiding together of witnessing and history is characteristic of the first period, when the most learned and apparently impartial books, often illustrated like the massive history of Hanotaux (1915–23), were no less influenced by friendships, relationships, or political commitments, all the more at a time when all these authors were well aware of the importance of their writings for the morale of the nation.

This merging of actors, witnesses, and historians defines the first historiographical configuration, which did not end at the Armistice but continued later on as politicians and diplomats followed in the footsteps of the generals. The historical narrative was just beginning, in the form of the collection and the critique of documents. In each issue, the *Revue d'histoire de la guerre mondiale* put side by side articles by historians, by witnesses, by generals, and by diplomats. The French *Revue historique* reviewed works of popularization, at times booklets sold at kiosks in railway stations, as well as the memoirs of the main actors, and historical studies. History had not yet emerged from its chrysalis.

In this configuration, it is important to recognize the pre-eminent role played by the series sponsored by the Carnegie Endowment for International Peace. In chapter 5 and elsewhere we will analyse this project in greater detail, but, for the moment, it should suffice to emphasize these particular points. This project was the largest single historical enterprise ever constructed. It was a 'comprehensive economic history of the war, the theme of which should be the extent of displacement caused by the war in the normal process of civilization' (Shotwell, 1924, p. 1). There were 132 volumes published on almost every belligerent nation and some neutral countries, through national committees composed of bureaucrats, businessmen, statesmen, as well as some economists and historians. The British committee included both Keynes and Beveridge, who was responsible for manpower and food supply during the war. The French committee was composed of Charles Gide, Charles Rist, Arthur Fontaine, and the historian Henri Hauser, who was during the war one of the advisors of the Minister of Trade, Etienne Clémentel. This series remains of the highest interest to historians, because of the position of their authors in scholarship and administration, and the documentation they personally had at their disposal.

The primacy of diplomatic questions

The main undertaking of this first configuration was the publication of full sets of diplomatic documents. In effect, contemporaries were haunted by a central question which dominated their work: that of war guilt. It is difficult today to appreciate the amplitude and intensity of this debate. The ordeal had been so long, so hard, so murderous, the cost had been so staggering, that everyone absolutely had to know why it had broken out and why it had lasted so long. Each nation was convinced of the justice of its cause. The Germans had been persuaded of the reality of the menace of encirclement which presented them with the danger of an aggressive France set on revenge and of Allies determined to block German access to the place she deserved as a robust world power. They clung to the notion that all they had done was to defend themselves. To them their defeat was unjust, all the more so since article 231 of the Versailles Treaty made them bear sole responsibility for the war. Arguments tending to minimize the significance of this article did not reach a population in a state of shock. Even before the historians began to intervene, two incompatible versions of the subject of war guilt lived side by side.

To establish the validity of their arguments, governments undertook the publication of official documents, not only on the immediate origins of the war, but on the whole field of international relations which determined the alliance system and then precipitated the war. Each government mobilized its professional historians to manage this task and to assure its objectivity. Of course, when the archives were opened in later years the views drawn from these documents would be corrected. But for the time being, these vast publications of diplomatic documents dominated the work of historians and absorbed their energies. As universities were weak institutions, professional historians were few in number; hence their role in the global historical literature was limited. They published fewer books than did actors, witnesses, and diverse essayists.

This general situation varied country by country. The French case is distinguished from others in two respects. On the one hand, the Faculties of Letters were weaker than elsewhere. They emerged effectively only from the 1880s; they had few students and graduated in history approximately 100 students each year. There were few Professors of history: fifty-five throughout the country, covering the history of every period and every nation. In the Sorbonne, Seignobos was the only Professor of the 'political history of modern and contemporary times'. On the other hand, this weakness was balanced by the exceptional importance given to the teaching of history in high schools. The teaching of history was obligatory in all secondary schools and was taught by specialized teachers, who numbered 620 in 1914. Such a huge historical event as the Great War could not remain outside the classroom. The teaching of this subject was launched officially in 1929, but even before that date the author of the most widely used textbook, Jules Isaac, completed in 1921 the classic text of Albert Malet, killed in the war, by adding a chapter of 100 pages in a separate volume, on the history of the war.[2]

Since French universities were relatively weak, historical enquiry about the war was centred on a particular institution run by the Ministry of Public Instruction under the supervision of a professional committee: the Library and Museum of the War, which rapidly became the Library of Contemporary International Documentation (BDIC).[3] This library was linked to the Society for the History of the War, which from 1923 published the *Revue d'histoire de la guerre mondiale*. This journal later became the *Revue d'histoire de la deuxième guerre mondiale*, and today (2004) is *Guerres mondiales et conflits contemporains*. The BDIC was directed by Camille Bloch, and a young *agrégé* in history,[4] Pierre Renouvin, who had lost his left arm in the Battle of the Chemin des Dames in 1917, served as librarian. As early as 1922, he was invited to lecture in the Sorbonne about the origins of the war (Renouvin, 1925b). He was elected to a chair in history in the Sorbonne in 1932. His professional and moral authority was above reproach. Editor of the *Revue historique*, dean of the Sorbonne from 1955 to 1958, chairman of the National Foundation of Political

Science, he directed the publication of French diplomatic documents. A member of the Institut de France, honoured by the highest degree of the Legion of Honour, Renouvin dominated the history of the Great War and that of contemporary political history until his retirement in 1964 and his death ten years later.[5] Neither in Germany nor in the United Kingdom did a single outstanding historian tower over the history of the Great War as did Renouvin. Across the Rhine, the war was too dark and too conflicted a memory; across the English Channel, it seemed too recent for historical analysis, and the Oxford English History abruptly stopped in 1914. There were exceptions, though. Cruttwell's military history of the war appeared in 1934, though it never approached Renouvin's work in stature.

Renouvin's reputation was definitively established by his volume 19 in the great series 'Peoples and civilizations' edited by Halphen and Sagnac, a parallel project to the many volumes published at the same time as the Cambridge Histories. Isaac, who did not share and sometimes criticized Renouvin's views, reviewed this book in the warmest terms. This book is, Isaac wrote, 'the first synthesis which can be considered as scientific. I would readily say that this book, respectful of the rules of the art, is a perfect example of the kind of historical writing celebrated in the French university, the methods and principles of which our masters Langlois and Seignobos have set out.'[6] This large volume (640 pages) has been re-published and updated in 1939, 1948, 1962, 1969 (776 pages in the 1969 edition). Its status as a classic rests on the breadth of its learning, the precision of its documentation, the rigorous nature of its interpretations, the clarity of its organization, and the fluidity of its prose. No one matches Renouvin's ability to explain the most complex situations in the simplest and most lucid manner. His intelligence was contagious, and his analyses are so easily understood as to appear self-evident. Not surprisingly, he was asked to write the section on the war in the textbook for higher education in the series 'Clio' on the eve of 1940 (Renouvin, Préclin, and Hardy, 1939). In 1965, he produced the volume on the war in the series 'Que sais-je?', which has an unparalleled status as an authoritative encyclopedia of knowledge.

Let us turn to *La crise européenne et la grande guerre*. It is a purely political, diplomatic, and military history. The economic and social aspects of the conflict are neglected. Only two pages are given to the 1917 strikes and the mutinies of that year. In total one paragraph dealt with the strike wave, twenty-six lines were sufficient for the mutinies and Pétain's response to them, and one paragraph was devoted to their causes (Renouvin, 1934, pp. 437–8). In the 'Clio' volume, published later, Renouvin enlarged his comments on the economic aspects of the war:

he devoted one and a half pages to economic mobilization, two and a half pages to the blockade and submarine warfare, and one page to economic 'weapons'. But he was much more laconic about the strikes and mutinies, with only a few words: 'In France, in May 1917, strikes in Paris industry coincided with mutinies which broke out in many regiments at the front. The crisis lasted more than three weeks; it had repercussions on the political situation' (Renouvin *et al.*, 1939, p. 564).

Renouvin's work was characteristic of a particular and widely shared approach to the writing of history. Bidou's massive study (1936) offered detailed treatment of the battles with beautiful maps, of whose quality the publisher was proud, but this book was equally spare in its treatment of economic and social themes. The mutinies were dealt with in a bit more than a page, and the author thought it sufficient to present General Mangin's account of their causes.[7] Bourget's *Petite histoire de la Grande guerre mondiale* (1932) is a short book, intelligent, well documented and nuanced, but exclusively military. The strikes and mutinies are mentioned only in passing. But the last chapter enlarges this perspective and speaks of the people's war, the awakening of a world consciousness leading to the creation of the League of Nations. Ironically, the last volume of Lavisse's great *Histoire de la France contemporaine depuis la Révolution jusqu'à la paix de 1919* (Bidou *et al.*, 1922) provides the least strictly military and political approach to the subject, with two chapters dealing with the impact of the war on 'national life'. Surprisingly enough, Seignobos comments upon the economic consequences of the war, on public debt, the growth of which is analysed and measured.[8] But there is nothing on the organization of the war economy or on the social problems it produced.

At this stage, the historiography of the war was still in its infancy; research was well under way, but only in the fields of military and diplomatic history, as a glance at the pages of the quarterly *Revue d'histoire de la guerre mondiale* will attest. This journal is well presented, with abundant space given to reviews of publications in this field. For instance there were reviews of Huber's work on population (1931) and of Picard's (1928) study of trade unionism during the war. Two central articles appeared in each issue, and at times extended over several issues, alongside collections of documents and memoirs. The two central articles were balanced, in that one was dedicated to military history, and one to diplomatic history.[9] There are no articles at all about economic and social aspects of the war. Similarly, the *Revue historique* virtually did not review the Carnegie series: of the thirty-seven volumes in the French series, only seven were noticed. Two were books by contributors to the review: Camille Bloch (1925) and Renouvin (1925a). Three were monographs on cities during the war

(Gignoux, 1926; Lhéritier and Chautemps, 1926; Masson, 1926), one was Peschaud's work on the railroads (1926), and one was Collinet and Stahl's account of the food supply of occupied France (1928). Neither Huber's work on demography, nor Picard on trade unionism, nor Oualid and Picquenard (1928) on wages was reviewed. The enormous resource of information provided by the Carnegie series was not yet of central interest to professional historians. The history of the war remained solely that of battles and of diplomatic exchanges. The only exception is that of a great thinker, open to modernity, Elie Halévy (1930), who provided a global interpretation of the crisis, in which war and revolution are inextricably linked. However Halévy had little influence on historians at the time.[10]

An historiography in its own context

This way of writing history helps us to understand the point of view of the journal *Annales*. Olivier Dumoulin and Laurent Mucchielli have shown that Bloch and even more so Febvre were excessive in their denunciations of the privileged position of political history, and of what they termed the history of mere events, since historians were already widely interested in social and economic history.[11] However, their critique was indeed well founded when we survey the history of the war. We have here a perfect illustration of this kind of history of 'mere events'. In defence of these historians, it is necessary to take account of the political context. The historians of the *Annales* school were rather distant from the political debates of this time. In 1940 Bloch would confess that 'we have been good workers. But have we been good enough citizens?'[12] In contrast, historians of the war hung on to an exposed position since, without any concession to political interests, they raised questions central to the legitimacy of the position of France vis-à-vis Germany. What was at stake in the writing of history was the making of foreign policy.

This preoccupation required the most rigorous use of historical criticism. Historians had to make 'a violent effort of objectivity'[13] in order to give to their interpretations a kind of authority well beyond that of other voices. In a context in which historical actors and witnesses spoke authoritatively, the essential task was to separate truth from falsity, the likely from the certain, and to compare different documents in the search for evidence. One of the best examples of the difference between professional history and history for the general public can be found in the accounts of the mutinies of 1917. The official interpretation given by Bourget (1932)[14] or Bidou (1936) explains the mutinies as the result of pacifist propaganda. Renouvin is much more prudent and critical. To him, more evidence is needed before these assertions can be accepted. 'It is difficult, when considering the origin of the mutinies, in the present state of documentation, to measure exactly what weight to attach to military and to political causes; but no one has yet proved that the movement was organized or hatched by a group of defeatist activists' (Renouvin, 1934, p. 437).

Historical objectivity is negatively defined, by the identification of what is not proven and can be discussed again. This caution is the very rule, the respect of which is even more necessary when historians are so close to the events they seek to understand. Neither Renouvin nor Isaac ever thought that he had to step back in order to write history. Only lazy or timid historians thought it impossible to write the history of recent events. Renouvin and Isaac were under no burden of constructing new concepts such as that of the history of 'present time', although they were much closer to the war in which they had fought than are those scholars of more recent times claiming to write the history of the 'present'. With respect to the war, they applied the same methods they had used for any other subject. But they retained a deep sense of the precariousness of their conclusions and of the vital necessity of continuing vigilance: not all documents were published; not all archives were open; and new documentation could transform what historians had previously stated. Historians provide interpretations, but they must be ready to modify them. 'We must offer conclusions which are never more than provisional' (Renouvin, 1925b, p. 14). Because it is rigorous, and alert to documentary evidence, history remains open: a work in progress.

The great omission: the soldiers

A final feature distinguishes this first phase of historiography: the absence of both combat and combatants. In this body of writing, we meet men of politics, diplomacy, we meet the generals, but not the men in the ranks. We see war from above, but never from below. The war in its material day-to-day reality, the war experienced and suffered by millions of men, is not yet a subject of historical enquiry.

In this first generation, in which actors, historians, and witnesses are braided together, the one form of evidence deemed of little or no interest or value is that provided by the soldiers themselves. They are literally strangers in this history which was written without them and in which they would hardly recognize themselves. There was a deluge of publications after the war in two waves, one in its immediate aftermath, and one between 1928 and 1934. In both waves there appeared innumerable books of letters, notebooks, diaries, memoirs, and novels. The public was interested in what they wrote, but historians were not. Even Renouvin, a disabled war veteran, wrote: 'The evidence of soldiers, the consultation of which is important for the understanding of the atmosphere of battle, can rarely give information on the conduct of operations, since their field of vision was too narrow.'[15]

Some of these witnesses, as we will see below, try to make themselves heard in different ways (Ducasse, 1932; Péricard, 1933). The most striking attempt was that of Norton Cru (1929) in his *Témoins*.[16] The meaning of this book is incomprehensible outside the context of this first historiographical configuration, dominated by documentary criticism, and a particular exclusion, that of the front-line soldiers. The critical method is decisive for any history of the war. For instance, historical criticism has established that the celebrated meeting of the Kaiser and others at Potsdam on 5 July 1914 was actually invented by an ambassador eager to push himself forward; the majority of the supposed participants were actually away from Berlin that very day (Renouvin, 1925b, p. 36; Fay, 1929, II, pp. 170–1; Schmitt, 1930, I, pp. 275–82). To Norton Cru, the writings of ex-soldiers had to be criticized in the same way in order to become historical material. He gathered together 300 books published in French, and he reconstructed in minute detail the military service records of the authors: were they where they said they were, and were they there at the time they affirmed? He traced improbable statements, improper modes of expression, in a hypercritical and suspicious spirit. He preferred to turn away from celebrated witnesses, like Barbusse and Dorgelès, rather than to risk distorting what he deemed accurate in terms of his own experience. It is easy to contest such a project today. But in the context of the time, this kind of criticism was the entry price soldiers had to pay to get into the historical record. Norton Cru's work is a somewhat desperate attempt of a man excluded from the official history to make his voice heard and to achieve belated recognition for the soldiers' role in a war which after all they and only they had fought.

This attempt, so revealing of the methods of the first historiographical configuration, failed. Renouvin did not hear nor did he learn from Norton Cru. It was not only that their perspectives were different – one looking at the war from above and the other looking at war from below. It was also a question of method or ethics. Cru made his own experience the ultimate criterion in the judgment of different witnesses. Just like most other historians, Renouvin thought that objectivity required him to exclude himself totally from the history he would write. To our knowledge, Renouvin never mentioned in his own historical work the war he had endured.[17] The commitment to maintaining a critical distance as a professional historian is the precise opposite of the position Norton Cru affirmed. Here is a real point of contention: how distant personally must an historian be from the event on which he writes? This question has more than one answer. In the first generation, the reply of Renouvin was dominant. It made it possible for him and his colleagues to write the first professional historical narratives of the war, while at the same time it made it impossible for those who had fought the war to be recognized in these narratives and to recognize themselves in them.

The discussion of the Great War in interwar Germany and Britain followed the same patterns as in France. In virtually every text, the war was treated as a political conflict on the grand scale, best viewed from above. This Clausewitzian bias was inconsistent with what might be termed a Tolstoyan emphasis on the will of the masses or Stendahlian irony on chaos as critical elements in determining the outcome of military encounters. Overviews such as that of Basil Liddell Hart, a war veteran who had been twice wounded, and who was a great specialist on military questions and a celebrated chronicler, were more about war rather than about warriors, more about patterns rather than lived experience, more about units rather than about isolated individuals trapped in the trench system (Liddell Hart, 1934). The move towards the decentring of the war narrative would come, but only after considerable time had passed and after a major expansion in the number of historians at work in and outside universities. Before the 1960s historical writing was restricted to a relatively small group of professional scholars. Thereafter the numbers engaged in the study of the Great War grew exponentially, and so did the literature they produced. The new literature, to which we now turn, opened up new perspectives on the history of the 1914–18 conflict.

The second configuration: social history

A general overview

The second half of the twentieth century was a period of massive expansion of higher education in all European countries and in the United States. One effect of this phenomenon was the expansion in the market among the broad public for historical works, in particular among people whose level of education had risen considerably. In addition, there was a massive increase in the number of people trained as professional historians and who received the doctoral degree in the subject. To publish their works and to meet wider demand, the field of historical reviews also expanded rapidly. National historical reviews, like the *Historische Zeitschrift*, or the *Revue historique*, are still active, but no longer dominate the field of historical publications. Specialist journals have proliferated,

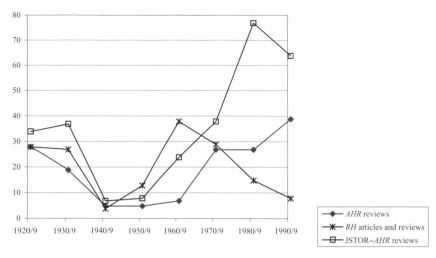

Fig. 1. A comparison of publications on the Great War in the *American Historical Review*, the *Revue historique*, and a group of Anglo-Saxon historical journals, by decade, from 1920 to 1999.

and as a consequence the likelihood of articles on the Great War appearing in national journals has probably gone down. There are other places in which such work can find a home.

In a study of historiography, this broad context must be taken into account, for the expansion of the tertiary sector created both readers and scholars. Writing about the Great War is not a special case; all historical study has expanded rapidly since the 1960s.

The following statistics provide some quantitative evidence on a phenomenon which also has a qualitative character, to which we turn below. Figure 1 is a comparison of the *Revue historique*, the *American Historical Review*, both national journals, and a cluster of eighteen Anglo-Saxon historical journals – excluding the *American Historical Review* – whose holdings have been digitized by JSTOR. The JSTOR data incorporate publications which date from the 1960s and later. Not surprisingly, the number of reviews in this cluster of journals increases rapidly. On the contrary, the emergence of new historical journals made it possible for the *Revue historique* to bypass books about the war in its section of reviews. Therefore the apparent decline in interest is no decline at all, merely a redistribution of publications in different professional journals. The two curves express the same evolution. The *American Historical Review*, which covered all facets of historical research, shows a three-part trend. The first is in the 1920s and 1930s, when interest in the Great War

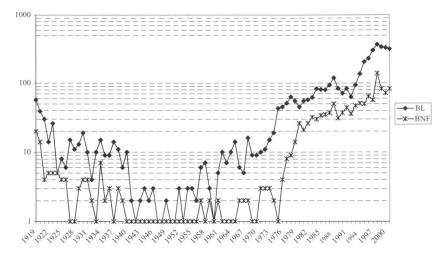

Fig. 2. A comparison in logarithmic scale of annual changes in the number of works on the Great War catalogued by the British Museum (British Library – BL) and the Bibliothèque nationale de France (BNF), 1919–2001.

is robust. The second is in the 1940s and 1950s, when interest wanes. The third is after the 1960s, when interest increases very rapidly.

Figure 2 is a comparison of the production of historical work over time, seen from another angle. We have collected data on the cataloguing by year of publication both by the British Museum (BL) (now the British Library) under the headings of 'World War 1914–1918'. These data include books published in all languages. For the Bibliothèque nationale de France (BNF), data include only works published in French. Both curves are instructive, though they are bound to reflect the zeal of librarians in seeking out works to catalogue. Here again we can see a three-part distribution, this time described in logarithmic terms so as to measure rates of change rather than absolute values. Before the Second World War, publications were numerous, though slowly declining. From 1940 to 1960, there is a trough. Thereafter the curves rise, though more rapidly in the case of the BL than in the case of the BNF. This third phase stabilizes in the 1980s, as a steadily rising field of publication.

In conclusion, these data describe processes which are not solely national in character. The historical profession writing about the Great War has expanded very rapidly in the last generation, and so have the journals which incorporate their research. But we must bear in mind that we see reflected here more general trends in the expansion of the academy.

It is likely that other historical subjects grow in terms of reviews and in books catalogued in national libraries in similar ways.

However, there are other non-quantitative differences which are particularly relevant to the writing of the history of the Great War. It is to those differences that we now turn.

The return of the excluded

The war that is discussed in this second phase of historical writings since the 1960s is not the same as the war described by the first generation of historians. This change can be exemplified in the case of France by the success of the book by Ducasse, Meyer, and Perreux (1959). These men were all veterans of the Great War, and not professional historians. Theirs is a history from below, as is indicated in their title, *Vie et mort des français 1914–1918*. This study has its own history. The authors had difficulty in finding a publisher. The firm of Hachette finally accepted their book, but on one condition: that they find a well-known personality to write a preface to the book. Since the three authors had all graduated from one of the most renowned schools of higher education, the Ecole normale supérieure, they asked their comrade Maurice Genevoix, permanent secretary of l'Académie française, who agreed to write both a preface and an epilogue to the book. Genevoix's name appeared on the cover of the book, and in letters larger than those given to the authors. The book was a tremendous commercial success, enabling Hachette to approach two of the authors to write books in its well-known series *La Vie quotidienne*, one about soldiers and the other about civilians in the Great War (Meyer, 1966; Perreux, 1966).

Vie et mort des français is a hybrid book. The authors are on the edges of the academy. They did not enter the academic profession, though they went through the training of the Ecole normale supérieure and the *Agrégation*. Only one of these authors was a teacher, but in a high school and not in a university. Having asked Genevoix rather than Renouvin for a preface, they seemed to have chosen literature rather than history. Their study is half a textbook for undergraduates and half an anthology of writers who served during the war. On the subjects of military operations or diplomatic intrigues, this book rests on secondary sources and offers nothing new. However, these amateur historians fundamentally changed the way the history of the Great War was viewed. Here is an invitation for professional historians to learn a bit of modesty.

What is new in this book and explains its success is its point of view, which is rather non-conformist, as Genevoix said in his epilogue. First, it is a global view, not limited to military or diplomatic history. The battlefield is clearly in the foreground, but economy and society are certainly part of the landscape. A chapter dealing with the home front indicated the vast gap which separated idealized images from the reality of the war, and the distance between the front line and the home front. Above all, the centre of gravity of this study is new: in place of a history of the French nation, we have here a history of the French people.[18] What they succeeded in doing was to merge a history from above with a history from below, told in vivid detail. The war they described was at one and the same time 'the war of the generals and the war of the soldiers'; they show that what is difficult is not the giving of orders, but carrying them out. 'The victor of the Marne is also the French soldier' (p. 44). In their narratives of combat, they set the stories of writers who served, giving their own book an entirely new and unknown tone, as well as an incomparable power. Genevoix is right when he said that this history of the war 'goes further and innovates. A "simple" history, for it has no pretensions of offering premature syntheses, but it does provide an objective and complete overview. Neither military, nor diplomatic, nor sociological, nor technically focused in any particular way, they leave to the specialists the tasks of more ample and detailed treatments. What they have deliberately aimed at is a "history of men at war"' (p. 11).

The social context

The reversal of perspective, which substitutes the point of view of soldiers and civilians for that of generals and diplomats, is part of a more general movement which requires further elaboration.[19] Some factors apply to the history of the Great War. Later wars, that of 1939–45, that of Algeria for the French, that of Vietnam for Americans, modified the perspective and questions asked about the Great War. It was well known that the settlement of 1919 did not last, and that early on contemporaries like Charles de Gaulle saw the 1914–18 conflict as the first phase of a new Thirty Years War.[20] The question of similarities and differences as between the two world wars became a central matter.

Secondly, a generational effect is evident. War veterans were above the age of sixty in 1960; they were close to retirement. This is precisely the moment for them to return to their youth in such an exceptional time, the memory of which they did not wish to lose. There is as well a vast market for their narratives through which they relived their early experiences. Publishers, emboldened by the success of *Vie et mort des français*, tried to exploit this new situation (Nobécourt, 1965; Boutefeu, 1966, etc.).

There are other factors in motion. Not only was the number of educated people growing rapidly, as we have already noted, but this expanding market was radically changed by the force of television. In the telling of the story of the war of 1914–18, here is a new and powerful medium, capable of reaching millions of viewers who do not need a long and painful apprenticeship to understand the war. The fiftieth anniversary of the outbreak of the war was the occasion for the commissioning of television histories of the war. In 1964 in Britain, the BBC asked noted historians, including Corelli Barnett, John Terraine, and later, with the assistance of Sir Basil Liddell Hart, to launch the new channel, BBC 2, by producing a long and important series lasting twenty-six hours. Their scripts provide a view of the war from above, but their images establish forcefully the war from below. When the series ended, the BBC received massive responses opposing the official view: the Great War, from this perspective, had been a massacre, the story of which had to be told through the soldiers' experience.[21]

In France, as well, a second channel was also launched in 1964. At the government's invitation, three historians wrote and produced three programmes, each two and a half hours in length, on the Great War, the interwar period, and the Second World War, a sensible distribution. The first programme was produced by Marc Ferro, a specialist on the Russian revolution (Ferro, 1967 and 1976), with a passion for cinema, at that time on the staff of the VIe section of the Ecole pratique des hautes études in Paris. This programme, *1914–18: the Great War*, is distinctive in three ways. First, it was a Franco-German production, and was broadcast in both countries simultaneously. Secondly, it was a presentation of film footage alone, without any interviews of veterans or historians. Thirdly, the perspective was firmly international. In both countries it had such a appeal that the film company Pathé, which did not initially intend to make a film production of this programme, distributed it in cinemas with great success.[22]

This programme marked the emergence of new sources in the historiography of the war. Starting from a script written by Renouvin, Ferro ransacked visual archives all over Europe, at least west of Moscow, and he found images of originality and power. The last sequence of the programme, for example, shows the jubilant crowd in Berlin on 11 November 1918. They are as yet unaware of the defeat and instead celebrate the revolution. In addition, this moment was one of the emergence of a new narrative mode. For to present film is not to offer images illustrating a text, it is to compose a narrative through images. The images dominate the words. In a short commentary, Ferro analysed the particular difficulties of this historical mode: the gaps in documentation, which cannot be filled by stock photographs; the risk of distorting history by the use of images the value of which is less than their beauty; the severe constraints of brevity which limit the commentary.[23]

The historian of the French communist party, Annie Kriegel, a co-author of the programme, emphasized the historiographical change of which this film is evidence.

Marc Ferro has well demonstrated that war, in the full sense of the term, is the product not only of strategic decisions, but also of decisions taken in the realm of the economy, society, politics and diplomacy. The war was also women working in the factories; it was diplomatic negotiations to win a new ally or to prevent a possible adversary from joining the other side; it was civilian rationing (perhaps somewhat over-dramatized with respect to France in 1916, at least in the eyes of those who lived in France in 1944). This conception of war as a global phenomenon is the source of the success of the film. The viewer literally sees the emergence of the revolution from the war. The February Revolution, the Bolshevik, the German revolutions. Is there a greater spectacle?[24]

The new vision of the Great War made possible by television was inevitably marked by the faces of individual men and women. This democratizing tendency of images underlay the most powerful Anglo-Saxon synthesis of the history of the war, A. J. P. Taylor's *The First World War: an illustrated history* (1964). Taylor was also the author of the volume of the Oxford History of England covering the years 1914 to 1945 (1965), but his illustrated history had an even greater impact as a best-seller, with more than 50,000 copies sold. Taylor's ironic prose extended to the captions he wrote for each illustration. Together, image and analysis transmitted an interpretation of the Great War which was cosmopolitan, democratic, and unillusioned about the outcome of the conflict. Taylor's *Great War* was a monumental waste of the goodwill and dedication of millions of men and women whose efforts and whose lives were thrown away by politicians and generals overwhelmed by a war they could not control. This populist vision of the Great War decentred the historical narrative and constituted a fundamental point of departure for all subsequent studies in the Anglo-Saxon world.

The Marxist paradigm

This second historiographical configuration was marked not only by the expansion of public interest, by the enlargement of available documentation, and by the emergence of new narrative modes. It is part of an intellectual context marked by the domination of Marxism since the end of the Second World War. The huge influence of Marxism did not make historians less rigorous, but it inspired their questions and helped frame their hypotheses.

The question of war guilt was central to the first historiographical configuration. For the second, it was the link between war and revolution: the failure of the Second International in 1914, the 'treason' of social democracy, the growth of the revolutionary movement. This point had been raised by Rosmer in 1936, but he was marginal in two senses. He was neither an historian nor a communist.[25] After the Second World War, such enquiries became more frequent. They were often more political in focus than social, as is evident in Annie Kriegel's doctoral thesis, *Aux origines du parti communiste français* (1964).

The Marxist paradigm adds a kind of obviousness to the explanation of the political by the social, and of the social by the economic. If one wants to find a global understanding of history, one must consider social classes and their relationships of agreement and conflict. It is at this level that the objective conditions combine with the choices made by individuals and groups. At this time, historical production was dominated by histories of social groups, such as *The making of the English working class* by E. P. Thompson, *Labouring men* and *Primitive rebels* by E. J. Hobsbawm or, in France, the magisterial theses of Maurice Agulhon on the Var, of Gabriel Désert on the peasants of Calvados, of Rolande Trempé on the miners of Carmaux, of Michèle Perrot about workers on strike, of Yves Lequin on the working class in Lyons, and so on. For this generation of historians, history is a story, the actors in which are social classes. At that time, all these words were self-evident.

As the political context favoured the study of the labour movement, and the ideological context favoured the study of the working class, it is easy to explain why historians of the labour movement became social historians of the war. Jay Winter (1974) and John Horne (1991, though the original PhD was 1980) began the study of socialism at war. In France Jean-Jacques Becker (1977) who dealt with the mobilization of 1914, had previously studied the 'treason' of social democracy and inquired into the reasons why anti-militarist activists were not jailed in August 1914 (Becker, 1973). Antoine Prost (1977a and b) who studied the veterans' movement, had already published a book on the French trade unions under the Popular Front. In chapter 6, we will comment on this flourishing of social studies, many quantitative in nature, which are characteristic of this second historiographical configuration. Some of them were centred on particular groups; others are devoted to the understanding of a national society as a whole and to its structural changes (Feldman, 1966; Kocka, 1973; Waites, 1987). Suffice it to say here that this evolution is noticeable in the general histories of the war which link together military and diplomatic events, public opinion, economic organization, and the soldiers' experience.

The synthesis of Marc Ferro (1969), for years without equal, is the first successful outcome of this evolution; the book is all the more remarkable in that it embraces all the belligerent nations. The author was entirely aware of his paradoxical position: 'It may seem impertinent to write a history of the Great War when one is the student both of Pierre Renouvin and Fernand Braudel', he wrote in his introduction. Renouvin in his preface registered this change and saluted the originality of this book:

It puts the emphasis on the psychology of the men of the first half of the twentieth century, on the analysis of their feelings and aspirations. Popular attitudes at the outbreak of the war, the forms of weariness when the conflict dragged on; the hopes this weariness gave to revolutionaries, eager to substitute civil for national war; the formation of broad movements of opinion, despite the 'mobilization of minds'; the effectiveness of those movements – such are the major themes of this book.

As an example of this new balance of interpretations and approaches, let us consider one study which became a textbook for French students of the period. In the series the New History of Contemporary France, a paperback edition, the twelfth volume was entitled *La Fin d'un monde 1914–1929* (1975). It was written by Philippe Bernard, an historian who died young. The origins of the war had been treated in the preceding volume in the series. Here 130 pages are devoted to the war, its consequences and the peace settlement; 30 pages are given to military operations; a bit less to political aspects; 15 pages, to the war economy as such, and 10 deal with civilian life. Neither the Marne nor Verdun nor the Somme has disappeared, but the history of the war has become more that of an economy, a society, and a state at war.

The reorientation of diplomatic and military history

In his preface to the synthesis of Marc Ferro, Renouvin wrote with his characteristic lucidity: 'From this perspective, military history remains in place . . . But diplomatic history has become of secondary importance, since the negotiations and manoeuvrings of chancelleries remained secret'. Renouvin was right, but the place of diplomatic history in this new configuration varied by country.

The new significance granted to public opinion, previously ignored by Renouvin until new documentation permitted an informed discussion of it,[26] in effect re-invigorated diplomatic history by shifting attention away from the question of war origins to the question of war aims. If patriotic mobilization forged the *Union sacrée*, war-weariness undermined it from 1917, and governments were obliged to say for what reasons, for what objectives, it was necessary to continue to fight. Social Democratic parties broke up, and growing minorities refused to go on with the war for imperialist objectives. Since the people were embroiled in this pointless butchery by the old diplomacy and its secret treaties, it became imperative to impose on governments a new diplomacy, in which discussions would happen in the light of day. The form of the diplomatic system determines its content (Mayer, 1959 and 1967). At once, the central role returns to domestic politics rather than diplomacy.

In Germany it was precisely through the question of war aims and the primacy of domestic politics that diplomatic history was re-launched. Since Nazism had blocked any critical study, an enduring question haunted Germany: did the Nazi period constitute a parenthesis in German history, an accident, or did it stem from an earlier tradition? Fritz Fischer's statement in his 1961 study *Griff nach der Weltmacht* is clear. Imperial Germany wanted nothing less than hegemony in Europe, by the construction of a powerful *Mitteleuropa*. This book precipitated a polemical debate of great intensity. Diplomatic history was revived and given new impetus. At the same time access to archives made it possible to complete and to correct previous interpretations. The earlier thesis about German responsibility for the war was confirmed.

France and Great Britain were unaffected by this debate. Renouvin found a confirmation of his earlier interpretation[27] in Fischer's book, which was translated into English with an introduction by James Joll (1967) and into French with a preface by Jacques Droz (1970). Droz summarized this German debate three years later (Droz, 1973). Renouvin's students enlarged the history of international relations by dealing first with public opinion and financial relations. Here we see the impact of the Marxist paradigm, which made war the consequence of imperialism, the final stage of capitalism. A series of dissertations on the history of international finance, a subject to which we shall return, undermined or refuted this hypothesis, further enhancing the decline of the Marxist paradigm.

Military history, at least partially, was also influenced by this new configuration, through which this branch of history discovered the common soldier. The opening of military archives permitted Pedroncini (1967 and 1968) to study mutiny in detail and to show their origins in the conditions in which soldiers lived. He also proved that the repression of this mutiny was not so severe. Hence he refuted two widespread ideas dear to different political milieux: first, on the right, the ghost of pacifist agitators; and secondly, on the left, the myth of systematic and blind repression.

A conference held at Verdun in 1975 (Association nationale du souvenir de la bataille de Verdun, 1976) revealed the depth of this reorientation of military history. Alongside thorough contributions on strategy and tactics, there were articles on the life and death of soldiers, public opinion, the press, and even the representation of the war in school textbooks.

In the Anglo-Saxon world, the London historian James Joll provided the most powerful reorientation of the diplomatic and political history of the war in Great Britain in the 1960s. A scholar of the Second International, Joll reviewed the diplomatic history of the July crisis in a strikingly new way. He presented the leaders of the major combatants as men who found themselves in July 1914 in a situation the outcome of which they could not predict. What they did was far from a Clausewitzian calculus of the rational. Instead they turned to a series of vague notions about honour or the inevitability of struggle which they had learned much earlier in their lives. Lord Grey, the British Foreign Secretary, responded not in terms of the ideas of 1914 but in terms of the code of honour he had learned in his English public school forty years before. Here were what Joll termed the 'unspoken assumptions' of 1914, the hidden motivation of men lost in a moment of great tension (Joll, 1968). *L'histoire des mentalités* had clearly crossed the English Channel to take up residence in the London School of Economics. It is but a short step from this perspective to the period when social and cultural history came to the fore as a central element in European historiography.

The third configuration: cultural and social

Why and how did history change?

Between the first and the second configuration, there was a break, a period of silence due to the impact of the Second World War. Between the second and the third configuration, on the contrary, there was no rupture. It is evident that there was a smooth transition, and many scholars passed easily from social to cultural history, for instance, as Jean-Jacques Becker, Jay Winter, and Stéphane Audoin-Rouzeau did. There was no real change of generations, but rather a shift of emphasis, a displacement of the centre of interest. This is the reason why this evolution was so rapid, as is clear from a glance at the subjects of two major international conferences: the first, held in Nanterre in 1988 on European societies and the Great War (J.-J. Becker and Audoin-Rouzeau, 1990), and the second held in Péronne in 1992 on war and cultures (J.-J. Becker *et al.*, 1994); from European societies to cultures in only four years.

In 1988, in a synthesis written for the public at large, Winter anticipated this shift. After four chapters on the politicians' war, the generals' war, the soldiers' war, and the civilians' war, each of which was divided into four chronological sequences, he wrote a chapter on the consequences of the war, and another about the memory of the war in literature, the arts, and cinema. Here he followed the path pioneered by Ferro, however more systematically and in a more formal manner. The use of many illustrations, mixing photographs of real life and some images and representations gave to the whole book a clear cultural dimension (Jay Winter, 1988). Eight years later, Jay Winter and Baggett (1996) produced a new television history in eight hours for the BBC in Britain and for the Public Broadcasting Service in the United States. They enlarged their visual project by offering in *The Great War and the shaping of the twentieth century* (1996) a general cultural history covering all combatant countries. Their introduction was explicit: within a chronological framework, here is a cultural history of military conflict. The aim of the authors was to explore 'the hopes and dreams, the ideas and aspirations, the exhilaration and the despair, both of those remote from power and of those who led them. Cultural history is the story of the way they made sense of the war and its consequences.'[28]

This evolution was rapid and relatively untroubled because it was a kind of continuation. Within social history, cultural history already existed, under terms such as 'mentality', 'opinion', or 'psychology'. Here we are not far from what cultural history terms 'representations'. At times cultural history informed even diplomatic history. The historiography of the war is here in no way original; it follows the same path as did that of the rest of the entire discipline since the 1990s. However, by this time, the transition has been interpreted as a transformation. It is evident that cultural history was already in existence, but was not recognized as such. Why was it that a continuity became a rupture?

One central reason is the delegitimation of the Marxist paradigm. The fall of the Berlin Wall and the implosion of communist regimes discredited more than their politics; it disclosed the prior collapse of an ideology, a set of ideas which claimed to be scientific in character. Marxism was mistakenly presented as the science of society *par excellence*; equally mistaken was the tendency after 1989 to treat Marxism as unworthy of discussion at all. By some absurd exaggeration, people using terms such as 'social classes', present in the work of conservative historians like Guizot well before Marx, have been classified as complicit in communist crimes and survivors of a vanished dark age. There has been a de-materialization of historical study, a turn towards ideas and representations as independent of material conditions. To escape from the naïve view that the superstructure reflects the substructure, many historians have ignored the substructure entirely. We see here a new kind of historical idealism. The collapse of Marxism has had an indirect effect as well on the study of economic history. This trend is evident in the overall decline of economic history and in the way in which scholars now disregard quantitative evidence, and have turned their backs on serial perspectives to consider the history of enterprises or corporations.

In Europe the crisis of the Marxist paradigm was one of the main reasons for the shift from social to cultural history. In the United States, where Marxism was much less influential, scholars expressed their interest in cultural facets much earlier. The seminal work of Paul Fussell (1975) *The Great War and modern memory*, inspired an entire generation of scholars interested in literary and cultural questions. In Britain, the military historian John Keegan's *The face of battle* (1976) helped reorient military history in such a way as to make central the question of the soldier's behaviour in battle, which is evidently an anthropological perspective.

With the decline of the Marxist paradigm, what changed is more than an approach to causality; it is an approach to history itself. Historians no longer try to provide global explanations for historical events or to study an entire society in all its dimensions. Through micro-history or what the Germans term the history of everyday life (*Alltagsgeschichte*), historians approach particular issues worthy of study in themselves. This is the point of origin of the renewed interest in the memoirs of individual witnesses, but for very different reasons than informed the work of Norton Cru. What makes sense today is not their objectivity, but precisely their subjectivity, and the question of how representative are they is now deemed meaningless.

In this third historiographical configuration, memory and identity are inseparable. Is this not the reversal of the materialist assumptions of the second generation, for which identities emerged out of social conditions? Is it a consequence of the overwhelming changes in technological and material life, which have destabilized prior conceptions of identity? At the end of the twentieth century, there was a powerful memory boom, one which created a sense of duty to remember the collective past. What is at stake is not only to remember what happened in the Holocaust, though that is of major importance, but also to find the elements of social stability in a widespread search for origins. Only those who have roots or foundations can be sure of their existence. For social agents, institutions, corporations, communities, commemoration is a way to affirm their importance and to perform their collective existence. Social identities are legitimized through commemoration. Here is one of the major characteristics of contemporary cultural life: identity is value.

This evolution has led the public to consider the Great War as part of their patrimony. As the survivors died out, there was a risk that the war would be forgotten. The business of remembrance ensured that that would not happen. Through constructing museums, exhibitions, and memorials – it is still the case that Great War battlefield memorials are being constructed in the twenty-first century – and through educational initiatives, the Great War remains very much alive. It is also present in family memory, and in the interest of families in reading about the war, in seeing its history told on television and in film, and in visiting museums and battlefield sites.

The domain of culture and the cultural paradigm

In this third historiographical configuration, in which culture occupies a central place, it is neither unified, nor unique. The widespread interest in patrimony as identity has coincided with the rediscovery of sites and objects which have considerably enlarged the repertoire of historical documents.

This enlargement began with the use of newsreels as documentary sources, for example in the work of Ferro in his film of 1964. Jay Winter and Baggett followed his lead and put alongside documentary films many other sources (1996). Many objects previously considered as mere curiosities or unimportant souvenirs became the subject of historical research. Historians studied photographs, postcards (Huss, 2000)[29], monuments, graffiti, church plaques (A. Becker, 1994), toys (Audoin-Rouzeau, 1993). George Mosse devoted a chapter of his book on the Great War to the subject of the 'trivialization of war'. His interpretation rested on his survey of domestic objects of all kinds, imprinted with images or messages about the war, and the kit that soldiers collected or made, or that merchants sold to them and to civilians alike.

The opening of the Historial de la grande guerre at Péronne marks this evolution in two respects. First, the museum reinforces the trend towards according a new importance to objects, the organization of which in space creates its own narrative (Audoin-Rouzeau, 1995a). The inauguration of the museum, the quality of whose design was universally praised, was the occasion for the convening of the conference on 'War and cultures' organized by the historical advisors of the research centre located in the museum itself. Secondly, by bringing together German, British, and French objects, this museum made it evident that a comparative approach was both meaningful and essential. This project has given the cultural history of war in France a decisive push.

Beyond this belated discovery of objects, historical enquiry turned its attention to new domains: the arts, science, medicine, literature, and the ways in which these fields were affected by the war. However, this kind of enquiry has gone deeper still, to pose profound and fascinating questions, more psychological in character, which seek to understand how men and women not only lived, but also felt about it. Our own society of comfort, of high technology, and of relative security, has difficulty in understanding how people managed to live through such an extreme situation. To refer again to the subtitle of the work of Duroselle (1994), the war is 'incomprehensible'; indeed his point is stronger still in French. The Great War was *the* 'incomprehensible'.

The shift in frameworks of thought and analysis has completely modified our interpretations of the war of 1914–18. During the interwar period, this conflict was seen as the last war; later on it became for some the first episode of a new Thirty Years War. Now it appears as the very foundation of a short, barbaric twentieth century, and those who survey this war have in mind both the monstrous Nazi genocide against the Jews and the enormity of Stalin's crimes. Was it not the case that the war of 1914–18 was the first experiment in totalitarian war and mass death? In the interwar years, historians could not pose this question; now historians can not avoid posing it. It is impossible to provide an answer to it through the history of battles, diplomatic history, or even social history.

Hence representations, feelings, emotions of men and women became of central interest to historians. Cultural history is a history of the intimate, the most moving experiences within a national community. It is a history of signifying practices; it studies how men and women make sense of the world in which they live. Hence the importance of mourning (Jay Winter, 1995; Audoin-Rouzeau, 2001), brutalization (Mosse, 1990), violence, as studied by the Historial and the Institut d'histoire du temps présent (Audoin-Rouzeau *et al.*, 2002), and of face-to-face killing (Bourke, 1999). Our contemporaries are fascinated by these subjects. Here the work of historians crosses disciplinary boundaries, and meets that of scholars in other fields, and in particular, in literature, who at times were there before (Fussell, 1975; Hynes, 1992; Pourcher, 1994; Trévisan, 2001).

But cultural history does not only enlarge the field of enquiry. It proposes other paradigms. The first configuration of the 1920s and 1930s explained the story through the decisions of individual actors; the second, by the force of social groups or classes. The third makes culture the driving force of history. Representations inform and cause actions. John Horne and Alan Kramer (2001) for instance have shown how German atrocities during the invasion of Belgium and France in 1914 were inspired by the image of irregular fighters of the war of 1870. When Ashworth (1980) described the material and psychological conditions of trench warfare, his purpose was not to move the reader but to make soldiers' behaviour and attitudes comprehensible. It is a kind of anthropology of this kind of micro-society, which front-line soldiers constituted. In a similar vein Len Smith (1994) explains the mutinies of 1917 by analysing the relationship between commanders and the men in the ranks, who saw themselves as citizens in uniform. Perhaps the best instance is that of Jean-Louis Robert (1989) in his study of Parisian workers during the war. In the 1960s such a subject would have required a Marxist explanation, in which objective conditions of work and wages would have been the foundation of social class. In fact, Robert showed how workers' demands arose out of their ethics.

It is important not to drive this argument too far. Obviously cultural history is the pioneering sector of research on the Great War. Indeed, this book is part of it. However, cultural history is not the only kind of history today. Recently published general syntheses, mostly in a national framework, hardly broach the subject of the anthropology of the war. But it is clear that they take into account that which has been established by the second configuration and even the third configuration of writing about the war. For instance, consider Duroselle for France (1994) or Moyer (1995) for Germany or general surveys such as Strachan (2001) or de la Gorce (1991). Here war is not defined only through alliances, negotiations, and battles, but through economies, finance, food supplies, and public opinion.

It would be difficult, though interesting, to analyse to what extent and in what ways this cultural change has affected the history of specific fields. A minimalist claim would be that books of political, diplomatic, or military history would now take into account some elements of cultural history. As we have already noted, there was cultural history within social history; ideas, representations, even misunderstandings were always considered by historians. It is impossible to say if George Henri Soutou (1989) would have put less emphasis on cultural aspects in his study of economic war aims, for instance in his interpretation of Bethmann-Hollweg's September programme of 1914, if he had written his book in 1969. A maximalist claim would be to state that the change is deeper and that the framework of all history has shifted in response to this cultural turn.

In conclusion, it is clear that the notion of historical configurations does not mean that one kind of history dominates all others. It is a question of emphasis. First, the emphasis was put on military and diplomatic history, then on social history, and later on cultural history. But all these types of history are present in each configuration. Their respective place and their weight change, as does their role in the overall interpretations offered.

Here is the reason why we have organized our book by sector or subject of analysis. Successively, we will examine questions associated with particular places. In each of these chapters centred on particular issues, the three configurations are unevenly represented. In the first configuration, diplomatic history (chapter 2) or military history (chapter 3) have a larger place than in the third configuration. The history of trench warfare (chapter 4), of war economies (chapter 5), or of workers (chapter 6) is much more important within the second configuration than within the other two. The third configuration is dominated by the home front (chapter 7) or of memory (chapter 8). But in each configuration, every kind of history is present. Finally, in the last chapter we try to adopt a transversal view in order to propose a more global interpretation of our history of the history of the war.

NOTES

1. The German usage of *Weltkrieg* may even have antedated the war. Thanks are due to Hew Strachan, who drew our attention to this point.
2. The series of history books used throughout France in high schools was known as 'Malet–Isaac'. These were textbooks on different historical periods, initially written by Albert Malet, whose name was retained by Jules Isaac even after Malet's death in the war. The phrase 'Malet–Isaac' became synonymous with historical volumes produced long after the war for use in secondary schools.
3. Joseph Hüe, 'De la Bibliothèque-Musée de la Guerre à la BDIC', *Matériaux pour l'histoire de notre temps*, 49–50, Jan.–June 1998, pp. 5–6.
4. The competitive examination for graduate students who want to teach in the best French public high schools – the *lycées* – is the *Agrégation*.
5. See Christophe Charle, *Les Professeurs de la faculté des lettres de Paris, dictionnaire biographique 1909–1939*, Paris, INRP/CNRS, 1986, pp. 181–3.
6. *Revue historique*, 1935–6, p. 412. Langlois and Seignobos established a school of historical writing through the publication in 1897 of their *Introduction to historical studies*, a book widely discussed and republished even now. Their standing was similar to that of Lord Acton in Britain.
7. Bidou, 1936, p. 517: 'The spread of the contagion from rear to front is evident, first and foremost among those troops stationed close to Paris.'
8. Seignobos apparently read Bogart (1919).

9. This division is apparent in the first issue, published in 1923: Charles Appuhn, 'Le gouvernement allemand et la paix. L'offre de médiation pontificale' and Colonel E. Desbrière, 'Le rôle du corps expéditionnaire britannique dans les opérations de l'été 1914'. It continued thereafter. For the five years from 1927 to 1931, this formula was not altered.

10. He presented these lectures to the French Society of Philosophers on 28 November 1936. See below, pp. 129–30.

11. Olivier Dumoulin, *Profession historien 1919–1939, un métier en crise*, Thèse de l'EHESS, 1983; Laurent Mucchielli, 'Aux origines de la nouvelle histoire en France: l'évolution intellectuelle et la formation du champ des sciences sociales (1880–1930)', *Revue de synthèse*, 4th series, 1 (Jan.–March 1995), pp. 55–98. See also Antoine Prost, *Douze leçons sur l'histoire*, Paris, Seuil, 1996, pp. 37 ff.

12. Marc Bloch, *L'Etrange défaite*, Paris, A. Michel, 1957, p. 218.

13. This expression is that of Jules Isaac, who insisted upon the need to be 'not too proud of one's self, and to adopt a violent and permanent constraint'. See Jacques Thobie, 'Jules Isaac et les origines de la première guerre mondiale', in *Jules Isaac, actes du colloque, catalogue de l'exposition organisé par l' Université de Haute-Bretagne, 28 novembre–10 décembre 1977*, Paris, Hachette, 1979, pp. 43–51.

14. Bourget, 1932, p. 77, attributed the mutinies to pacifist or defeatist propaganda, 'in large part financed by the enemy and encouraged by the example of the Russian Revolution'.

15. Renouvin *et al.*, 1939, p. 609.

16. On Norton Cru and the genesis of *Témoins*, see Rousseau (2003).

17. On this point, see Annette Becker's and Jean-Jacques Becker's remarks, in Véronique Sales (ed.), *Les Historiens*, Paris, A. Colin, 2003, 'Pierre Renouvin', pp. 104–18.

18. *L'Histoire de la Nation française* was the major work of Gabriel Hanotaux, fifteen volumes published between 1920 and 1929 by Plon-Nourrit. *L'Histoire du peuple français*, edited by Louis-Henri Parias, was published in four volumes by la Nouvelle Librairie de France between 1951 and 1953. The fifth volume, *Cent ans d'esprit républicain*, was added in 1964. Therein the war of 1914–18 was treated by François Bédarida.

19. For example, there is a parallel movement turning the history of the French Revolution into the history of revolutionaries, with the thesis of Albert Soboul (1958), which explicitly opposes history from below with history from above. See the introduction to the abridged edition of his thesis, *Mouvement populaire et gouvernement révolutionnaire en l'an II* (1793–4), Paris, Flammarion, 1973.

20. This phrase was explicitly used by de Gaulle in a radio broadcast from London, on 18 September 1941; see his *Discours et messages, 1940–1946*, Paris, Plon, 1970, vol. I, p. 103.

21. See Daniel Todman, 'The Great War in British popular culture, 1914–2000', PhD thesis, University of Cambridge, 2001.

22. We are grateful to Marc Ferro for furnishing us with this information.

23. Annie Kriegel, Marc Ferro, and Alain Besançon, 'Histoire et cinéma: l'Expérience de "la Grande Guerre" ', *Annales ESC*, 1965, no. 2, pp. 327–36.

24. Ibid., p. 331.

25. Christian Gras, *Alfred Rosmer (1877–1964) et le mouvement révolutionnaire international*, Paris, Maspero, 1971.
26. See Renouvin's paper delivered to the 1967 conference on 1917, published as 'L'opinion publique et la guerre en 1917', *Revue d'histoire moderne et contemporaine*, 1968, pp. 4–23.
27. See his review, 'Nouvelles recherches sur la politique extérieure allemande (1914–1945), I. Les buts de guerre de l'Allemagne d'après les travaux de Fritz Fischer', *Revue historique*, 228, 1962–3, pp. 381–90.
28. Winter and Baggett, 1996, p. 11.
29. The research of Marie-Monique Huss had begun much earlier. See her contribution to Wall and Winter, 1988, pp. 329–67, 'Pronatalism and the popular ideology of the child in wartime France: the evidence of the picture postcard'.

2   Politicians and diplomats
Why war and for what aims?

The first questions to be asked about the war are who was responsible for its outbreak? Why did it occur? For what reason? What possible explanation was there for the cataclysm? However, as years passed, new questions arose. In particular, that of the belligerents' war aims came to the fore.

The quarrel over responsibility

The mobilization of national historians

Article 231 of the Versailles treaty states: 'The Allied and Associated Governments affirm and Germany accepts the responsibility of Germany and her Allies for causing all the loss and damage to which the Allied and Associated Governments and their nationals have been subjected as a consequence of the war imposed upon them by the aggression of Germany and her Allies.' Even if, taken literally, this article only defines the legal responsibility of Germany on which reparations rested, it was viewed by the winners and above all by the losers as a moral statement, one which was not diluted by any other article of the treaty. Deemed to be the aggressors, the German nation was responsible for the war. For them, this was an entirely unjust accusation; more than that, it was scandalous and completely unacceptable. They termed it 'the Versailles Diktat'.

Throughout the interwar years, the question of responsibility for the war, of the *Kriegsschuldfrage*, was of capital importance. In international affairs, German war guilt justified France's claim to reparations and a policy of firmness which led to the occupation of the Ruhr by her army in 1923. On the contrary, the thesis of shared responsibility between the Allies and the Central powers inspired more benevolent reactions towards the many complaints which the Weimar Republic voiced. Furthermore, the thesis of French and Russian responsibility for the war, advanced by some authorities in Britain and the United States, justified a degree of wariness concerning French exploitation of the question of reparations and security in order to justify her own aggressive foreign policy.

The issue of war guilt was no less important in domestic politics. In Germany, the Versailles Diktat was rapidly brushed aside by public opinion, even if it was formally accepted by the most determined advocates of Franco-German rapprochement. In France, the thesis of sole German responsibility for the war was contested by pacifists who pointed to the part played by the nationalist right led by Poincaré during the July crisis. Here was an enduring point of conflict.

Not surprisingly, in every country academic historians were mobilized to justify the positions of their government, backed by national public opinion.[1] Historical work of this kind had already begun during the war.[2] As early as 4 August 1914, the German government published a white book of documents in order to show to the German socialists and to neutral countries that Germany had entered the war for defensive purposes alone. The armistice gave such work a decisive impulse. In Germany, on 13 November 1918, Karl Kautsky, a former leader of the Independent Social Democratic party, was asked by the Provisional Government to take on the task of publishing official documents on the origins of the war. He was aided in this effort by well-known historians. However, his position was not that of the majority of the Provisional Government. He accepted the idea that the Kaiserreich was responsible for the war (Kautsky, 1919), while the new government had refused to accept article 231, and had insisted on publishing in June 1919 a note stating its rejection of it.[3] The Kautsky committee was reshuffled, and at the end of 1919 it published four volumes of documentation supporting the government's position.[4]

A much more methodical and effective means of exculpating Germany from war guilt, however, was that of the Ministry of Foreign Affairs, which created a particular office for this purpose. At the core of the diplomatic service, this office succeeded in preventing the publication of even-handed accounts, such as the report the enquiry committee created by the German National Assembly had produced.[5] In 1923, the office created a periodical, entitled 'the war guilt question' (*Kriegsschuldfrage*) in order to give its interpretation a wider audience. The key role within the office was played by a military officer, not by an historian. A. von Wegerer was the editor of this journal. He published many books reiterating his position (Wegerer, 1928), so that on the eve of the Second World War he appeared to be an authority even among historians, by publishing a massive book on the origins of the war (Wegerer, 1939). Wegerer's case is one of many examples of the blurring of the border between historians and other writers, a striking feature of the first historiographical configuration of writing on the war.

The pillar of the German attempt to justify German policy before the war on the basis of rigorous historical research was the rapid publication of the forty volumes of diplomatic documents under the title, *Die grosse Politik der Europäischen Kabinette 1871–1914*. This monumental task was overseen by the historian, von Thimme. After 1945, the opening of German archives made it possible to expose the biases in the way this series was put together, and to raise doubts about its supposed objectivity. The United Kingdom and France also published extensive collections of their diplomatic documents, but later on and at a slower pace. As for the Bolsheviks, they were delighted to accuse the Czarist government of imperialist intrigues, and they published a 'black book' of documents from the Czarist archives, exposing the imperialist promises that were made, and the planned division of the future spoils of war among the Allies after victory.

In France, the 'Library-Museum' of the war was created with somewhat different objectives. It was a research centre, the aim of which was to produce a documented, objective, and rigorous history, according to the highest standards of the historical profession. It was headed by an archivist, Camille Bloch, not a general. The head of its German department was an *agrégé* in philosophy, Charles Appuhn, who was very well informed about the diversity of German opinion (Appuhn, 1926). Pierre Renouvin was appointed as librarian in this research centre. We have already noted the role he played in the publication of French diplomatic documents as well as in supervising historical research on the war. He provided abundant evidence supporting the thesis of German responsibility in the lectures he gave in the Sorbonne in 1922 and which he published a few years later (Renouvin, 1925b). In subsequent works, he confirmed this analysis. Bloch's study (1933) was even more damning of Germany.

In contrast, the French pacifist left wing indicted the peace settlement and the supposed theory of German war guilt. A group of people with diverse political commitments had launched during the war a society for critical and documentary studies of the conflict, Société politique d'études critiques et documentaires de la guerre. After the Armistice, it continued its work and chose as its central target 'Poincaré la guerre' (Poincaré the warmonger) (Morhardt, 1924; Société politique d'études critiques et documentaires sur la guerre, 1926).[6] Some historians, like Jules Isaac, took a more even stance between the two sides. In short, the debate raged on. To show the full contours of this debate, a brief sketch of the July crisis may be useful.

The July crisis

On 28 June 1914, Archduke Franz-Ferdinand, heir to the crown of Austria–Hungary, was murdered in Sarajevo by a Serbian nationalist student. One month later, Poincaré, the president of the Republic, and Viviani, head of the cabinet, fulfilled a long-scheduled commitment to visit St Petersburg. France and Russia had been Allies since 1893. On 23 July, Austria delivered an ultimatum to the Serbian government, leaving it only two days to reply. Russia indicated she would protect the Serbs, while advising them to act cautiously. On 25 July, Serbia accepted the ultimatum with one reservation only: she refused the participation of Austrian policemen in the enquiry into the assassination. Austria considered this response a refusal; her ambassador left Belgrade and she mobilized eight army corps. Then Serbia decided to mobilize the whole of her army. A regional war seemed imminent.

To prevent it, Great Britain proposed, on 26 July, the convening of an international conference. Germany refused this offer. On 28 July, Austria declared war on Serbia. The next day, Poincaré and Viviani, who were at sea and out of reach, disembarked at Dunkirk. The Russian decision to mobilize on 30 July provoked immediate German mobilization; and Germany declared war on Russia on 1 August. France mobilized to support her ally Russia, but the United Kingdom remained uncommitted. Berlin asked her to remain neutral, and Paris asked her to act on the terms of the Entente Cordiale, agreed in 1904. From London's point of view, the key issues were respect for Belgian sovereignty and the status of the Belgian coast. On 31 July, the British government formally asked Germany and France whether they would respect Belgian neutrality, guaranteed by all the powers in 1839 and 1848. The German answer was equivocal, the French one positive. On 2 August, Germany asked Belgium for permission to pass through her territory. This request was rejected. The German army entered Belgium two days later. On 4 August, Great Britain went to war against Germany and decided to send an expeditionary force to the continent.

Different emphases produce different interpretations of who was responsible for the war. French historians point to the desire of the Austro-Hungarian Empire to settle accounts with Serbia, by a war limited to the region, a war which would prevent the Dual Monarchy's disintegration under the pressure of her many nationalities. Serbia did constitute an obstacle to Austrian influence in the Balkans, and some of her virulent nationalists threatened Austrian interests. This was the reason why Austria deliberately framed its ultimatum to Serbia in a form she had to reject, as any other sovereign nation would not have accepted the intrusion on her own national territory of policemen from a foreign and hostile country. Furthermore, Austria made it impossible to avoid war by declaring it as soon as 28 July, whereas her complicated process of mobilization would not permit military engagements before 12 August. Germany supported Austria, accepting the risk of a European war, for she knew that Russia would not let the Austrians crush the Serbs. In this regional conflict, Germany believed that the balance of forces would never be better for her than at this time. The German naval programme, developed over the previous decades, had been realized; the modernization of the Russian army, though, had not yet been achieved. Germany suggested on 28 July that Austria accept the British proposal of occupying Belgrade as a protective measure, but this conciliatory statement was a ruse, and its main objective was to prevent Britain from going to war on the French and Russian side.

The breach of Belgian neutrality – to Bethmann-Hollweg a 'scrap of paper' – was of central importance in this analysis, for it emphasized the decisive role of the German general headquarters in Germany's preparation for war. Army commanders, and therefore the Chancellor himself, were bound by their war plans. In case of a war with Russia and France, the Schlieffen plan, their only plan – they had no alternative proposal – consisted in crushing France in a few weeks before facing the numerically larger Russian army whose mobilization would take longer. A rapid victory against France could not happen without the German army passing through Belgium to destroy the French army. When the Kaiser and the Chancellor, Bethmann-Hollweg, accepted the only plan the generals had conceived, they put Germany in the wrong. Hence the conclusion: 'Only Germany and Austria' wanted the war. 'They did not envisage either discussion or compromise; they did not accept any other solution than the resort to force . . . As far as the *immediate* origins of the war are concerned, this is the fact which dominates the entire debate' (Renouvin, 1925b, p. 214).

German arguments (Wegerer, 1928 and 1939) tend to assert the complete innocence of Germany. This thesis is supported even by celebrated historians such as Delbrück (1929). The general framework of this analysis was the picture of a rapidly expanding Germany, encircled by threatening neighbours, and which was refused vital space and a legitimate part in the colonial division of the world; in this environment, her policy was simply an act of self-defence. In such an explanation, the pressure placed from the beginning of the crisis on the German government by the General Staff is of little account; on the contrary, the recommendations of prudence given by the German to the Austrian government are emphasized. This analysis stresses the responsibility of

Russia: by deciding to mobilize her army entirely, she made it inevitable that Germany mobilized as well and went to war. This school of thought did not take account of the fact that the German attack on Belgium and France was essential to the Schlieffen plan: otherwise, with a different strategic plan, Russian mobilization would not have led to such radical consequences. Finally, this analysis indicted French diplomacy for not pushing Russia to compromise; France only reaffirmed her previous commitment to support her ally. The French ambassador to St Petersburg, Maurice Paléologue, is among the main targets of this criticism, for his interventions on the side of confrontation, when Poincaré and Viviani were at sea on their way back from Russia. For Great Britain, her degree of responsibility, in these arguments, comes from government indecision at the end of July: by hesitating, Lord Grey let German officials believe that Great Britain would remain neutral. Had this been the case, there would have been an even balance of military power between the belligerents, and a chance for Britain to act as an honest broker, and to bring the crisis to an end.

French pacifists did develop arguments pointing to Allied responsibility for the war (Morhardt, 1924). From this point of view, Russia was an autocratic regime which pursued clearly imperialistic objectives. French political leaders, above all Poincaré, by renewing the Franco-Russian defensive alliance in 1912 had turned it into an offensive one. In this scenario, Poincaré is supposed to have convinced the Russian ambassador to Paris to launch a war which would give back to France her lost provinces, and which would permit Russia to control Constantinople and the straits. After the war Poincaré refuted these arguments, though without convincing the pacifists (Poincaré, 1921; Gérin and Poincaré, 1930). Their claims were not based on evidence, but fit in to their sense of a system of secret diplomacy operating outside the French political system. No one in the French Parliament knew the text of the Franco-Russian agreement; no one knew about the diplomatic correspondence on the eve of the war, nor the reasons why a peace-loving ambassador in St Petersburg was replaced. His successor, Paléologue, was accused of having reinforced Russia in her aggressive stance, at the very time when Germany tried to limit the war. Hence he made the international war inevitable, and both France and Russia could not evade bearing decisive responsibility for the outbreak of the war. An American historian, whose arguments were often used by French pacifists (Barnes, in Société politique d'études critiques et documentaires sur la guerre, 1926), went so far as to refute the argument over German violation of Belgian neutrality. He stated that had Germany not invaded Belgium, Britain and France would have done so themselves.

Isaac's analysis (1933) outlined an intermediate set of conclusions. He described different levels of responsibility, attributing to Germany and Austria the major responsibility for the war. But he thought that France and Russia had some lesser responsibility as well. He criticized Renouvin for underestimating the hardening of the Franco-Russian alliance in 1912 and the interventions of the Russian ambassador to Paris as well as those of Paléologue in St Petersburg. France did not ask the Russians to moderate their position when it would have been useful to do so. War became inevitable when the Russian general staff persuaded the Czar to order total mobilization, because a partial mobilization would have endangered Russia at the beginning of a war. In his later work, Renouvin took into account some of these criticisms, in particular about Paléologue; but he stood by his central thesis that the Central powers were primarily responsible for the war. He admitted, though, that the Allies did not do everything possible to prevent the war: France did not push Russia hard enough towards moderation; Great Britain did not state clearly and as early as possible that she would not remain neutral if Belgium were invaded. Since the 1930s, Renouvin's analysis has continued to inform French high-school textbooks in history, while in the 1920s these textbooks had treated the war in a more patriotic and chauvinistic manner.[7] This thesis that Germany bore the major responsibility for the war, although a responsibility shared in part by other powers, has been confirmed by Fischer (1961). Even after the so-called Fischer controversy, which we shall discuss below, seventy years after Renouvin examined this question, we have come full circle back to his position, published only five years after the end of the conflict. One can only admire how scholarly and cautious he was, and how well his conclusions have stood the test of time.

Historical objectivity and political compromises

It is remarkable to what degree historians were able, so soon after the war, to treat with rigorous and extensive documentation issues of profound political importance for contemporary domestic and international affairs. Hence several questions arise: what conditions made this historical achievement possible? Are all questions, however significant their contemporary echoes, open to historical analysis?

First of all, it is evident that some subjects of great controversy were not considered to be historical in character. Thus the peace settlement, which was universally discussed, was not studied as an historical phenomenon. The war had indeed happened; thus its origins were a closed subject. The peace treaty was just beginning to unfold, and how it would be put into effect was still an open question. Pacifists argued that the treaty was too harsh to Germany and claimed it was necessary to revise it. The core of the discussion concerned article 231 and reparations, which Keynes said were beyond Germany's capacity to pay. His *Economic consequences of the peace* (1919), written after he had resigned from the British delegation to the Paris conference, stated the core of this argument, which we shall consider again in chapter 5. Keynes thought French demands were exaggerated, and that it was absurd to insist on a schedule of repayment of the costs of the war over thirty years. With wit and brilliance, he told the disastrous story of the peace negotiations, and provided unforgettable portraits in vitriol of the key participants. On the other side, there were those who were alarmed by Clemenceau's acceptance of a united Germany, represented by the revolutionary government in Berlin, rather than a set of divided German states, including Bavaria. At the very least, these intransigents insisted, there had to be a buffer state between Germany and France on the Rhine. As Bainville put it, the treaty was too mild as well as too harsh (Bainville, 1920).

The question as to whether either Keynes or Bainville was right is not specifically an historical one. No one could decide between them on the basis of a critical analysis of the documents. Evidently we have entered another terrain, that of economists and politicians, many of whom published justifications of their positions, not only about what had happened but about what had to be done in the present and future. Some provided negative images of their adversaries (Tardieu, 1921; Nicolson, 1933). Thus these studies, while providing much important information, are not historical in character. They are open political essays. Even the later study of Etienne Mantoux (1946), which is historical in character, is constructed polemically to refute Keynes's thesis about a 'Carthaginian' peace. But when Mantoux wrote his book, the question of the application or revision of the treaty was outdated; it was no longer an open political question, and therefore could be a subject of historical analysis (Birdsall, 1941; Luckau, 1941).

In this first configuration of writings about the war, the question of war origins never fully escaped from political argument. Historians' conclusions were inevitably marked by their nationality; they would immediately be treated with suspicion if they were unfavourable to their own countries. In this atmosphere, American historians had something of a privileged position. No one could accuse the United States of responsibility for the war. And both early American neutrality in the conflict, and President Wilson's crusade for a 'new diplomacy' seemed to place most Americans 'above the battle'. German diplomacy saw very early the advantage to be gained by mobilizing friendly American scholars who would provide outside confirmation of their position on the war guilt question. They facilitated the work of such historians and contributed to the distribution and the translation, in particular into French, of their books (Mombauer, 2002).[8]

Three American studies of the period were immediately translated into French: Barnes (in Société politique d'études critiques et documentaires sur la guerre, 1926), later Professor at the New School, leaned towards the Central powers; Fay (1929), Professor at Harvard, favoured the thesis of shared responsibility; Schmitt (1930), Professor at the University of Chicago, placed the primary responsibility on Germany and Austria–Hungary. The French debate followed these three studies. Isaac (1933) devoted an entire book to these arguments, and concluded that if, as Renouvin stated, the Central powers had 'imposed war' on Europe, Europe was hardly reluctant to follow suit.

Thirdly, French historians made clear distinctions between those subjects on which discussion rested on documentary proof and those subjects which remained open due to the lack of full and critically assessed documentation. This distinction enabled there to be a degree of pragmatic conciliation between scholars who differed fundamentally on some points but who could agree on some others. Thus the field was open to a kind of diplomatic discussion or negotiation of historical issues. In 1935, for instance, at the initiative of the President of the German Association of high-school history teachers, a conference was convened in Paris on the teaching of history in the two countries. Among the French delegation were Renouvin, Isaac, and the general secretary of the National Union of Primary School Teachers. The objective was to find an acceptable formulation of the historical narrative for both French and German teachers.[9] The two delegations could only agree on compromise statements which each side could interpret in its own way. Consider these two: 'The available documents do not permit us to attribute in 1914 a premeditated desire for a [European] war . . . on the part of any of the governments and peoples.' 'In every country there were belligerent currents of opinion' (Isaac, 1938). Of course, the Nazis rejected these statements. The effort at reconciliation was renewed in 1951, when Renouvin met a German historian, Gerhard Ritter, whose anti-Nazi credentials were above reproach – he had even been imprisoned. They did not reach a much greater degree of agreement than had their predecessors in 1935. Differences remained, despite the appearance of the three fundamental volumes of Albertini (1942–3) – a distinguished journalist turned historian[10] – who concluded from new evidence that German responsibility was established, though Albertini had strong words to say about Poincaré.

From diplomatic history to the history of international relations

Immediate and deeper causes

All historians recognized the absurdity of reducing the question of the origins of the war to the role of several ministers, generals, and diplomats. Everyone recognized the need to place the July crisis in a context which renders it intelligible. Renouvin's work – indeed, this is its force – is structured by a dual conceptual framework: immediate causes, deeper causes, which imply our departure from the narrow world of diplomatic exchanges and negotiations in which traditional history was imprisoned (Pingaud, 1938). Renouvin launched an appeal for the study of the deeper forces at work in history,[11] through which *diplomatic* history can become the history of *international relations*. This is the source of the great originality and success of his *Histoire des relations internationales*, which, for the war, follows his earlier line of argument (Renouvin, 1955–7).

In a study published in 1934, Renouvin spent little time on the deeper causes of the war. He reviewed them rapidly in passing, evoking in order 'affective and psychological' causes, 'material causes' – the arms race – and 'economic causes'. Thereafter, the study of deeper causes has become a constant theme of discussion and debate, which takes on different forms in different places and times. In Britain, the question is whether the war was a matter of deliberate choice or whether it arose out of a series of errors and miscalculations. A. J. P. Taylor, who never ceased to dwell on the absurdity of the war, construed with no little irony the outbreak of war as a reflection of railway timetables (Taylor, 1969). The technical constraints on railway mobilization changed the way war came about. Once the wheels were set in motion, they could not be stopped; however peaceful the leadership of the country was, its army had to be ready for war on time. More flexible war plans could have avoided the war: without them, war arose out of miscalculation, a constant element in history and in contemporary life.

After a detailed analysis of the belligerents' war plans, Kennedy (1979) modified this interpretation. The plans made necessary by the increasing complexity of operations and the use of more sophisticated techniques acted as constraints, since the general staffs saw them that way. To them, as for the political elite, inflexibility was a virtue. Total war arose not from a miscalculation; compromise was ruled out from the start. The objective was absolute victory.

The discussion of war by design or war by miscalculation was bypassed by the opposition between the *causes* of the war, and its *origins*, as

Renouvin had put it. Causes, always seen as immediate causes, seem trivial when applied to such an earthquake; origins are always set in a longer and more profound temporal framework. For example, Joll (1984), in his *Origins of the First World War*, after a chapter on the July crisis, dealt with the alliance system and the military, political, economic, and colonial facets of the situation. But this framing of the question broadens into a more profound consideration of the epistemology of history, embracing determinism and contingency, as we see in the reflections of the philosopher Raymond Aron.[12] Every time an historian weighs the force of those conditions which made an event happen, he has to control the 'retrospective illusion of fatalism'. This is a contradiction which the historians of the origins of the war could not resolve, because it is not possible to resolve it. After a long discussion on the deeper causes, they always return to the irreducible character of the contingent in the process of the outbreak of the war. As Renouvin put it (1934, p. 180), not a single one of the deeper causes of the war constituted a sufficient explanation of its outbreak. In the search for a better explanation, we must turn to 'the orientation of national politics, to the action of governments, which at the end of the day, were the events that counted'. Fifty years later, Joll echoed this position (Joll, 1984, p. 205):

The question whether war was inevitable, or at least that particular war at that particular date, is not one which can be answered except in terms of individual responsibility. In spite of all the forces making for war, and in spite of all the evidence we now have about the will to war of certain sections of the European, and especially the German, ruling class, and about the domestic pressures to which they were subjected, we still feel that a war a few years later might have taken a different form and had a different result. Moreover, a study of the individual decisions of 1914 . . . shows that the consequences were not those which were expected.

What was absurd to Taylor becomes here the discrepancy, the lack of fit between anticipation and outcome. Between the calculations about the summer of 1914 and the reality of that time, a yawning gap exists:

If some of the belligerents achieved the goals for which they went to war – the French recovered Alsace-Lorraine and the British ended the German naval challenge – the price turned out to be much higher than almost anyone in 1914 had dreamed. And those countries which had more ambitious aims – the German drive for international hegemony, the Russian drive to Constantinople, the Austro-Hungarians' desperate bid to keep their decrepit empire intact – found that their ambitions turned to defeat and ruin, and those members of the governing classes who had believed that war might consolidate the state and end the fear of revolution had to face the fact that war only produced a result it was intended to prevent.

Undoubtedly politicians did not imagine in 1914 that the war they had unleashed would become the 'Great War'.

French historiography

In this second configuration, French historiography was dominated by the Marxist paradigm and the *Annales* school, which discredited the history of mere events. Hence this kind of history, which was now deprived of its political dimension, could only lose the central position it had held before 1940. It sought its revival in the search for the deeper and more frequently cited causes of the war: economic and financial causes, imperialism, the last stages of capitalism, in Lenin's phrase. Historians at work in this vein did not share the same hypotheses: some hoped to confirm the Marxist position, others wanted to refute it. But in any event, it was important to examine economic interests and alliances and to study in precise cases how they influenced the outbreak of the war.

Under the supervision of Renouvin and his successor at the Sorbonne, Duroselle, young French historians undertook research based on new archival sources. Ambassadors' dispatches had been studied again and again; to find out something new, it was necessary to explore other sources, such as the consular reports and the commercial services of the Foreign Ministry, those of big business, and in particular of banks. Many 'grand' dissertations were launched, and they came home a dozen or so years later according to the rules of the game in the French academy: Poidevin (1969) on financial relations between France and Germany; Girault (1973) on French investment in Russia; Thobie (1973) on French interests in the Ottoman empire. Others explored parallel enquiries: Miquel (1972) studied public opinion and the Versailles Treaty; Bariéty (1977) and Artaud (1978) wrote on reparations and inter-Allied debts, which played such an important role in the failure of the treaty. Some wrote about the United States from varied points of view (Nouailhat, 1977; Kaspi, 1978). Similarly there were a number of studies of economic and business history, in which war always plays a significant part.

These findings were important, but did they modify the historiography of the war of 1914–18? These authors offered subtle periodizations, they showed the differences between industrial and financial capital, and the ways in which there were national colorations in the outlook of these interests. They showed, however, the interlocking nature of national economic interests, while no one argued that these interests played a decisive role in the outbreak of the war. This does not mean that there were no economic causes of the war, but it made it impossible to claim that they were of decisive importance.

Economic and financial questions are not at the origin of the declaration of war between Germany and France. Obviously political and strategic factors played the decisive role, but economic issues contributed to the worsening of the general climate between these two states, and thereby, to facilitate their rupture. (Poidevin, 1969, p. 819)

Imperialism, in short, is not the simple political translation of economic interests.

The German controversy over the work of Fritz Fischer

This orientation of research in international relations was particular to France. It did not exist in the same way in Great Britain or the United States, where the Marxist paradigm, although present, was an insignificant social force. In Germany, there is no parallel to France; the trauma of the Second World War was of a different order. With the crushing defeat of 1945, with ruins everywhere and with staggering losses, with the division of Germany into two states, there was also the shadow of the Nazis and the horrors they had brought about. The main historical issue behind all thinking about the First or the Second World War was to understand why and how did Nazism dominate Germany. Was it an accident of history or the outcome of long-term trends? Here the old question of continuity or rupture takes on an existential dimension.

In post-Nazi Germany, the conditions of historical research were radically transformed in the west. Political constraints imposed by the Nazis on universities disappeared. To be sure, the elitism of the university Establishment continued, as in other countries, to exercise a degree of social control, but research was free. The archives were open, and the volumes of *Die grosse Politik* were no longer the major source for historians, who discovered at times that these documents had been carefully selected and bowdlerized in order to confirm official interpretations.

In the 1950s, some German historians began to explore the continuities in the German drive for world power between the First and the Second World Wars. But it was Fritz Fischer who first, in an article in 1959, and then in his book, *Griff nach der Weltmacht* (1961), radically revised the historiography of 1914. His later work and that of his students confirmed and hardened his interpretations (Geiss, 1963).

In this discussion, the question of war aims played a central role. Fischer set out to analyse the war aims of imperial Germany. The war guilt question was no longer at the centre of the enquiry, though the arguments about German responsibility in his book are extremely strong. This was at one and the same time new and scandalous to German historians, but it rested on a huge documentary base. Due to the opening of the archives,

Fischer was able to use a wide and rich range of documents to set out an interpretation of great moral power, unsurprising in a man who had trained in theology. For instance, he showed that, as early as 5 July, the German government pushed Austria to confront Serbia and to present her with an unacceptable ultimatum. But what interested Fischer above all was the political project of the German ruling elite: for what aims did they engage in a limited war and why did they accept the risk of a European war?

Such a question led to a profound revision of the historiography of the war. While in his public statements Bethmann-Hollweg took a moderate stand, in order not to alienate the Social Democrats and weaken national cohesion, actually he pursued quite an ambitious expansionist policy. This argument rests in large part on the 'Peace programme' he framed on 9 September 1914, during the Battle of the Marne. The central concept is that of *Mitteleuropa*, a customs union which would include Austria–Hungary, as well as France, Belgium, Holland, and Denmark. Germany would also extend its influence in the east through a number of buffer states, notably Poland, which would protect her from Russia. In the west, Belgium would become a vassal state, economically controlled, stripped of Liège, Verviers, and possibly Anvers, and dominated by German garrisons at strategic points. The Belgian Congo would become the centre of *Mittelafrica*. France would lose Belfort, the western side of the Vosges, the fortresses of the Hauts-de-Meuse and the iron mines of Briey-Longwy, considered indispensable for the German steel industry. In addition, Germany would take the coast from Dunkirk to Boulogne, and a sizeable indemnity sufficiently heavy to prevent rearmament for twenty years. As a whole, despite some adjustments according to circumstances, this programme corresponded to the desires of the Ruhr magnates and the Prussian Junkers. It was supported by the General Staff and informed German policy until 1918.

Fischer's book gave rise to a debate of surprising ferocity. Fischer and Geiss, along with Berghahn (1971), contradicted the dominant historiography, by interpreting the expansionism of the Third Reich as a continuation of the expansionism of the Kaiserreich. Hitler and the Nazis were no longer an exception, a parenthesis. This argument was totally unacceptable to an historian with impeccable professional and political credentials, Gerhard Ritter. His study of militarism, his masterpiece, showed how the military establishment had gained a stronghold on policy, and had transformed, through the Schlieffen plan, a defensive war against Russia into an offensive war against France, which necessarily implied the violation of Belgian neutrality. For Ritter, Bethmann-Hollweg was the very incarnation of civilian power, and of its moderation and its desire to control the military (Ritter, 1954–68). It is evident why much of the debate turns on the character of the Chancellor, and particularly on the image presented by his diaries, published posthumously with corrections, by one of his principal confidants, Kurt Reizler (Erdmann, 1972).

Perhaps the importance of Fischer's books lies elsewhere, in the inversion of systems of interpretation. From his perspective, the war is explained by the interplay of different German political and social forces on the Emperor and the Chancellor, rather than from external pressures. The primacy of foreign policy is superseded by the primacy of domestic politics. Fischer gave a new and enlarged form to a position advanced a decade earlier by Kehr,[13] who had already suggested that the aggressive diplomacy of Germany was aimed at the reduction of internal social tensions. By placing the emphasis on the social dimensions of foreign policy, Fischer was responsible in part for the shifting of questions which characterized the historical configuration of 1950 to 1980.

Shifting emphases

Outside Germany, the subject of Hitler was less all encompassing. But historians knew, as did everyone, that the peace of 1919 did not last. This intensified interest in the peace settlement more than in the origins of the war. The Cold War presented the Soviet threat as appearing at the same time as new popular democracies emerged. The risk of communist subversion in Italy and France, after their liberation in 1944–5, seemed similar to the revolutionary upheaval of 1919–20 in Europe. Elie Halévy was the only one in the interwar years to bring together the subjects of war and revolution; his influence was posthumous. These questions renewed the study of the political history of the war as well as informing its social history, more than its international history.

The studies by Arno Mayer (1959 and 1967), which were more influential in the Anglo-Saxon world than in France,[14] show this new configuration of interest in war and revolution. His focus was on the 1917–19 period, though he set it in a wider context. In every combatant country, the pre-war period was marked by an intensification of internal conflict, as evidenced by social strife and electoral contests. Some saw war as a way of overcoming these tensions. Mayer describes a reversal of the position of the economic and social forces at work. At the beginning of the war, the political and economic constraints necessary for waging it benefited the forces of order, and this was represented in every country by a kind of social truce. But the longer the war went on, it developed precisely those political forces which favoured public control of foreign policy and a peace settlement founded on liberal principles and not pure force. Diplomats and politicians discovered that it had become impossible to keep secret their war aims. They had to take account of public opinion in order to preserve the social truce necessary for a war which demanded so many sacrifices.

The rupture emerged in March–April 1917 when the question of war aims was publicly posed, both by the United States from a position of strength, and by Russia from a position of weakness. Brest-Litovsk and Wilson had a converging impact: they forced the Allies to take a principled stand on war aims. In effect, there was a confrontation between the *old diplomacy* based on national interest and the will to power as principles, and on secret exchanges as its method, as against the *new diplomacy*, openly discussed, whose principles would rest on a rejection of imperialism and on the right of all people to self-determination and the practice of democratic rule. This confrontation is the dividing line in every country between social patriots and pacifists. Foreign policy, its guiding principles and its methods have become fundamental issues at stake in domestic politics.

In the same manner as did Renouvin but from a different point of view, Mayer's work points to a pronounced enlargement of the field of diplomatic history, which in effect is a point of entry into general history itself.

The analytical framework of conventional diplomatic history simply must be enlarged to accommodate the complexities of international relations in an age of mass and crisis politics, in an age of international civil war. Furthermore, its scope must be broadened in order to show the impact of the dialectic between revolution and counter-revolution on the national and international level upon the processes of diplomacy. Thirdly, diplomatic history must abandon its national or bilateral perspective in favor of a multilateral, comparative, and transnational approach (Mayer, 1967, p. 30).

From this new perspective, the Treaty of Versailles has a new centre of gravity. Older interpretations focused on the Franco-German conflict; for Mayer, the most important element was the absence of Soviet Russia from the deliberations. It did not withdraw from Europe as did the United States; Russia was excluded, and placed in diplomatic quarantine to prevent the spread of its revolutionary 'infection'. At once the question as to whether the peace settlement was too harsh, whether a more conciliatory peace might have changed things, loses its pertinence. The two post-war periods were dominated by the struggle against Bolshevism, in the light of which the participants in the post-war settlements organized the world.

The history of international relations thus shared many of the same central concerns as did the social history of the period. But if war and revolution were braided together, if the central questions were why the war did not come earlier, and why it ended with this treaty, then the debates over war aims become of critical significance. Here the work of British historians has been of importance, in describing the contingent nature of the unfolding of the question of war aims (Stevenson, 1982; French, 1986). There was a fundamental difference between the nature of the war aims developed by the Central powers and those advanced by the Allies. This subject has been explored by David Stevenson (1982) from the perspective of domestic as well as foreign policy. The task of defining war aims was much more difficult for the Allied powers than for the Central powers. Among the Allies, no single power played the same leading role as Germany did on the other side. The very preservation of the alliance was a French war aim. In the democratic countries, the discussion was much more intricate, involving the different political parties, than it was in Germany, where the government had a much broader field in which to manoeuvre.

But these statements of purpose were also part of an elaborate world of diplomatic exchanges, to which replies had to be framed and published. In effect, 'normal' diplomatic history went on as it had done before. There were a number of independent initiatives, in particular from the Vatican, some from other sources, but none came to fruition, in part because the gap was too great between stated war aims and those which were discussed secretly within government circles.

From 1914 to 1916, the central aim of the two sides was to destroy the power of the other, but from 1917 on, not for any intrinsic reason, but because of the need to maintain the domestic political truce, and because of the political implications of the Russian revolution and the American entry into the war, war aims became everybody's business. They mattered too on account of the staggering nature of total casualties registered by 1917. Surely, the public thought, there had to be some destination, some point at which each side could claim that we are fighting the war for this and precisely this cause, and will cease fighting when it is achieved. By 1917 the public mattered much more in international relations than ever before; the re-mobilization of the second phase of the war forced governments to pose as standard-bearers of popular causes, and these were defined as war aims.

This subject has been explored thoroughly by Georges-Henri Soutou (1989) from the economic point of view. His thesis provides a fresh look at well-known documents and adds to them much new material informing an authoritative account of the economic war aims of all the belligerent powers. By doing so, he undermined Fischer's central thesis, showing that the 9 September programme is not as significant as Fischer said it was. This programme, which Niall Ferguson (1999) analyses as an angry answer to the British entry into the war, is above all for Soutou a moderate response to more extreme plans of German annexation, as we will show in chapter 5. On the other hand, Soutou increases the importance of French economic war aims in their overall thinking about the postwar settlement. As early as June 1916, France received British backing for her control over raw materials and a kind of economic hegemony in Europe.

Against this backdrop, it is hardly surprising that the victorious powers arrived at the peace conference of 1919 with very limited preparations. The historiography of Versailles has been subject to significant reinterpretation. The Keynesian critique of reparations has been contested by Feldman (1993) and by Ferguson (1999), who showed that Germany could indeed pay, despite her protestations to the contrary. For some scholars, the treaty was the least bad compromise available at that difficult time (Sharp, 1991; Stevenson, 1991; Boemeke, 1998; Macmillan, 2002). It was necessary to conclude the negotiations in a few months, since it was impossible to keep their armies in uniform. Demobilization was urgent and unavoidable. Civilians made hungry by the blockade had to be provisioned. Last but not least, the Allied governments were preoccupied by the revolutionary turmoil which they had to contain. Negotiators, constrained by their domestic troubles, could not have done any better. The contrast here is between the expectations of a radically new peace, represented by Wilson and initially supported by European public opinion, and the realities of the peace treaty, which was bound to look like the old ways in slightly new clothes.

Consider the contrast between the peace France accepted in 1871 and the peace Germany rejected in 1919. France paid a heavy indemnity, and did not contest the terms of the settlement. Forty years later, Germany refused both to admit to having been defeated and to the terms that that defeat had imposed unwillingly on her. Here is the source of a massive weakness in the peace settlement, one which lasted throughout the interwar years. Stevenson argues that had the Allies preserved a united front, they could have managed to limit the danger of such a settlement. Instead of strengthening the peace, the Allies managed in the years following the signing of the peace treaty to weaken it further. But the division of the victors enabled Germany to recover her standing as a military power, and ultimately to launch a war.

In her study of *Peacemakers*, Macmillan confirmed this revision of older interpretations of the peace settlement. It is too simple to say that the

Second World War emerged directly from the Versailles Treaty. The decisions of policy makers between 1919 and 1939 and the world economic crisis played their roles as well. The major weaknesses of the peace settlement lie elsewhere. Her emphasis, and that of Krumeich (2001) on other contradictions, provided a new interpretation of Wilson, Lloyd George, and Clemenceau in this period. It was impossible at one and the same time to construct a world order out of the French desire for security, the British commitment to her empire, and Wilson's belief in self-determination. In effect, Clemenceau obtained for France those measures which were supposed to protect her from any future form of German revision. Lloyd George's and Jan Christiaan Smuts's imperialist vision was also recognized, but the results did not correspond to their hopes. The British empire became weaker; the Allied attempt to destroy the Bolshevik revolution failed, even though a free Poland resisted a Soviet invasion in 1920. Wilson suffered a double defeat, first a domestic one, in his failure to get the Treaty of Paris ratified, and secondly, through the concessions he gave to Lloyd George and Clemenceau, as well as his own reservations about the nature of self-determination for the non-white world. By refusing to include in the treaty the principle of racial equality, these peacemakers set in motion developments which transformed the face of the entire world, and in particular that of Asia. The 4 May movement in China, out of which the Chinese Communist party emerged, as well as Japanese expansionist imperialism, were responses to the manner in which the Americans and the European powers treated them at Versailles. Turmoil in Egypt and in India was a direct result of the 'betrayal' of Wilsonian principles in the peace treaty of 1919. After a reading of Macmillan, it is possible to suggest that in Versailles were the seeds of the Pacific War of 1941–5 as much as the European war of 1939–45.

Unspoken assumptions

Cultural history provided a new impulse for the study of the origins of the war. In his inaugural lecture at the London School of Economics in 1968, James Joll suggested the utility of an understanding of public opinion and collective mentalities for international history. In his *1914. The unspoken assumptions* (1968) he called for a reconstruction of the ideas and the preconceptions of political figures as well as ordinary people, or in the words of Lucien Febvre, to understand their mental furniture. His conclusion was 'It is only by studying the minds of men that we shall understand the causes of anything' (p. 24). Fifteen years later, at the end of his *Origins of the First World War* (Joll, 1984, p. 205), he wrote 'In order to understand the men of 1914, we must understand the values of 1914, and it is against these values that their actions must be measured.'

In some ways, Joll's programme has been realized, notably by Düllfer and Holl (1986). It is interesting to see that this enquiry into national opinion has been the work of historians from different nations. Historians of one nation have explored the *mentalité* of the enemy. Gerd Krumeich (1981) dealt with the debates on the French Three Years' Law in a German thesis published not in French but in English. He showed that the French government promoted a campaign of fear in order to secure the passage of the law. Their argument was that France would be inundated by the newly reformed German army, capable of a surprise attack before the French could mobilize their reserves. Just after the passage of the law, the government's majority was threatened by the results of the election of 1914. In July 1914 Poincaré could have thought that time was not on his side or that of the national interest and that in a few months' time the French army would be weaker and the Russian ally less steadfast. The image of a profoundly pacifist France needs some modification, but the core of it rests intact nonetheless.

The first occasion for a comparative analysis of collective mentalities on the eve of the war was a conference held at Rouen in 1979. There Poidevin supplemented Krumeich's argument by showing that there had been an increasing fear of Germany in French public opinion after Agadir, due to the strength of French subsidiaries of German companies selling France material produced in Germany.[15] In Britain, there was little concern for a land war, and the defence of the realm was confidently placed in the hands of the Royal Navy. It was at this moment that Norman Angell advocated a new kind of pacifism, derived not from moral views but from material calculations. War is a mistake, because it does not pay. It was not only that war had become more and more expensive but because victory would not bring the victors the benefits they had foreseen. In Germany, Wolfgang Mommsen noted the force of opinion favourable to war, which the government both stimulated and then claimed that it was incapable of resisting.

An imperialist enthusiasm favourable to the use of force, presented as a necessary, even a positive element in the life of a people, began to develop. On the other hand, and as a kind of reaction, there was also a sense of fatalistic resignation with respect to a world war which would develop sooner or later. This idea of an inevitable war . . . had its own dynamic and soon became . . . a kind of fatalistic expectation of war.[16]

Actually, many elements of German opinion inclined towards war. In his course on politics, published posthumously in 1911, Heinrich von

Treitschke presented war as part of a God-given order and the normal means of politics. Friedrich von Bernhardi's views were widely celebrated in 1912, though the great liberal newspapers and the Social Democratic party criticized him for saying that war was inevitable, desirable, and legitimate.

> Force is the great legislator, and the great trial will be judged by war which is the measure of force, and which always makes the biologically correct judgment . . . Without war, one would see depraved [*verkommen*] races of inferior value [*minderwertig*] overwhelming all too easily the sane elements which are the bearers of the germ of the future; a general decadence would result.[17]

Here is a test which all peoples must pass. Mommsen (1990 and 1995) analysed this nationalism which invaded German public opinion, and in particular that of the lower middle classes and the bourgeoisie. These people wanted a firm hand in politics, because they were persuaded that the Great Powers would not take into account German interests except if they believed that she was ready and willing to go to war. Other German scholars worked on similar themes, such as Klaus Vondung (1980).

Thomas Lindemann (2001) followed the path opened by Joll in 1968 in the London School of Economics. He analysed the role of *Volkische* Darwinian ideas in the outbreak of war of 1914, and traced them back to their intellectual elements and their appeal. He went further, in posing the question as to how a political situation is perceived in the terms set by an ideology and its preconceptions. From his point of view, social Darwinism not only created a climate favourable to war, but it was responsible for errors replete with serious consequences. As many Germans and their leaders thought that a state composed of many races was necessarily fragile, they underestimated the capacity of Austria–Hungary to resist the tensions it faced. Edouard Benès or Tomas Masaryk counted on reforms rather than on the implosion of the double monarchy. The idea of radical racial antagonism between Germans and Slavs convinced Germans that Slavic Russia would necessarily attack Germany and that southern Slavs necessarily would join Russia in ethnic solidarity, despite many indications of their desire for autonomy. Williamson's research has confirmed this interpretation, in showing that in the case of Austria–Hungary the distinction between domestic and foreign policy is meaningless, and how no one in 1914 seriously envisaged a breakdown of the Dual Monarchy (Williamson, 1991).

Christophe Charle (2001, pp. 235ff.) placed this set of representations in its political and social context and showed how what he termed the 'class ethos' (or what others call 'culture') made it impossible for there to be real negotiations between French diplomats, who came through the Republican meritocracy into the upper class, and the diplomats drawn from the aristocratic ruling class of Germany:

French leaders, as much as German leaders, did not want nor could they play the same game as that of their adversaries, because it required that they adopt their world view. One could possibly offer some concessions, but from the French point of view, one could not accept the Germans' superior arrogance, nor from the German point of view, the French egalitarian practice of haggling. From both sides, these attitudes are rooted in two political cultures, two ethos of class, and still deeper, in two opposing social dynamics (pp. 240–1).

France's proposals were not interpreted as being the product of a demo-cratic and rather pacific society, which German diplomats held in con-tempt. They were mere duplicity. The image each had of the other pre-cluded the acceptance of the overtures each side proposed.

In a certain sense, this narrative follows a well-established path. For many years historians have accepted the need to understand the political decisions men take by reference to their ideas and their beliefs. But what is new is in fact two-fold. First there is the linkage between the mentalities and cultures and the supposedly rational world of policy making. These mediations are long, complex, indirect, and they involve not only intelli-gence but emotions and moral assumptions. Secondly, there is a filtering of reality which distorts the perception of a situation at the very moment when people in charge believe they are analysing it objectively.

David French (1986 and 1995) had shown how strategic choices at the end of 1914 had been the result of British perceptions of the way an unanticipated stalemate had emerged on the Western Front. Since the price of breaking that stalemate was so high, Churchill and others thought up a new alternative strategy, centred on the Ottoman empire and the Middle East. In addition, preconceptions fatally flawed British plans, since they were based on a view of the decadence of the Orient, and could not imagine that the Turks would defeat them. This 'Orientalism' cost the lives of tens of thousands of Allied servicemen, who died in the trenches of Gallipoli.

Brock Millmann (2001) provided an example of this kind of analy-sis which goes beyond diplomatic history, through his examination of the role pessimism played in the development of attitudes within British opinion and leadership in the aftermath of the Battle of the Somme. Almost everyone, except Haig, was pessimistic, and the war went on because to make peace while German forces were still on French soil was

to admit defeat. Final victory was more complete than they had anticipated. After the Somme, what he terms the 'defeatists' thought that the
war had been lost, and that the losses of life were so staggering that the
difference between victory and defeat was merely a matter of degree,
and not kind.

At the end of this survey, it is striking to see to what degree historians'
views have changed as the social and historical context of their writing
evolved. In the aftermath of the war, what appeared to be a crime was
something done by men who had to be identified and punished. The
First World War was the first war to be configured as a crime, rather
than built into the nature of things. This criminalization of war was,
from the cultural point of view, astonishing and unprecedented, since
it made war to a degree illegitimate. This normative statement, which
itself was full of contradictions related to the imperialist attitudes of the
winners and their willingness to countenance military intervention in
Soviet Russia, faded rapidly in the interwar years. Over time, the notion
of war guilt, while still present, became less acute. All states, all governments, all peoples shared, to different degrees, some responsibility for
the catastrophe which they had been unable to foresee or to prevent.
Even worse, the Treaty of Versailles was unable to prevent its recurrence.
What had been deemed a crime had become a collective error, the elements of which had to be disentangled in order to comprehend how it had
come about.

Today, war is imagined in the shadow of the Holocaust and the Gulag.
What links them is the acceptance of mass death, so characteristic of the
twentieth century (Mosse, 1990). War was indeed the seminal catastrophe
of that century. As a result, those who presided over the first act of this
collective catastrophe of the twentieth century appeared to be puppets
blown about by the events they had set in motion. Here is a story different
in kind from that of Hitler and Stalin, who murdered millions knowingly
and without the slightest intention of doing otherwise. The Holocaust and
Stalin's mass murder were not tragedies, in the classic sense of the term,
but rather crimes against humanity. The leaders of 1914–18, in contrast,
managed to achieve precisely the opposite of what they had intended.
They made choices for war in July 1914, but how free were their hands
and minds? And once the war was set in motion, no one could stop it,
however much individual leaders wanted to wish away their fate and that
of the people whose hopes of a peaceful life they by and large betrayed.
Cultural history here takes on the form of a meditation on destiny. Given
what the men of this time were, what they thought and what they believed,

they could not have done otherwise. In this historiographical context, we face once again the interminable dialogue between liberty and necessity in human affairs.

NOTES

1. Camille Bloch and Pierre Renouvin, 'L'article 231 du traité de Versailles, sa genèse et sa signification', *Revue d'histoire de la guerre mondiale*, 1–1932, pp. 1–24.

2. Droz (1973) and Mombauer (2002) have analysed how the historical debate on the war guilt question evolved from 1914 to the Fischer controversy and beyond. Their books are both historiographical accounts of this particular issue. Interestingly, the first initiatives towards an historiography of the Great War both chose this issue as their starting point.

3. It was signed by the historians H. von Delbrück and A. Mendelssohn-Bartholdy, the sociologist Max Weber, and Count Montgelas, a retired general, and probably written by a senior civil servant in the Ministry of Foreign Affairs, in charge of the diplomacy surrounding the *Kriegsschuldfrage*, von Bülow.

4. *Die Deutschen Dokumente zum Kriegsausbruch 1914*, Berlin, Deutsche Verlagsgesellschaft für Politik und Geschichte, 4 vols.

5. It was only published in 1967.

6. Most pacifists were unfettered by such diplomatic manoeuvres. Morhardt, though, did receive German subsidies; on this point, see Gerd Krumeich, '80 ans de recherche allemande sur la guerre de 14–18', in Maurin and Jauffret, 2002, pp. 25–37, esp. p. 26.

7. Hubert Tison, 'La mémoire de la guerre 14–18 dans les manuels scolaires français d'histoire (1920–1990)', in Becker *et al.*, 1994, pp. 294–312.

8. Mombauer (2002); Holger Herwig, 'Clio deceived: patriotic self-censorship in Germany after the Great War', in Wilson, 1996, pp. 87–127. See the version of this paper in Jay Winter, Mary Habeck, and Geoffrey Parker (eds.), *The Great War and the twentieth century*, New Haven, Yale University Press, 1999.

9. The pacifism of these teachers made them very attentive to the nationalism in textbooks, a point which helps to account for the publication of this encounter in *L'Ecole libératrice* on 15 May 1937. See the annex to Isaac (1938), for the reports of Renouvin, Isaac, and Mantoux on this meeting.

10. Albertini was editor of the *Corriera della sera*, and died before these volumes appeared. See his posthumously published *Venti Anni Di Vita Politica*, Bologna, Zanichelli, 1950.

11. The notion of deep causes came from Henri Berr in an article in the *Revue de synthèse historique* (Aug.–Dec. 1921), cited by Annette and Jean-Jacques Becker, in Sales (ed.), *Les historiens*.

12. Raymond Aron, *Introduction à la philosophie de l'histoire, essai sur les limites de l'objectivité historique*, Paris, Gallimard, 1938.

13. Kehr, 1965, which is a collection of his earlier articles.

14. André Kaspi reviewed these two works together at a much later date in *Revue historique*, 1974, 2, pp. 517–18.

15. Raymond Poidevin, 'La peur de la concurrence allemande en France avant 1914', in *1914: les psychoses de guerre?*, 1985, pp. 77–84.

16. Wolfgang Mommsen, 'Le thème de la guerre inévitable en Allemagne dans la décennie précédant 1914', in *ibid.*, pp. 95–123.

17. Friedrich von Bernhardi, *Deutschland und der nächste Krieg (1912)*, cited by Karl Ferdinand Werner, 'L'attitude devant la guerre dans l'Allemagne de 1900', in Poidevin, *1914*, p. 25.

3   Generals and ministers
Who commanded and how?

Introduction

The vision of the battlefield we have formed over the past century is in large part a legacy of the reflections of those who directed the war. Both in general headquarters and in ministries of state, command decisions were taken, primarily on three levels: on grand strategy, on the unfolding of particular military and naval campaigns, and on logistical problems, covering both manpower and material. The balance between civilian and military authority in these decisive areas of the waging of war was unstable. And this shifting political terrain is one on which the major actors had much to say in the interwar period. Blaming the other side was an unavoidable part of the unfolding military history of the war. Since generals and politicians were responsible for the way the war was waged, the subject of leadership and command in the historiography of the Great War must be treated as requiring comment on both the military history of the war per se and the structure of civil–military relations during the conflict.

We can distinguish three periods of historical debate in this field. First, between the two world wars, there was a 'heroic' period, during which battle was conceived generally in nineteenth-century terms. Then, in the 1960s and 1970s, there was increased interest in questions of command under the pressures of industrialized war. Finally, in the 1980s and 1990s, there ensued a third period, one in which there was much greater division of opinion and contested interpretations. In these years there emerged especially in Britain the notion of the 'learning curve', describing the hypothesis that Allied command slowly but surely learned to master this new battlefield of industrialized warfare, to the point that they were able to achieve the victory of 1918. Defeats and failed offensives there were, to be sure, but, both on the level of high command and further down the chain of command, the Allies finally learned how to break the stalemate and thereby win the war. In this third period, national differences in the writing of military history are palpable. The term the 'learning curve' was a British invention hardly evident in French or German writing on the subject of command in wartime. The vehemence of the debate in this field is also a characteristic of British historiography, in which the issue of command has been central to more general questioning of the futility of the war itself.

The first phase: heroic histories

Victories and defeats

The first period, which covers the interwar years, is essentially a history of campaigns and battles. The volume of publications on the military history of the Great War began during the war itself and took on some of the characteristics of a deluge in the early 1920s. In this first period, much of this work concentrated on the history of particular battles; the larger the scale of the battle, the greater the volume of historical commentary on it. These works were overwhelmingly of two kinds: heroic histories of how victory was achieved; and operational and strategic histories as to how staff officers had conducted operations. It was history in the grand style, written with a sense of the epic dimensions of the events described. Much of it was also official history, written with a didactic purpose, for the enlightenment of future staff officers. Its capacity for dispassionate criticism of the main players in this story was, therefore, limited.

This *parti-pris* character of historical writing in the interwar years extended clearly to the sphere of civil–military relations. The memoirs of the central political figures all addressed the question of the responsibility they bore for the unfolding history of battle during the conflict. A characteristic example of this stance is that of the French Minister of War, Paul Painlevé, and his book *Comment j'ai nommé Foch et Pétain* (1923). Not surprisingly, in virtually every case, the blame for shortcomings or errors lay elsewhere than in the pages or performance of the author in question. This highly personalized history of the military effort of each combatant country produced much of a polemical nature. Most of these books were based on the author's memories or on his access to papers not in the public domain. Despite some notable exceptions, in this period we remain largely on the level of military history as the domain of great men in uniform or in 'frock coat' – the dress of cabinet ministers – deploying millions of soldiers on a giant chess board; the outcome was checkmate Germany in November 1918.

A second dimension of historical reflection on the battlefield of the Great War was more nuanced, though it still reflected a top-down approach. It was the tendency to use history to prepare for the next round. Analysing the reasons for victory or defeat had both operational and political consequences, of which authors and readers were well aware at the time.

Within this first configuration, one element is particularly evident. It is the tendency of writers who are not professional historians or soldiers to flood the marketplace with books on Great War battles. If anything proves that academics are at best partners in the ongoing public conversation on the meaning of the Great War, it is a brief glance at the range of books which appeared from the Armistice of 1918 onwards about military matters. This 'white noise' of scholarship included much of little value, but it did describe a reading public with a seemingly unquenchable thirst for books about the war. And that meant initially and primarily books about battle.

The fact that these works were written for targeted populations, and in particular for different national populations, is evident throughout this book. Battlefield history in its first phase is the history of great men leading national armies in decisive encounters, whose names became household words – the Marne, Verdun, the Somme, Tannenberg, Gallipoli. This is epic history on a grand scale.

The treatment of the Battle of the Somme by Gabriel Hanotaux is exemplary. The families reading his work were French and therefore had no particular interest in the British side of the battle, which is treated as a minor facet of French operations (Hanotaux, 1920, p. 370). In precisely the same way, the British battlefield handbooks of the period virtually ignored the French participation in the engagement. It is as if the Allied forces operating north and south of the river Somme were occupying different universes.

The war and national identity

Here we encounter one of the most striking features of the first phase of the military history of the war – its essentially national character. The story of the diplomacy of war-making and peacemaking was intrinsically international. The history of war production and of the vicissitudes of civilian life raised issues of a very similar kind in all combatant countries. But military history was the stuff of national character, and therefore not amenable to trans-national or comparative treatment.

The dozens of official histories of military operations, written by and for the high commands of all major combatants all suffered from this form of national or imperial myopia. Essentially, all official histories – like most military commanders during the war itself – underestimated the force and tenacity of the other side. The subject of these works was the orchestration of the nation in uniform. Command was measured by victory alone, understood as the successful mobilization and deployment of the human and material resources of the nation. The other side of the equation – the relative capacity of the enemy to exercise military power – was never treated with the same care as the examination of the national story. This form of national military history may have arisen from the scarcity of sources available about the enemy's war effort, but whatever its origins it produced a series of national histories which glorified the side for which it was written and denigrated the other.

Hanotaux's 1923 history of the Battle of the Marne is a case in point. Why did the Germans fail in their objective? 'This war', he wrote, 'appeared as an error and the chastisement of a people without will who, in the name of a false discipline and in step with the exclusively materialist character of its politics and its organization, was abandoned to the hands of bureaucrats, pedants and dueling instructors [*traineurs de sabre*]' (Hanotaux, 1915–23, II, p. 409). Why did the French win the battle? Because France was a very different country, with a different approach to war. The history of battle here is the lens through which readers are invited to examine the national character of their own country.

One historian whose work exemplified this approach to military history was the Australian official historian, Charles Bean. Bean had accompanied the Australian Expeditionary Force in its landing at Gallipoli and throughout the doomed campaign in Turkey in 1915. He was the general editor of the Australian official history of the war and author of the key synthetic works about what were termed the 'Anzacs at war'. His military history is the chronicle of the birth of his nation (C. E. W. Bean, 1934). Here he helped account for the fact that a complete defeat was the scene of noble sacrifice, worthy of an independent nation. Once more, the role of British troops, or French troops, or the Turkish enemy, formed the backdrop to what was essentially a national foundation myth.

A different set of constraints operated when military history was set the task of explaining German defeat. In October 1919, the military history section of the German army was transferred to the new *Reichsarchiv* in Potsdam. The assignment faced by these 100 now-retired army officers was to write the official history of the German army in the Great War. The national archive was part of the Ministry of the Interior, which appointed an advisory board of soldiers, historians, and politicians to help oversee the task. But the old guard in the military history section of the National Archive were determined to keep the amateurs out. And in that task they succeeded. They decided to deal with the 'strictly military' facets of the war, and to exclude its social and political history entirely. Consequently, the series of volumes they produced were both dull and unbalanced. Out of twelve volumes, six dealt with 1914; two, with 1918. How the seeds of defeat were to be discovered in this manner is a mystery (Pöhlmann, 2002).[1]

There was a more sinister side to this 'tilt' in the history of the war, one which crudely contradicted the myopia of the military historians in the *Reichsarchiv* responsible for these volumes. It is the inclusion of reflections on the 'stab-in-the-back legend' in the last volume of the series. If the army was betrayed by radicals and Jews in the home population, and thus had victory snatched from its hands, then the military history of the war could not be written without scrutiny of its civilian and domestic determinants. Such logic escaped these authors, and the large reading public which was thereby fed toxic accounts of the end of the war of great use to the enemies of the Weimar Republic (Bessel, 1993).

These historians were merely following the lead of the former high command of the Kaiserreich. On 19 November 1919, Field Marshal von Hindenburg was asked to testify to the Reichstag about unrestricted submarine warfare. Instead he read a prepared statement affirming that the German army had been stabbed in the back by the home front. He repeated this calumny a year later in his memoirs. When German military historians followed suit, they were honouring their old leader, and preparing the way for his ultimate political act – the handing over of power to another Great War veteran, Adolf Hitler. Here the dangers of the heroic element in military history took on lethal dimensions, for what were the historians who conveyed the 'stab-in-the-back legend' as history doing, if not returning with Hindenburg to the Nibelungen saga? 'Like Siegfried', Hindenburg wrote, 'stricken down by the savage spear of treacherous Hagen, our weary front collapsed' (Hindenburg, 1920, p. 403).

There are several notable exceptions to this kind of political conservatism in the writing of military history in the interwar years. Cruttwell's survey of the military history of the war is judicious (Cruttwell, 1934), as indeed are parts of the multi-volume histories constructed after the war for the instruction of later generations of soldiers in different armies. The British series provided much interesting and insightful discussion of tactical and logistical questions, and it extended to a parallel official history of the navy. The French series, in contrast, is a mere compilation of documents without any general overview at all, even of a single battle. As Cyril Falls put it in his survey of war books, the French official military histories constitute in sum 'one of the most inhuman documents that one can imagine' (Falls, 1930, p. 146).

Much more interesting than official histories and more controversial than Cruttwell is the work of Basil Liddell Hart (1930 and 1934). A wounded and decorated veteran, fiercely independent of both the military and the university establishment, Liddell Hart provided a number of acute critiques of British command as a whole, and mobilized these opinions to spread his doctrine of mechanized warfare, dominated by rapid breakthroughs, a war of movement of the kind Guderian waged in 1940. With Liddell Hart's work, we begin the phase in which the careers of Douglas Haig and Lord Jellicoe were subjected to intense and continuous interrogation. That period is with us still.

The second phase: the history of command

The evolution of the debate

The second period, that of the 1960s and 1970s, was marked by a more vigorous contestation of command than the first period. In the 1960s, the history of battle took on a different character. The epic dimension was still there, but by this time archival records enabled historians to contradict heroic history and to replace it by a grayer, more nuanced, more heterogeneous portrayal of command. Controversy still surrounded the history of command, but whether in the portrayal of Philippe Pétain, or Douglas Haig, or Erich Ludendorff, the story of their military performance was embedded in a much broader and more sophisticated technical framework than was available to the historians of the 1920s and 1930s. Participants' history, in the first phase of writing about the military history of the Great War, gave way to professionals' history. The huge expansion of the documentation available on civil–military relations also brought out much that had been veiled about the bitter struggles over control of the waging of war that took place throughout the conflict. The political history of legislative and executive participation in major command decisions laid the groundwork for later reinterpretations of the military history of the Great War.

In this second phase, the range of documentation available was broadened considerably by the advent of military history on television. This kind of evidence expanded exponentially the audience drawn to military history, which had been considerable before. But the emergence of televised history brought the history of battle and of command onto a new level. The sheer chaos and superhuman scale of battle became obvious when viewers could see a landscape no single mind or leader could fully control.

These forms of official history as apologia were ripe for academic revision after the Second World War. But it took several decades more for a different kind of military history to emerge. The breakthrough of the

1960s and 1970s was achieved by historians who were not participants in the conflict and who were able to deploy archives in such a way as to turn national legends into documented historical narratives. Battle was no longer a test of character, but of staggeringly complex organizations and the inevitably limited vision of the men who led them. Again, the national perspective predominated, but it did so in a way which enabled historians to evaluate command in the Great War as an unprecedented and virtually impossible challenge, to the military and political elite alike.

Biographical history

The resulting scholarship enlarged our understanding of high command in several important ways. First Guy Pedroncini's studies of high command and in particular of Pétain's generalship (1971 and 1974) showed the significance of caution and patience in the deployment of men in the field. The *élan vital* so highly praised in the first generation of writing about French battlefield history was complemented now by an admiration for judicious delay and a defensive posture, especially after the disastrous Nivelle offensive of 1917. Pedronicini's account of Pétain's handling of the mutinies of the spring of 1917 is consistent with this more subtly etched portrait of his period in command.

Similarly John Terraine published a series of works defending the reputation of Field Marshal Sir Douglas Haig on the grounds of his professionalism and sangfroid (Terraine, 1963). Corelli Barnett provided vivid accounts of many First World War commanders in his pathbreaking *Swordbearers* (1963), a work which did not hesitate to point out the limitations of the men entrusted with command. These two important studies were based largely on published memoirs and accounts of the war. Their work therefore pointed back to the first configuration, but came one year before the ending of the fifty-year rule restricting access to the official archives. Barnett by and large shared Terraine's point of view: military history is best written in large biographies. It is the history of great men and lesser men thrust into a tempest they could not control. Barnett retraced the history of the Great War through the personalities of four commanders in chief: Moltke, Pétain, Jellicoe, and Ludendorff. Moltke and Ludendorff were gamblers, who gambled everything and lost everything. This is how Barnett described the resignation of Ludendorff: 'At this point, the war ended just as it had begun, by the disintegration of the personality of the man who in effect was the commander in chief of the German army' (Barnett, 1963, p. 374).

Admiral Jellicoe, the man who failed to destroy the German high seas fleet at Jutland was 'a sailor with a flawed cutlass', flawed because of the decadence of British society, so mired in the culture of gentility. Only Pétain got it right. He saw that no single offensive would win the war, but that victory would come to those who were able to wait and who then could apply overwhelming force on a wide front. In comparison to Pétain, Nivelle was a fool, and a criminal fool at that. Here is Barnett's dismissive reference to the circumstances which led to the Chemin des Dames offensive. The failure of British sea power at Jutland left no other course than to persist in the war on the Western Front. Nivelle, a man of charm and verve, convinced the politicians that he could win. They both were disastrously mistaken. Barnett concluded: 'in despair men turn to quacks who promise them their dreams' (Barnett, 1963, p. 218).

This profoundly individualistic form of writing military history had many attractions. Sensitive to the larger and political context, Barnett turned military history into a branch of biography, and he personalized the history of the war to such an extent that we totally lose sight of the structural reasons for victory and defeat.

The weakness of this strictly biographical approach to the history of military operations was thoroughly exposed by the British historian Norman Stone, the scholar who opened up the military history of the Eastern Front. Stone argued that the defeat of the Russian army had structural rather than ideological causes, and that the weaknesses of command were minor matters compared to the incapacity of the country to survive the pressures of modernization needed to wage total war (Stone, 1975, pp. 299–301). His analysis of the Brusilov offensive of 1916 starts out in the way Barnett's history did. It is a history of high command. But Stone shows that, from 1916 on, the fault lines deepened in the structure and in the logistics of the Russian army. Stone's expertise in the economic history of the war – what Barnett termed 'the audit of war' – is what separates his work from that of other scholars in this field. The Russians produced adequate supplies of munitions, but their transportation system could not deliver what the army needed. Here is the central point: it is primarily distribution and not production which determines the material strength of armies. The Russian army progressively could not mobilize even minimal levels of supply. Precisely because it had to modernize at great speed to wage an industrial war, the Russian economy collapsed while doing so (Stone, 1975). The beneficiaries of this disaster were the Bolsheviks, who, to paraphrase Lenin, seized power the way one plucks a ripe fruit from a tree. The history of great men can rarely reach this level of explanation. Stone showed effectively how command was a prisoner of the war machine it attempted without success to deploy.

Political leadership and military strategy

Precisely the same set of constraints operated on the level of political responsibility for the way the war was waged. None of the major political leaders of the war – Asquith, Lloyd George, Wilson, Poincaré, Clemenceau, Bethmann-Hollweg, among others – had direct military experience, though they were all well aware of the direct responsibility they bore for the outcome of military campaigns launched with their approval, tacit or explicit. The hesitation of successive Ministers of War, Lyautey and Painlevé, faced with Nivelle's strategic plan, is a case in point. As late as 6 April 1917 Painlevé called Nivelle to a meeting in Compiègne, chaired by President Poincaré, to take the final decision on whether or not to launch the offensive on the Chemin des Dames. Despite open criticism from Nivelle's own commanders, who like Pétain doubted the feasibility of the plan of attack, the politicians authorized it. When the memoir literature gave way to the archivally backed historiography of the war, it became evident that civilian authorities were no better at solving the stalemate of war than were the generals.

One of the pioneers in this field was Paul Guinn, whose 1965 study of British strategy and politics between 1914 and 1918 rested largely on published sources. His primary view is that the politicians abdicated their responsibility for mastering strategy, and left the key decisions to Sir Douglas Haig and his liaison officer with the Cabinet, Sir William Robertson. In part this was due, Guinn showed, to Haig's political sophistication. He drew on his friendships with the King and with prominent press barons to threaten implicitly any minister who would challenge his strategy or authority. Headlines would appear the day after such a challenge to this effect: 'Inexperienced politicians responsible for the deaths of thousands of British soldiers.' This threat effectively meant that Haig could not be fired. And indeed he outlasted all of his critics.

The literature on the German case showed roughly the same situation. Technically, the Kaiser appointed army chiefs. Bethmann-Hollweg, the Chancellor, had virtually no say as to strategy or tactics. When the commander in chief von Moltke had a nervous breakdown after the failure of the Schlieffen plan, he was replaced in late 1914 by Falkenhayn, not through political but through military pressure. The same was true when Falkenhayn went in mid-1916, when Verdun was devouring the German army as much as the French. Thereafter, as Gerhard Ritter showed, political constraints on strategy and on logistical questions were virtually non-existent in the slide towards defeat and the collapse of the Kaiser-reich. Ritter's magnum opus *Staatskunst und Kriegshandwerk; das Problem des 'Militarismus' in Deutschland* was published in four volumes between 1954 and 1968. The third volume dealt with what Ritter termed 'The tragedy of statesmanship' during Bethmann-Hollweg's chancellorship, between 1914 and 1917, and the last volume dealt with the general problem of German 'militarism', defined as the elevation of military values and the pre-eminence of military thinking in affairs of state. These, he believed, had led to disaster in the Great War. This work was translated into English (though not into French) at the end of the 1960s, and has had an influence on much subsequent scholarship. The Canadian scholar Martin Kitchen followed much of Ritter's lead in his 1976 book, as did Afflerbach in his biography of Falkenhayn (1994). No segregation of military and political history here (Mommsen, 1995; Chickering, 1998).

It is important to examine Ritter's notion of militarism to appreciate its influence and its limitations. In 1953, he presented a lecture to the annual German Historical Congress in which he summarized his views. As Berghahn put it later, to Ritter, militarism was both:

1. The one-sided determination of political decisions by military-technical considerations replacing a comprehensive examination of what is required by *raison d'état* – which comprised both the military aspect of state policy as well as the moral code; and

2. 'the one-sided predominance of militant and martial traits in a statesman's or nation's basic political outlook' to the extent that the most important task of a state is neglected which is 'to create a durable order of law and peace among men, to promote general welfare and mediate continuously in the eternal struggle among divergent interests and claims in domestic affairs and between nations'.[2]

The significance of this definition lay in its narrowness. It clearly applied to the ruling military class of Germany in the Great War, but the notion of 'militarism' Ritter advanced was specifically restricted to the realm of politics. Militarism was a deformation in the relationship between the state and the military, but it was not a German invention. And if anyone had any doubts as to the political slant of his writing, Ritter added that the really explosive mixture arose out of the blend of militarism and the masses. Another way of summarizing his outlook is to say that Ludendorff plus the French Revolution equals disaster. It was not the militarism of the army that ushered in the Nazi revolution, but the militarism of the mass movement represented by the Nazi party.

For our purposes, the most important element of Ritter's thesis was the way it prepared the ground for the intervention of Fritz Fischer (see pp. 46–8). Fischer demolished the boundary between the militarism of the state and the economic dreams of the country's industrial and financial elite (Fischer, 1961, 1969). At roughly the same time Gerald Feldman's account of the relationship between army, industry, and labour in wartime Germany made it impossible to isolate militarism from every corner of German life. His study of the mediating role of Colonel Bauer with industrialists and the new Fatherland party provides a portrait of a sinister figure, whose activities symbolized the way German militarism captured all the major institutions of the wartime state (Feldman, 1966). The Third High Command (OHL) succeeded in escaping from the control of the Ministry of War by creating in late 1916 a new War Office (*Kriegsamt*), a huge bureaucracy headed by General Groener, under the pretext of implementing Hindenburg's ambitious armaments programme. This programme was instigated in part by industrialists who wanted state subventions to construct new factories. Colonel Bauer was their intermediary. However this programme was totally unrealistic, and provoked a crisis of coal supply and transportation as well as the expansion of an inefficient bureaucratic system parallel to the old one. The general crisis of the German economy and society was in large part the outcome of this invasive militarism (Feldman, 1966).

The French situation was very different. Georges Bonnefous provided much evidence as to the lively exchanges that went on in France between the high command and various wartime leaders, especially Clemenceau. Here the question of the independence of the army command to wage the war the way they wanted to wage it was not answered in an unequivocal way (Bonnefous, 1957). The American scholar J. C. King showed even earlier (1951) how difficult it was for general officers to escape from the intrigues of parliamentary politics. The dispatch of General Sarrail to command French troops in the Greek theatre of operations is a case in point; despite the support he received from some well-placed individuals in the Chamber of Deputies and in General Headquarters alike, and despite his popularity, he was sent to Greece.

Naval warfare

The historiography of the war at sea has not been as contested nor as voluminous as that of the war on land. But there are a number of key elements in the configuration of naval warfare which intersect with key debates on the way the war was waged.

In the first historiographical period, many books on naval warfare were published in the epic nineteenth-century mode we have observed when dealing with land warfare. This heroic phase of historiography was evident in the voluminous treatments of the war at sea in official histories. In the 1960s, this archaic form of historical narrative was superseded by the first true classic on the sea war, Arthur Marder's *The war at sea* (Marder, 1961–70). This study in five volumes was published from 1961 to 1970, on the basis of several decades' work in the papers of 'Jackie' Fisher, the First Sea Lord and architect of the Royal Navy in the Great War. Marder published Fisher's diaries in three volumes between 1952 and 1959 (Marder, 1952–9). Marder's achievement was monumental, unparalleled in the work of military historians in any other combatant country. For in no other country was the fleet as significant as the defender of the realm, and in no other country did the survival of the nation so evidently depend on sea power. British history in this domain contrasts very strikingly with French historiography.

Marder analysed the development of the Royal Navy at a moment when it was challenged as never before by the development of the German High Seas Fleet, and charted its passage through the dangerous waters of the war. His is history of the grand kind, told from the viewpoint of the quarterdeck and the Admiralty. But his mastery of the archives was unmatched, and through it he was able to show how the Royal Navy made an indispensable contribution to British victory in the war.

His treatment of the Battle of Jutland is a case in point. The encounter between the British and German High Seas Fleet in 1916 was a critical moment. On the one hand, the German fleet inflicted heavier damage on the Royal Navy than the other way around; on the other hand, when the German fleet disengaged, the Royal Navy still controlled entry and exit to the Baltic, where the German navy remained penned up until the end of the war.

Who won the battle, the 'greatest' in history to date, in terms of the number of capital ships engaged and what was at stake? Marder sifts the evidence and reaches an authoritative conclusion. This was a qualified victory for the British fleet. Yes, the Royal Navy had not won a clear victory, a Trafalgar. Such a victory could have led to the speedy end of the war, in that it would have lifted any possible threat of invasion of the British Isles, freeing many more troops for immediate overseas duty, and opening the German ports to British naval bombardment. But that was not to be. Instead, Jutland was a British victory not because of what it changed but because of what it did not change: 'From the strategical point of view, which is what really matters, the Grand Fleet was, without a doubt, the winner . . . *The British control of the sea communications was unimpaired* . . . Not only was the British sea command unimpaired, but the results of the battle ensured that it would remain unimpaired' (Marder, 1952–9, III, p. 252). Marder's interpretations carried weight on other episodes too. When considering Churchill, First Lord of the Admiralty responsible for the Gallipoli debacle in 1915, Marder does not pull his punches. Churchill was to blame for planning a naval operation at Gallipoli before an adequate army was available to seize territory. Due to 'Churchill's impetuosity', in deciding to force the Straits of the Dardanelles by naval power alone, tens of thousands of Allied soldiers died for nothing (Marder, 1952–9, II, p. 261).

'Jackie' Fisher and Tirpitz were the two dominant figures in the history of sea power in the period of the Great War. The literature on Tirpitz is much more heavily contested, and two lines of argument emerged in the aftermath of the great debate over Fritz Fischer's interpretation of German pre-war and wartime grand designs for world power. The first was developed by Volker Berghahn (1971), who showed how much Tirpitz's vision was circumscribed by the need to stabilize the domestic position of the regime. His challenge to British mastery of the sea through the Naval Law of 1898 and the subsequent building spree which produced the Imperial Fleet had both a domestic and a geopolitical destination. Berghahn's position was clearly stated in the subtitle of his book, which described the Tirpitz plan in terms of its role as a 'domestic political strategy' (Berghahn, 1971). Jonathan Steinberg came to similar conclusions. Tirpitz really intended to build a deterrent to war; but Tirpitz's memorandum of 15 June 1897 setting out his vision shows that he indeed 'intended to wrest naval hegemony from the British. Hence it cannot be considered a defensive move' (Steinberg, 1965, p. 201). These works reinforce the interpretation of the way the military leadership of the country courted disaster before the war and reaped the whirlwind at its end. Secondly, though, Tirpitz has his defenders. A much more conservative and lenient verdict on his approach to pre-war policy and wartime strategy may be found in the work of the German scholar Michael Salewski (1979). His caveats about the interpretation of Berghahn and Steinberg, following Fischer, are judicious, but do not shift the overall balance. Tirpitz like the German high command were gamblers at heart, and they had their eyes fixed as much on the domestic as on the international scene.

The same gambler's mentality can be seen in the decision to wage unrestricted submarine warfare in 1917. The gamble was clear: to bring Britain to her knees in mid-1917 by cutting the Atlantic lifeline of food and essential supplies before the United States, provoked by the U-boat campaign to enter the war, could make a difference to the outcome.[3] The fate of this desperate strategy was a near thing, but the convoy system ultimately enabled the British and the Allies to withstand the threat of underwater attack (Halpern, 1994). Here too there is evidence of the degree to which the civilian authorities in Germany were eclipsed by the military and naval command (Michalka, 1994, pp. 384–66). Bethmann-Hollweg's attempts at finding a negotiated peace in the spring of 1917, after the first Russian revolution, were literally torpedoed by Tirpitz and the naval staff. The Chancellor resigned, leaving the field of command, and of war policy, open entirely to the military. The disastrous outcome of this turn of events is evident in much of the historical literature which has followed Feldman's 1966 study of the German war economy, which we will discuss in chapter 5.

The low point of German thinking on the naval war came at its end, when Admiral Scheer decided to launch one last suicidal attack on the Royal Navy in November 1918. German sailors' lives were to be sacrificed so that the honour of the German navy would be preserved. The outcome was that sailors doused the boilers, and *Götterdämmerung* never took place. Instead, mutinies broke out, leading directly to the German revolution and the end of the Hohenzollern regime (D. Horn, 1969). What price glory indeed?

Questioning strategies

Despite the different configurations of each national case, there are some striking parallels in this second phase of the historiography of the Great War with respect to the history of the battlefield. By the 1960s the emphasis had shifted in historical writing. The history of command, both military and civilian, became the history of the frustrations and failures attending four years of stalemate on battlefields scattered throughout the world. Here we move from personalized history, as written during the first phase, to the history of immovable objects. The sheer scale of the challenges faced by commanders and their political 'superiors' dwarfed any attempt to portray the war in heroic terms. Whoever had the last say about battle, the struggle for mastery over this new kind of warfare was tough, protracted, and without unblemished heroes.

Television history visualized this historiographical turn. We have discussed in chapter 1 both Mark Ferro's 1964 French television documentary and the BBC series of the same year. The scripts of both productions were professional and concise, but what conveyed the war was not words but images. In the French case, the public hardly needed reminding of how intractable was the landscape of the Western Front. The name 'Verdun' conjured up a series of images of unimaginable hardship. But in the British case the power of the imagery used in the 1964 BBC series suggests it confirmed and legitimated a more general sense already common in the British populations that, whatever the justification for waging war in the first place, the Great War was a monument to futility. In the decade of the Algerian and Vietnam wars, this message helped create an environment in which a much more complex, politicized, and divided historiography of battle emerged. At the same time, the torrent continued of publications of general military histories, written by men and women outside the academy who profited from the opening of new archives and other sources.[4]

Battlefield history renewed?

Contrasting national historiographies

In the 1980s and 1990s, the military history of the Great War entered a new phase. The efflorescence of interest in the conflict among social and cultural historians presented military historians – generally marginalized in the historical profession – with a particular challenge. It was how to reclaim the battlefield as an historical space on which they could speak with privileged authority (Beckett, 2001). Some were suspicious of the 'pacifist' tendencies of social and cultural historians; military historians could therefore reassure the general public that their subject was alive and well, and that it was in the hands of those who were professionally competent to master it. Military history thus became more overtly politicized than it had been in the previous two periods of writing. Despite several attempts to build bridges between 'right' and 'left' (Strachan, 1998 and 2000), each camp continued to contest the supposedly ideologically driven character of the work of the other camp.

A central argument deployed by the self-proclaimed 'new' military historians in Britain was that the record of command during the war described a 'learning curve'. We shall analyse this argument below. Suffice it to say that this interpretation is entirely absent from the French and German historiography, in which scholars examined the evidence surrounding the responsibility of individuals for success of failure in particular operations. The partisans of Joffre and Gallieni contest who 'won' the Battle of the Marne, just as firmly as the partisans of Joffre and Lanrezac point towards each other to find the blame for the bloody Battle of the Frontiers in 1914. Ludendorff and Hindenburg are given some or little credit for victory in the Battle of Tannenberg, constructed not by them but by Colonel Max Hoffman before they arrived on the scene. Falkenhayn is defended or attacked for his own claim that the Battle of Verdun was intended as a battle of attrition; after all, his army had failed to destroy the French artillery on the left bank of the river Meuse, and by this failure, ensured that the German army as well as the French would be 'bled white'. Pétain saw what Nivelle could not see: the need to develop a strategy of limited gains in place of thinking about a single breakthrough. And Ludendorff rewrote his account of the campaigns of 1918 to construe German defeat as the outcome of the treachery of the home front.

Haig also rewrote the history of his campaigns; he even rewrote his diaries. The intensity of the debate on command in the Great War in Britain, however, is far greater and more violent than its counterparts on the continent. Haig's portrait was removed from his Oxford college, by a decision of its Fellows who served under his command and considered his way of waging war to be simple butchery. In France or Germany, the issues were constructed differently. There compulsory military service was long-established; the army that Haig 'squandered' was initially made up of volunteers, who bore the brunt of his campaigns. And there the standing of military genius, from Napoleon to the elder Moltke, was a relatively uncontested part of national history. In Germany, command failures were recognized and sanctions followed. The younger Moltke was replaced after he broke down in the aftermath of the Battle of the Marne, as was Nivelle, despite his protests, after the failure of the Chemin des Dames offensive. Defeat was indeed personalized in the case of General Samsonov, who committed suicide after the disintegration of his army at Tannenberg. But the British debate was harsher, possibly because in Britain the shock of her losses was so great that the question of command and its failings led immediately to configure the deeper and more lasting question of the futility of the war itself.

The difference between British and continental historians extends as well to the subject of civil–military relations. In Britain, the question was treated in terms of the failure of the civilian leadership – Asquith and Lloyd George – to control the conduct of the war. Whenever there was a divergence of opinion, the liaison officer between Haig and Asquith or Lloyd George, General Robertson, maintained the dominance of the General Staff over questions of how to conduct the war. In Germany there was no contest. The three high commands (OHL) of Moltke, Falkenhayn, and Hindenburg and Ludendorff made war, and the political leadership of the country saw their task as enabling them to get on with it. Even in 1918, a strong opposition turned silent when the prospect of victory on the Western Front was in the balance. In France, with the exception of the autumn of 1914, the two chambers of the government did not relinquish control over the army and the financing of the war effort. In sum, the German army escaped from political controls, and to a degree absorbed them by 1917–18; the British army largely made its own way as well, despite the trappings of civilian control; in France, the army remained more or less under the control of the Republican state.

These differences are evident in the literature surrounding command in the Great War.

The 'learning curve'?

Military historians in Britain, facing a particular challenge from cultural historians, counter-attacked those who believed that the war was futile and who indicted the multiple failures of command in the great set-piece battles of the war. The riposte took two forms. The first was to argue from results. The war was won, Peter Simkins and John Terraine argued, by the British army in the field – note the narrow national focus yet again – and, whatever the horrors of earlier campaigns, Haig was right. He had worn down the German army by repeated British campaigns, which though they did not realize their stated objectives, did degrade the enemy's capacity to survive an extended industrial war of attrition.

The second argument deployed by the 'new' military historians was that the record of command during the war described a 'learning curve'. The commanding generals made major mistakes, to be sure, but those errors were steps on the way to mastering a battlefield that no one had ever seen before. By 1918 the British (and the French) had found an answer to the problem of immobility. One important element of this solution was effective counter-battery fire, which helped break the Hindenburg line in October 1918, leading directly to the end of the war (Griffith, 1994; Travers, 1984, 1992).

These two lines of argument have not gone unanswered. In a series of studies, the Australian historians Robin Prior and Trevor Wilson (1992, 1996, 1999) have found weaknesses in the claim that there was a learning curve. If such a phenomenon existed on the Western Front, they argued, it was an astonishingly uneven one. On 1 July 1916, Haig tried to do too much: the thrust was too wide and too deep and the artillery barrage had not obliterated German defences. The result was disaster. On 14 July, the objectives were more limited, and success more substantial. But thereafter, the older, failed approach resurfaced. It is as if there was progress in mastering the battlefield – and the enemy defences – but then it was nullified, by a return to older and inadequate operational ideas. Alongside the learning curve, there was an unlearning curve as well (Keith Simpson, in Bond, 1991, pp. 143–62). The American scholar David Woodward showed how shrewdly Haig blunted criticisms of his command decisions by mobilizing allies in every corner of the Establishment, from Buckingham Palace down (Woodward, 1983). If Haig had learned anything during the war, it was how to protect his flanks from his political 'masters'.

The Israeli historian Martin van Creveld provided a powerful answer to the 'learning curve' approach in his book *Command in war* (van Creveld, 1985). His claim, applied to the Great War, alongside examinations of other earlier and later conflicts, is that the best command is that which accepts and works within the limits of the high technology of the day. Commanders should assume that communications of whatever kind will break down, and therefore operate on the basis that no fixed plan of campaign can be realized. Thus the Schlieffen plan had no chance of success, since von Moltke, 300 kilometres away from his advance units probing the Allied dispositions near the Marne in 1914, had no idea what was happening. That is why Lieutenant Colonel Hentsch had to go and see for himself, and thereafter to issue the order which changed the war, that of retreat from the Marne. That is why General Haig's 27-page order of the day for the first day of the Battle of the Somme bordered on lunacy, since it assumed that he could control the battlefield, whereas it controlled him and annihilated a large part of the British infantry which went over the top on 1 July 1916. Command failure was based on arrogance, and on rigidity; command success, on flexibility and improvisation. But even when improvisation was tried, as in the Michael offensive of March 1918, the inevitable breakdown of supply lines, stretched to their limits after three and a half years of war, as well as the sheer exhaustion of the mass of the German army, made defeat inevitable. Ludendorff, the master of the adage 'first we break through, then we shall see', could not convert operational flair into strategic power. Thus the hundreds of thousands of German casualties in the 1918 offensives did nothing to change the balance of forces on the Western Front. The result was, from the German point of view, catastrophe.

This focus on the supply war helps account for the historiographical shift towards seeing the intersection of political and military elites as the key to the unfolding of strategic initiatives in wartime. Guy Pedroncini's account of Pétain's rise to command in the war (1974) showed how his replacement of Nivelle was not simply a matter of a failed offensive, but a reflection of powerful political conflicts which did not submerge in wartime (J. J. Becker, 1988). This is the theme as well of Fabienne Bock's more recent study (2002), wherein she shows the persistence of legislative review of all levels of strategic, tactical, and operational matters. The work of these parliamentary commissions, their role for example in the development of heavy artillery, the importance of which was underestimated by the Ministry of War for ideological reasons, suggests that the shift of power away from the legislature and towards the executive that took place in most combatant countries was successfully resisted in France, and resisted in ways which had meaning in terms of how the war was fought.

Pétain revisited

Pedroncini (1989) examined another facet of the evolution of French strategic thinking in the period prior to the launching of the German offensive of March 1918. His interest was in the politically explosive question of the 'second line'. After the failure of the Chemin des Dames offensive, and after the collapse of the Russian war effort, liberating dozens of German divisions for combat on the Western Front, it was apparent that a new approach was in order to the disposition of the forty divisions which constituted the French strategic reserves. Pedroncini showed that in late 1917 Pétain found a new way of framing the battlefield, which both helped to anticipate a future German attack and to marshal French reserves in such a way as to prepare a decisive counter-offensive. This prediction of what would take place in 1918 leads Pedroncini to claim that Pétain should be acclaimed not only for being a miser with the lives of his men, but as a sophisticated planner of the counter-attack which led to German capitulation in November 1918.

Foch among others was dead set against the notion of the second line. There was nothing objectionable in Pétain's attempt to shift the emphasis away from the front line and towards what Pétain termed 'the army's wider field of battle' (p. 262). What was impossible for Foch to accept was that this new optic justified – and perhaps even required – that French troops would retreat in the face of a German attack and thereby voluntarily give up French soil to the invader. The logic of Pétain's idea was that such a flexible defence would enable French troops to retake positions lost in the first phase of action. Here he was simply following the development of German tactics, implemented after the battle of the Somme and before the Chemin des Dames. But it was one thing for the German army to accept the loss of their front-line emplacements, and to retreat to their second line, and another for the French to do the same thing.

Pétain stood his ground. In January 1918, he gave these instructions to the Second and the Fourth armies. 'We have not taken sufficient account of the terrain. We do not have sufficient divisional strength to wage a defensive battle on the front line. We must therefore manoeuvre and let the terrain work for us . . . It is impossible to manoeuvre if everyone defends the front line' (Pedroncini, 1989, p. 263). Pedronicini terms this approach 'revolutionary'. It was not only a departure from the canons of French military thinking which had dominated the disposition of forces throughout the war. It also coincided with the needs of the moment when the German army actually attacked two months later.

Pedroncini makes Pétain a master of both offensive and defensive strategies. It is hardly surprising that he contrasts Pétain's sagacity with a 'lack of imagination' in Foch (Pedroncini, 1989, p. 417). It was Pétain after all who wanted to delay the Armistice until the German army was broken in the field (1989, p. 420). Perhaps then, Pedroncini speculates, the future – not only the future of Europe but also of Pétain – might have been different.

Perhaps. But what matters as much as the specific interpretation Pedroncini offers is the biographical character of this part of his work. Like Corelli Barnett, Pedroncini writes of strategy and tactics within the framework of a great clash of personalities. He has his champion, and champions always have enemies, which become those of Pedroncini as well. Some were in uniform; others were politicians. Pétain had to resist them all, and so, Pedroncini argues, resist them he did, thereby ensuring the victory of the nation he served. His work is judicious hagiography, based on perhaps unparalleled knowledge of the French military archives, but it is hagiography nonetheless.

There is no such unfettered admiration in the writings of German or British historians about generalship in the Great War. Terraine (1963) referred to Haig as the 'educated soldier' (rendered in its French translation as 'le soldat de métier'), and tried to conjure him up as the saviour of his nation, but his message fell largely on deaf ears. The bitterness of the casualties he accepted as part of the price of victory never left the debate about his role in the war. Thus views on Haig were closer to those about Nivelle than about Pétain in the historiography of the 1914–18 conflict. Both Haig and Nivelle promised victory through a 'knock-out blow' that never came. Pétain promised something different: tenacity, patience, the coordination of forces, and a flexible front. That is why his role in 1914–18 escaped the controversy that still haunts the name of Sir Douglas Haig.

Persistence and limits of the argument over responsibility

Haig is not the only figure to come in for criticism on the British side of the lines. Historical accounts of the political leadership have been caustic as well. The manner in which Lloyd George undermined and finally displaced Asquith as prime minister is a perennial theme in the literature. The braiding together of political and military debates during the war is the theme of a number of studies by the British historian David French (1982, 1986, 1995). He showed clearly how Lloyd George benefited from his key position in industrial mobilization to seize the initiative from the prime minister, Asquith, an initiative which led directly to his replacement of Asquith as prime minister in December 1916. Mobilization on the home front, of which Lloyd George was the master, was never far from broader debates on strategy and war aims. The great strength of David French's series of books is his capacity to see that the term 'strategy' itself evolved very rapidly during the war. In Britain the term referred to the deployment of fleet and forces in 1914. Within a year, it had been transformed to connote economic mobilization. Lloyd George's appointment as Minister of Munitions in May 1915, and the creation of a coalition government with Labour party members at the same time, announced the new strategic agenda. The war had not only to be fought; it had to be provisioned and paid for. From that moment on, the British state was engaged in strategic negotiations; the political leadership had to distribute goods and resources as between military and civilian claimants. 'Strategy' was the outcome of that set of choices, and the armed power of the state was set by them (French, 1982, p. 173).

So far so good; but the discussion did not stop there; supplying arms is one thing, controlling their deployment is another. The failure of the Gallipoli campaign, as we have noted above, was directly that of Winston Churchill, First Lord of the Admiralty, who had to resign his cabinet post. Here was a constraint on war policy which faced both Asquith and Lloyd George. As Guinn showed (1965) neither man was able to remove Haig, a man who treated politicians with contempt. Lloyd George had serious doubts about the plans for an attack in Flanders in 1917, but he approved it nonetheless. This third Battle of Ypres was popularly known as Passchendaele after the rubble of a village British and Canadian forces 'captured' in November 1917, six months after this bloody failed offensive had been launched. Who was responsible for this catastrophe? Haig, to be sure, but in the last instance it is Lloyd George who must bear the responsibility for this lamentable battle. Where is the learning curve here? A year after the Battle of the Somme, the British army repeated the mistakes of frontal assaults on heavily fortified German positions near Ypres. The history of British strategy is that of the displacement of responsibility for failure, an evasion evident in the memoirs of political and military leaders alike (Prior and Wilson, 1992, 1996, 1999).

This tendency to imbricate military history within the political and economic history of the war is one on which we shall reflect in later chapters. But it is significant in signalling the way in which military historians in recent years have moved outside the narrow confines in which the history of command had been set in the interwar period and beyond. One instance of this broadening of perspectives is the chapter on the people of France during the war in the *Histoire militaire de la France* (Pedroncini, 1997). It is clear that a purely military history of the war, defined as the history of battle alone, is now a thing of the past.

The controversy is an ongoing one. John Terraine and Corelli Barnett went on and on writing scathingly of Haig's detractors, who do not see that he waged war as it had to be waged and he won it. One of the most ferocious attacks on Haig as a commander was written by the British historian Denis Winter (1991).[5] Denis Winter's account is as damningly negative as Terraine's is defiantly positive. When historians talk about Haig, tempers rise. When a new BBC television series appeared in 1996, entitled 'The Great War and the shaping of the twentieth century', written by one of the authors of the current book, it was excoriated by Barnett in the popular press as pacifist claptrap, left-wing politics dressed up as military history. The force of the critique suggests something about the emotion this subject still excites, and the politicized nature of the polemics surrounding the Great War.

There are voices in between the opposing camps, to be sure. Hew Strachan's magisterial first volume of a projected three-volume military history of the Great War takes a position somewhere between the prosecution and the defence (Strachan, 2000). He has the advantage that few British military historians have had of deploying German and French sources with the same fluency as the British. But to date (2005), he has not reached 1916 or 1917, when the real collisions of historical interpretation occur. Peter Simkins of the Imperial War Museum sees Haig's faults as real, but diminishing over time. In tactics, in techniques, and in his capacity to leave his subordinates sufficient space to vary their responses to battlefield conditions, Haig's command did indeed describe a 'learning curve', the destination of which was victory (Simkins, in Bond and Cave, 1999, p. 97). Other scholars have followed this line of argument (Sheffield and Till, 2003); others remain unpersuaded.

In all this literature, though, we see one major flaw in the historiography, whatever its national origins. It is the tendency to analyse one commander or one army in isolation. There were exceptions, to be sure. As early as 1924 Charles de Gaulle published an account of his understanding of German ideas about war, an understanding fed by captivity in a German prisoner-of-war camp and his reading of the German press throughout the war.[6] He saw in the domination of the civilian authorities by the general staff the cause of German defeat. Others shared the simple assumption that if there was a 'learning curve' it was never developed by one army on its own. The thrust and riposte of trench warfare, as much as the major set-piece battles, were binary operations at least, and frequently involved multiple command structures. The international history of battle, as shared by men on both sides of the line, thinking about a set of common problems and a shared predicament, is yet to be written.

NOTES

1. Markus Pöhlmann, 'Yesterday's battles and future war', in Chickering and Forster, 2003, pp. 229–30.
2. As cited in Volker Berghahn, *Militarism. The history of an international debate 1861–1979* (Leamington Spa: Berg, 1981), pp. 55–6.
3. Holger Herwig and David Trast, 'The failure of Imperial Germany's undersea offensive against world shipping, February 1917–October 1918', *Historian*, 33 (1971), pp. 611–36.
4. There are many such publications from which to choose. In French, there are the successive volumes by Koeltz (1928, 1930, 1966), Gambiez and Suire (1968–71), Contamine (1970), Miquel (1983), Doise and Vaïsse (1989). In English, there are multiple works by Peter Liddle (Liddle *et al.*, 2000) among many others.
5. No relation to one of the authors of this book.
6. Charles de Gaulle, *La Discorde chez l'ennemi* (Paris: Berger-Levrault, 1924).

4   Soldiers

How did they wage war?

In the celebrated verse of *El Cid*: 'Combat ceases when soldiers disappear', Corneille reminded us that war is first and foremost about the men who wage it. This is not at all evident when reading the innumerable volumes published on the war since the Armistice and throughout the interwar years. The ordinary soldier was forgotten in these works.

This act of forgetting was not inevitable. Most of these historians had themselves fought in the trenches. For one well-known author of school textbooks, Jules Isaac, who was concerned with the pedagogical message he would transmit, and more worried about pupils than scholars, soldiers' experience would be included in the narrative of the war. He devoted one page to this purpose out of about 100 pages in the supplementary chapter he added in 1921 to the textbook for the final year of secondary school. He insisted on adding to his name that of the author of the immediately preceding issue of this textbook, because he had died in combat. Henceforth this textbook, commonly used in French schools, was known as the 'Malet–Isaac':

Depressing in its monotony, repellent in its multiple heavy duties, trench warfare was a war of endurance, in which armies, these national armies composed of men of all social classes, were struggling and suffering more than any professional army had ever struggled or suffered. The infantry above all went through the worst ordeals. In certain sectors, the fight was so atrocious that the front-line trenches and the communications trenches seemed dug out of human remains. Thousands of men had their feet frozen during winter nights and suffered evacuation, and at times amputation. The mud became so deep that one could become entrapped by it, and that when they left the trenches, infantrymen seemed to have been transformed into blocks of mud. Imprisoned and actually buried alive in their trenches, having only a hole in the ground with a bit of rotten straw as a shelter and for sleep, separated from the external world by an impassable barrier, day and night on the alert, exposed to death in the most hideous forms, soldiers of this terrible war – warriors in spite of themselves – seemed to have passed the limits of human resistance. (Isaac, 1921, pp. 1107–8)

Professional scholars did not share this point of view. In his major study of 1934, Renouvin did not write a single line on trench soldiers. Isaac points to this omission in his review of this book, with a kind of caustic irony:

There is one character whose total absence is surprising: the ordinary soldier, or the people in arms . . . This war which the historian lived as a soldier, and the memory of which obsesses us, has been cleaned up; the trooper with his stinking companions – blood, mud, garbage, rats, lice – have been left behind, and we now see it entering into history, as a war should with officers and general staffs.[1]

A history of the war without soldiers

The reasons for an exclusion

Trench soldiers were not forgotten; they were excluded. Let us neglect the Eastern Front: the majority of historians have neglected it for many reasons. But even on the Western Front, in which we are primarily interested, the soldiers played no part in what most professional historians of this time considered as history.

First, historical research at this time took a global view: to understand battle, one had to understand manoeuvres, as they were presented in French textbooks dealing with the Napoleonic wars with their battlefield maps. The left wing retreats, the right wing is in a poor position, Napoleon attacks in the centre. In this logic of army corps which advance or retreat in a defined space, soldiers are only pawns who do not count, and they are manoeuvred in the proper sense of the term. Their accounts are of no value, because their point of view was too limited to understand what was going on and what they were doing. How can they help the historian to understand war? Renouvin said it clearly, in his brief review of the work of Péricard (1933): 'Of course, this contribution is important only for the history of combat: the soldiers whose narratives M. Péricard has collected knew nothing of the conceptions of the high command.'[2] Or once more, in a bibliographical commentary of a textbook for university students, Renouvin insisted that 'The soldiers' accounts, the consultation of which is very useful for an understanding of the atmosphere of battle, can hardly give any information on the conduct of operations, since the horizon of these witnesses was too limited' (Renouvin et al., 1939, p. 609). Stendhal had put the same point earlier, when showing his hero Fabrizio passing through the Battle of Waterloo without the slightest idea as to what was happening.

But it was also that 'the atmosphere of battle', as Renouvin put it, was not yet an object of historical study. It may provide an element of local colour, which makes the narrative come alive, but it explains nothing important. Serious history is uninterested in trivial questions about material life or what it deems to be personal matters. Its proper object is the life of states and societies, of 'peoples and civilizations', to cite the title of the celebrated collection in which Renouvin had published his classic study of 1934. This is civilization in the noble sense of Paul Valéry who saw the meaning of the war in this phrase: 'we civilizations, we know from henceforth that we are mortal'. It would take a long time before the conditions of material life, housing, clothing, food, and drink entered into the domain of history, and before sentiments, emotions, and perceptions would enter as well. In the interwar years, literary scholars were deemed to be in charge of this domain, for example in the study of religious sentiment, to cite one great work still of general interest, which accepted the title of 'literary history'.[3]

What the soldiers had to say, their testimony, does not yet belong to history, but rather to literature or to psychology. When Renouvin revised his book, he added developments on the evolution of the world, economic, social, and political movements, on religious or intellectual life. He took into account the memoirs of soldiers as forms of literature, notably the works of Barbusse and Dorgelès, which had very wide success. He refers as well to the critique of these works which Norton Cru published in 1929, and which we shall refer to below, in a dismissive manner.

Even if we adopt all the conclusions of Norton Cru, whose attitude was often hypercritical, he raised doubts about the historical value of these war books, and not about their literary value. [Even if they are not always accurate], they retain an interest as psychological documents. (Renouvin, 1934, rev. edn 1969, p. 726)

In a way, this approach is outdated; it configures the war of 1914 with words, concepts, and patterns forged to explain nineteenth-century warfare. The Great War was entirely different, a war of masses, fought by conscript armies. The only precedent for it was the U.S. Civil War of 1861–5. Historians of the war of 1914–18 had not yet understood this difference. They had to describe the trenches, so characteristic of the Great War, but their descriptions had no trace of reality. They traversed the landscape without showing us those men who lived and died there. Trench warfare was seen as a kind of siege warfare across a gigantic line. For instance, in the volume of the great history of contemporary France, directed by Lavisse (Bidou et al., 1922), one chapter is devoted to trench warfare. The text opens with a geographical description of the front, then cites one particular sector of the front to explain the organization of the trench system: the first, second, and third lines, the communication trenches, shelters, and forward posts. It ends with an analysis of trench warfare in the language of regimental diaries or military communiqués. The trenches were not places where men lived and died; they were mere defensive organizations.

Underground histories

The indifference of historical accounts towards soldiers was matched by a reciprocal indifference on the part of soldiers towards history. They were interested above all in war novels and narratives. In this first historiographical configuration, public interest in this kind of war literature was intense. Parents, friends, wanted to know 'how it was'; they wanted to see the front, where the action was, and from where they had been excluded. Veterans – approximately half of the adult male population in France – wanted not to be forgotten. Some turned away from a too difficult past, but others were vitally interested in books recounting the battles in which they had fought. Families as well as veterans devoured histories of the war, in particular those which were illustrated, for instance collections of post cards. The same interest attracted tourists towards the battlefields – the first Michelin guides dated from 1919[4] – where both veterans and their families went on pilgrimage by coach.

Alongside the historical literature and the memoirs of the 'great' figures, politicians, diplomats, or generals who historians thought had something to say, because they took a broad view of the war, a huge additional literature appeared filling whole libraries, and of which some titles enjoyed enduring success. For instance, there was Barbusse and Dorgelès, and some others like Genevoix, whose reputations were established more slowly. A first wave of publications begins during the war itself in France. The highest literary prize in the country went in 1915 to *Gaspard* by René Benjamin, a book entirely inaccurate and rapidly forgotten. The following year the prize went to Barbusse for *Under fire*, which presented an entirely different picture of war, 'for civilians, a revelation, for soldiers, an act of revenge' (Ducasse *et al.*, 1959, p. 490). In 1917, the prize went to Malherbe for his *Flame in hand*, and in 1918 to Duhamel for *Civilization*. The following year, another literary prize was given to Dorgelès's *Wooden crosses*. In Germany, Ernst Jünger published his *Storm of steel* in the same period. In the middle of the 1920s, there was something of a lull, though there are some exceptions in England, for instance Ford Madox Ford's tetralogy *Parade's end* (1924–6) and R. H. Mottram's *Spanish farm trilogy* (1926–28); but on the whole, publishers thought that the public was no longer interested in the subject of war. The success of Erich Maria Remarque's *All quiet on the Western Front*, immediately translated into many languages, opened a second wave of publications, illustrated by books such as, in France, *La Biffe (Infantry)*, by Jacques Meyer, or *Fear* by Gabriel Chevalier, or in Britain, by Robert Graves's *Goodbye to all that*, R. C. Sherriff's *Journey's end*, Richard Aldington's *Death of a hero*, and Siegfried Sassoon's *Memoirs of an infantry officer*.

Academic distinctions place this work within literary production, and it has been analysed as such (Rieuneau, 1972; Riegel, 1978). Historians had no concern for literature, which they might include only in their last chapters on intellectual, literary, and religious life. Thus they ignored this particular body of war literature and what it showed. Hence the critical importance of some transgressive 'smugglers' from the literary world who were interested in history in progress. Three works published in France in these years illustrate how the soldiers were smuggled back into history.

The first book is an anthology of writers on the war (Ducasse, 1932).[5] The legitimation of the narrative rested on the status of the writer, and the social standing it conferred on him. But at the same time, Ducasse, a Protestant high-school teacher, was careful to include only witnesses of incontestable authenticity, which Ducasse himself determined by reference to his own personal experience. Literary skill did not always go along with such authenticity. Here are Ducasse's words:

Most novelists flattered the public's taste and confirmed their traditional conceptions of a melodramatic and gallant war: jovial pleasantries among the soldiers, the perfidy of spies, killing at close range, 'in a man-to-man fight where blood flows abundantly'. An athletic and sporting war for some; and to others, 'hateful murders by brutes drunk on ether'. (Ducasse, 1932, I, p. 6).

Thematically organized, these two volumes were made up of extracts, some long and some short, of the principal French writers on the war. The care to provide ecumenical coverage and to respect sensibilities is evident. Ducasse presents extracts from the work of about seventy authors. They are of varying interest, significance, and accuracy. However, as he had carefully chosen these extracts, he could include all the authors who appealed to him. He thus provided a portrait of the soldiers completely at variance with the patriotic image pleasing to civilians, citing Boasson, 'No bellicose nationalism could survive the realities of Verdun' (II, p. 47).

The second initiative was that of Péricard (1933). It was a product of the collaboration of a severely wounded veteran and publisher, Durassié, and of Péricard. This writer had been made famous by the preface Maurice Barrès wrote to his narrative about the war, *Arise! The dead!*

(*Debout les morts*), a work among the least trustworthy of its kind. Not surprisingly his work was not in Ducasse's anthology. Péricard was the first to appeal directly in the newspapers for individual soldiers to send him their accounts of the war. He received 6,000 replies, and used about half of them to compose his *Verdun*, a kind of mosaic following a chronological and geographic narrative of the battle.[6]

War literature and historical evidence: Norton Cru

The third initiative was that of Jean Norton Cru (1929 and 1930). We have already noted in chapter 1 his effort to turn war accounts into historical documents by criticizing them, sometimes over-criticizing them. But if we set aside this exaggerated criticism, which was itself a clear reaction to the exclusion of war experience from the historical narrative,[7] Norton Cru's books are not far from those of Ducasse. They denounce the exclusive emphasis on military facts, which has given a false idea of war.[8] In order to provide a true one, Norton Cru systematically analysed more than 300 soldiers' novels, memoirs, and letters published in French. He not only established a matrix of good and bad testimony, according to his own experience, but also provided many citations of passages he thought the most revealing of the war the soldiers endured. Hence his book is much more than an annotated bibliography, such as that of Falls (1930) on war books; it is a vivid picture of the war, very close to those of Ducasse and Isaac. He offered no concessions to those he considered excessive, as well as to those he considered pacifist or nationalist. He rejected on one side 'ponds of blood', 'piles of bodies', and on the other 'chauvinistic puff', 'elegies about baionnettes', 'soldiers burning to go into face to face combat'. On the contrary, he puts the emphasis on soldiers' hardships, and the misery of their material existence, on the harshness of a ravaged battlefield, on its stinking pestilential smells, on the haunting calls of distress and cries of agony, on the soldiers' minds, their fear and their courage, their solidarity and their individualism, their obedience and their revolt. Through this method, unprecedented and without a successor, Norton Cru presented a picture which today remains stunning.

Norton Cru, however, did not achieve his aim. The historical profession remained unpersuaded by his critical rigour. Renouvin wrote a long and favourable review of his work: 'This is a *new* book in the true sense of the term', but in conclusion he found that Norton Cru's critical approach was excessive,[9] and not worth taking into account. For historians like Renouvin, soldiers' narratives were related to history in the same improbable way that café music was related to that of concert halls.

The reintegration of the soldiers

Life and death of Frenchmen

The reintegration of soldiers within the history of the Great War was not accomplished by historians. They remained loyal in the 1950s and 1960s to the model of history developed by Renouvin, who retired only in 1964. One might have thought that the *Annales* school would have broken with this kind of history, but it was hardly interested in the contemporary period and looked down on 'mere events'.

The success of *Vie et mort des Français* (1959), arose out of the encounter between eye-witnesses to war and part of the public. On the one hand, soldiers were more aware of war novels than any historian of war literature, and were troubled about dying without passing on their message. On the other side were those both young and old who obviously were eager to hear about the war. We have already noted the difficulty in finding a publisher and the surprising success of this book.

The source of this success lay in the stance adopted by the three authors. Instead of presenting themselves as witnesses, and speaking from their own experience, as they had done in the past, they tried to tell a story which was well known but this time which had room for men and women, for the French people. The narrative is marked by the techniques of journalism, through the insertion of soldiers' accounts in the story, and they knew war literature so well that they always found an apposite account to confirm what they had to say. The work is based on secondary sources sufficiently rigorous to enable them to avoid commonplace errors,[10] and by their insights into other theatres of military operations and the evolution of international events. Duroselle was right when he said, in his long bibliography, that for him 'this book is the most remarkable on the whole subject' of the war (Duroselle, 1994, pp. 477–8).

Encouraged by this success, and aware of the fiftieth anniversary of the war, publishers produced many works destined for the general public which at the very same time was beginning to discover the war through television. We have no need for additional comment on books such as *La vie quotidienne des soldats* (Meyer, 1966), the study of civilian life by Perreux (1966), *Les fantassins du Chemin des Dames* (Nobécourt, 1965), or *Les Camarades* by Boutefeu (1966), which drew upon more than 300 unpublished personal accounts for which he had appealed in the press. The same situation may be seen in Britain through parallel works. First, there is Martin Middlebrook (1971), whose narrative of the first day of the Battle of the Somme rests on more than 400 personal accounts. Then there is the book edited by Georges Panichas (1968), which brings together personal statements by prominent veterans of different belligerent nations. One of the characteristics of the historical landscape of these years was the restoration to those who had fought the war of their own history while there was still time to do so.

Towards a history from below

Trends both within military history and social history help account for the inclusion of the soldiers' experience within professional historical writing. On the side of military history, Pedroncini (1971) could hardly write his thesis on the conduct of the war from May 1917 to the Armistice without reference to the mutinies and the way in which Pétain overcame them. After all, how can one write a history of mutinies without mutineers? The opening of the archives of the war permitted him (1967 and 1968) to revise this history and to put an end to the legend of the decimation of French units punished for the mutiny. In addition he provided a sociology of the mutineers which underscored the importance of rural workers (Pedroncini, 1967, pp. 194–231). In more recent years Christophe Charle has returned to these statistics, and has found that the place of workers among mutinous units was greater, especially when we take into account the exemptions from front-line service which diminished their number in the army (Charle, 2001, pp. 259–60).

Another military source became available for historical research at the same time: the archives of military censorship of soldiers' correspondence, which provide much information on the opinion and attitudes of soldiers. These reports are hard to use but of great value. Until now, however, historians have hardly explored them, with the exception of Jean-Noël Jeanneney, in an article on 1917 and a doctoral thesis by Annick Cochet.[11]

Social history at that time was defined by the priority it gave to the ruled rather than to the rulers. It did not have to go through the same process of reorientation as did military history. On the contrary, what had to be done was to go beyond the analysis of social groups established by economic solidarities, social classes, in order to become interested in a group knit together – but to what extent ? – by a common experience. It had above all to find new angles of investigation, that is to say, in the historiography of this time, to find new sources. For instance, Renouvin asked a young historian who had proposed to write a thesis on the subject of 'the Great War in French society between the two wars', do you have any archives? As the student looked rather embarrassed, Renouvin continued, 'you can see me again when you have found some archives'. He came back, having located the archives of the National Office of Disabled Veterans, and the outcome became *Les anciens combattants et la société française* (Prost, 1977a).

This thesis put the veterans, to be sure after battle, at the centre of this kind of history, which the academy appreciated. More than the experience of the war, evoked in one chapter only, it discussed mainly the long-term effects of the war upon those who fought in it and the role they had played in French society thereafter. Through this sociological approach, Prost emphasized the difference between disabled and able-bodied men, the numbers of disabled men, the political importance of their claims, and the strength of their associations. This study was completed by a linguistic analysis. At that time historians tried to be scientists, and linguistics was above all seen as a science within the humanities. These linguistic methods showed how the patriotism of most veterans was the opposite of nationalism and combined with a deep pacifism. The history of the inter-period was modified, and in particular the history of the fascist temptation. The pretence of the Croix de Feu, a right-wing group, to speak for the veterans was exposed for what it was: a mere imposture. This thesis enriched the history of the war only on the margins, through its study of the care of the wounded by the military administration during the war.

In the same year, Jean-Jacques Becker (1977) provided another illuminating treatment of the soldiers, this time not about combat but about their mobilization.[12] Becker treated the soldiers before their experience of battle. His study was a political history focused on public opinion. Before Becker, historians drew conclusions from press reports of the departure of troops from the Gare de L'Est in Paris to conclude that there was a general patriotic enthusiasm for the war in France. Becker undertook a national enquiry based on accounts written by primary school teachers from six French departments, the reports of Prefects, and the daily press of thirty-six provincial towns. All this evidence converged. As was expected at the time, Becker used linguistic and quantitative methods. He counted the frequency with which certain words appeared in his documents: 'calm' and 'resignation' were much more frequent than 'enthusiasm'. The war was greeted first with gravity as an event which interrupted the flow of work and days, and which entailed risks. Enthusiasm came later, when soldiers came together, and this was more an urban than a rural phenomenon. The history of mobilization was thus entirely revised.[13]

The only study which dealt explicitly and uniquely with soldiers of the Great War was that of Jules Maurin (1982). His perspective was fully sociological, and his method resolutely quantitative. At this time, computerized research was in its infancy, and Maurin put his data on perforated cards, wrote his own computer programmes, and produced his own calculations on large computers. In effect he mined a serial source, the dimensions of which had put off other scholars. These are the conscription registers, in which are found all the relevant data on every soldier: personal information – his parents, his address, his profession, etc., and military information – his service record, his wounds, his disciplinary record, sometimes his death. Such a vast array of data could only be selectively treated. Maurin dealt with two contrasting areas of recruitment near Montpellier: Béziers, on what was termed the 'red' vineyard region of Languedoc, and Mende in the 'white' mountains of this region, very Catholic and conservative. The result was a sociological picture of the soldiers of the Great War of great richness and variety.[14] These data enabled Maurin to provide a full account of a specific cohort of men from two separate regions. The percentage of private soldiers in the infantry killed on active service was very different in the two regions: 22 per cent of the men from Mende were killed, compared to 17 per cent from Béziers. Of course since they belonged to different regiments, the soldiers did not fight on the same fronts and at the same time. Things are not so simple, however, and as the rule of recruitment of regiments by region was abandoned, soldiers from all regions merged at the front. On the whole, workers in the vineyards and shepherds from the mountains fought the same war. If the number of deaths was not as numerous in the two cases, it is possibly because they did not fight the war in the same way. Here is a perfect invitation to caution among those who would rush to generalizations about the war.

Other interventions in this field were scattered. The opening of the colonial archives enabled Meynier (1981) to expore the case of Algerian soldiers and Michel to study that of black soldiers from Senegal (1982). The experience of trench warfare is not at the heart of these studies of colonial and African soldiers. They are, though, very instructive about the way in which the French army exploited these soldiers. A conference organized at Verdun in 1996 had as its focus the question of the professionalism of these colonial troops (Carlier and Pedroncini, 1997).

The experience of the trenches

During the same years, Anglo-Saxon historians, not so enslaved by archives, undertook a history of the experience of combat which rested in large part on soldiers' accounts, and letters published or preserved in the Imperial War Museum in London. The originality of this work was not in its documentation, even if the opening of military archives permitted the exploration of what the staff thought about the morale of the soldiers. The change was one of perspective.

The pioneering work is that of John Keegan (1976), a book which was translated into French sixteen years later. The reason why Keegan's book is so original is that it posed a universal question and gave particular answers. The question is, how is battle possible? Why do human beings engage in it, when the most natural response to its terrifying character is to put down your weapons and flee? This question was posed by a British historian teaching at Sandhurst, the Royal Military Academy, at a time when the British military had to construct a future for itself remote from its imperial greatness. This was all only twenty years after the Suez fiasco, when Britain recognized it was no longer a world power. To review the history of battle is to review a critical chapter of national history which seemed to have come to an end. Keegan's conclusion was that battle in the twentieth century had reached a level of terror that made it impossible to endure. This existential dimension set his work apart from that of all previous military historians in Britain.

Keegan's 'face of battle' encounters the whole of the battlefield: the armies, plans, preparations, bombardments, and so on, with careful attention given to different sectors of the front, the dimensions of no-man's-land, the efficiency of the artillery preparation, and the enemy's behaviour. He considers the wounded, citing instances of truces to remove them from the battlefield. But at the centre of his analysis, we find men trapped in a terrifying situation, who nevertheless went on fighting.

What battles have in common is human: the behaviour of men struggling to reconcile their instinct for self-preservation, their sense of honour and the achievement of some aim over which other men are ready to kill them. The study of battle is therefore always a study of fear and usually of courage; always of leadership, usually of obedience; always of compulsion, sometimes of insubordination; always of anxiety, sometimes of elation or catharsis; always of uncertainty and doubt, misinformation and misapprehension, usually of faith and sometimes of vision; always of violence, sometimes also of cruelty, self-sacrifice, compassion; above all, it is always a study of solidarity and usually also of disintegration – for it is towards the disintegration of human groups that battle is directed.[15]

Keegan embraces the whole of the battlefield. In the case of Ashworth (1980), the focal point is more distant and the framework is narrowly focused on the soldiers in the front line. In Ashworth's analysis, there are active sectors, where the question is to kill or to be killed, and other quieter sectors, where the rule is rather live and let live, a phrase in use since 1915. He is interested in unofficial and tacit truces, of varying size, and of varying motives, sometimes entailing a kind of reciprocity in not sniping or shelling in order to remove the wounded or to receive provisions. As a general rule both camps understood spontaneously that it was wise to let sleeping dogs lie; sometimes officers deliberately broke such truces. But trench warfare also entails combat in multiple forms. Sniping units were specially formed in the British army – grenadiers, sappers, and so on.

Ashworth like Keegan focused on British soldiers in combat and highlighted the special characteristics of this army. Alongside the professional army and its regiments, with long traditions and its officer corps manifesting all the elements of social class comportment and deference, the British Expeditionary Corps was formed, overwhelmingly composed of volunteers, who collectively were known as Kitchener's army, after the first wartime Minister of War (Simkins, 1988). More than a third of these battalions were raised by associations and local notables in towns and cities, whose inhabitants paid for their training, their equipment, their uniforms. Some of these 'Pals' battalions' were composed of friends committed to serving together, as they had worked together in commerce, in the mines, in factories. Others had joined the same sporting clubs and associations, or they had gone to the same schools. Many Pals' battalions were composed of workingmen, but ex-public schoolboys formed others, such as the Artists' Rifles, where men from more privileged social classes became officers. This social structure of voluntary recruitment brought to the army the habits of social deference which, as Keegan noted, fitted a different social order. Officers and men lived in entirely separate worlds. The French army in contrast was marked by its democratic aspects, its egalitarianism, the comportment of its leaders, paternal and approachable: 'rank was not a barrier in this army' (Fuller, 1990, p. 49).

Home leave was hard to come by in the British army in France and Flanders early in the war. After all, there was the English Channel to cross. The base camps in which they lived before or after going up the line became a society with its own distinct rules and associational life, quite distinct from those of the French and Germans alike. The British Expeditionary Corps transposed to the continent the forms of sociability familiar at home. The same social divisions existed, with the public-school ethos in evidence on the one side, and the elaborate schemes built up to occupy the men out of the lines drawing on popular practices of entertainment and leisure. British trench journals, studied by Fuller (1990), show how British men in uniform drew on their love of music hall and of football, the working-class sport *par excellence*, not as inflected by social class or regionally limited as cricket or rugby. Alongside football leagues, there were cinema, concerts, and theatrical entertainments of all kinds. 'Playing the game' was the rule, as much in the trenches as in the base camps, where not surprisingly volunteer soldiers from all over Britain brought with them their civilian habits and tastes.

One of the distinguishing features of the British historiography of trench warfare is the way it is firmly grounded in labour history. This may seem surprising, since on the continent labour historians were slow to come to the Great War, and when they did so, they chose subjects largely outside the military arena. The question driving forward much research in Britain is how to square two facts. The first is that Britain was in 1914 arguably the most class-conscious nation in Europe, if not in the world. The second is the record of loyal service by 6 million men in British forces through four years of war. Where did the militancy of the British workingman go? Why was the British army the only major force which avoided a mutiny during the conflict?

The answers scholars offer are varied. The first is to suggest that the British did indeed mutiny. Dallas and Gill (1985) point to a breakdown of discipline at the base camp at Etaples in September 1917, triggered by a brawl between military policemen and soldiers from different units in the British, Canadian, and Australian forces angered by the rough treatment handed to them by military police who never saw the front lines. The Honourable Artillery Company were called to restore order, but the men who rioted, and who stole whatever drink they could find in the neighbourhood, had returned to camp on their own. This event, though, was hardly a mutiny, since it occurred in the middle of the third Battle of Ypres or Passchendaele, and in no way affected the movement of troops or their disposition.

The question as to why the British did not mutiny is, therefore, still an open one. Fuller's work suggests that a kind of loyal indiscipline which marked industrial life in Britain was transferred directly to the army. Winter (1988) suggested that the more industrialized a workforce, the more likely it was to accept the 'rules of the game'; the more peasants in an army, the greater the likelihood of mutiny. Ashworth's interpretation is in line with this argument, since the 'live and let live system' bears a striking resemblance to the time-honoured British practice of working to rule, or doing just enough to fulfil orders, but not one jot more. Here the claim is that workers tolerated an unjust order in peacetime and did the same in wartime. Discipline was a reality, but it was consistent with popular contempt for the staff and their upper-class ways. Lyn Macdonald's series of compilations of what one of her books terms 'voices and images of the Great War' shows the richness of this working-class culture gone to war (Macdonald, 1978, 1988, 1993, 1998). The cadences of the men and women whose records she has published are remote from those of the war poets. Stoical endurance is their mainstay, and a kind of patriotic insouciance which persuaded them that, being British, they could not possibly lose the war. A similar study in stoicism was appropriately entitled 'Death's men' by Denis Winter (1978). A 'cheerful acceptance of fate came from a relatively static, tradition-oriented people', Winter wrote (1978, p. 234), men whose gallows humour made their hardships a bit less intolerable.

Bill Gammage's (1974) study of Australian soldiers points towards the same conclusion, though for different reasons. The men of the Anzac regiments could not stand the deference to authority they observed in some British units; their informality and indiscipline were their greatest strengths. One incident captured the distinction. An Australian officer addressing his men before being inspected by a British staff officer begged them not to call him 'Alf', his nickname. Informality meant self-respect, producing one of the finest fighting units in the war. Their origins were urban and industrial, though they took on the pose of men of the outback, the vast prairies of the Australian countryside.

In both British and Australian scholarship, what is evident is the way in which forms of loyalty to one's mates and stoical acceptance of harsh material conditions, both important facets of working-class culture, were translated into military efficiency in wartime. The opposite was the case in the Russian army (Wildman, 1980) and in some German units. The diary of Seaman Stumpf informed Horn's (1969) account of the German naval mutinies of 1918. Loyal, patriotic young Germans lost their faith in the war and in their officers after tolerating years of miserable conditions not shared by those of higher rank. That is why they refused to go to battle in November 1918 in a hopeless encounter of use only to the high command, desperate to rescue the honour of the navy at the end of the war. Deist's account of the 'soldiers' strike' of 1918 showed too how exhaustion, hunger, and social discontent led ordinary men by the summer of 1918 to surrender. Why should they throw their lives away in a war which could not be won?[16]

The Italian case is midway between the two camps. The Isonzo front was a mixed terrain, with rocky escarpments presenting a very difficult landscape to defend. In October–November 1917, Italian forces were routed at Caporetto, and the remnants of the army fled west in disarray. In some communities, where strike activity had been severe in 1917, the desperate plight of the Italian army intensified hostility to the war. Here was a revolutionary crisis in the making. What is extraordinary, though, is how the Italian army and state were able to survive this crisis, and to avoid the fate of the Russian army, which simply disintegrated after the failure of its last offensive in July 1917. In 1918 the Italian army regrouped, and, with Allied assistance, held the line and pushed back the Austrian and German forces until they capitulated (Isnenghi and Rochat, 2000).

The work of Len Smith (1994) on the French army is a major contribution to this literature. Here he returns to the study of the mutinies of 1917, begun by Pedroncini, but from a different perspective. Smith's work is both broader and narrower in focus. He chose one infantry division, the Fifth under Mangin, in part because this unit was strongly affected by mutinies, and in part because it was possible to follow its movements throughout the war. Without claiming the status of micro-history, Smith's book is nevertheless an ideal instance of what it can provide. By analysing in detail one case study, he was able to explore fully many issues which evade studies of a more general nature. By placing the mutinies within a broader chronological framework beyond 1917 alone, he has been able to unravel the system of social relations out of which the mutinies arose.

For Smith, soldiers and officers engaged tacitly in a form of implicit negotiation, in which junior officers acted as informal mediators. Commanders could not simply do what they wanted to do. They had to deal with what the men in the ranks believed they were able to do; they had to take account of the soldiers' inertia or ill will, or at times their bellicosity. Here is what the American scholar Jim Scott terms the hidden transcripts which govern the relationship between the dominant and the dominated, whose silent veto or modification of the fiat of their superiors corresponds strikingly with the pattern of behaviour of the Fifth Infantry throughout the war.[17] Keegan's book has elements of the same argument, based on the principle of proportionality. From the earliest days of the war, there was a considerable distance between what was asked of soldiers in battle, in terms of its costs – effort, danger, mutilation, death – and the value of the orders of the day. In Smith's work we see an instance of this key point. From one angle, an incident in which units of the Fifth division panicked on 18 September 1914 appears obscure; but from another angle, their actions took on a clear meaning. They simply had refused that day to launch a new offensive. Smith follows the Fifth division sector by sector, and shows how the drastic reduction in hopes about what attacks could yield, in the stalemate of the Western Front, led soldiers to believe that they were caught in a deadly trap. They had no choice between being where they were, among those who suffered like them, or defeat. Between June 1916 and April 1917, the division's military courts had found fifty men guilty of desertion; their sentence was to go back up the line, which indicated to every soldier that going up the line was a punishment.

In this context, the mutinies of 1917 were indeed political, but not in the sense understood by political activists outside the army. Soldiers aimed at – and succeeded in – making their commanders understand the 'policy' they wanted; that is to say, they emphatically expressed the unwillingness of the army to be sacrificed in futile offensives. Those who mutinied did not shoot their officers and go on a rampage, as in Russia. The limited nature of these French protests was evident; what their actions said was that the first concern of command at every level must be to avoid the irreparable: French soldiers must not be ordered to fire on their fellow soldiers. Here was a strike in military form, and understood in these terms, as both a strike and a civic protest as well. Soldiers demanded that their officers, in whom they had confidence, transmit their demands to the government, since the men in uniform had not ceased to be citizens and voters. Smith puts great weight on this point: on the difference between French citizen-soldiers and those who served in other armies. It is their citizenship which defines the resistance of the men in the ranks of the French army to further butchery of the kind entailed by the Chemin des Dames offensive. The profound consent these men had to the Republic set limits on their disobedience, but it also set limits beyond which the command could not go as well. Consent was real, but profoundly conditional.

This rich analysis of the experience of war has anthropological elements in it. It treats the men in the trenches as a kind of micro-society, with its own rules of behaviour to which it is committed, and with its own internal conflicts and fluctuations. This is a work whose comparative character is implicit. By focusing on the soldiers on one side, the other side is always there as a point of reference or similarity. The presumption here is that the experience of trench warfare was not fundamentally different in the different armies, even though a more openly comparative history could produce surprises.

Combatants between consent and coercion

French historiography in the 1980s

French historians came later to study the experience of war in a way their Anglo-Saxon colleagues had done since the 1970s. Several reasons may be adduced for this delay of about a dozen years. The tyranny of the archives on academic history is a point to which we have already alluded: the trenches were not places where official documents were produced. Then there is the nature of academic divisions in France, which may have made history turn in on itself. And there is the way these questions and approaches were more evident in the study of the middle ages and the early modern period than the twentieth century. But there was more.

First there is the matter of ideological reticence. To be interested in combat was politically suspect. This deep prejudice was rooted in interwar pacifism, which treated with suspicion everything associated with the army and which saw even in passive defence the militarization of society. The French left did not get along with the military, who returned the compliment, and who despised democracy in ways which were evident in the insults inflicted by the generals on Deputies mobilized in 1914–15. Most historians, like most intellectuals, were men and women of the left. But this was not all. The war in Algeria probably played a role here too, by persuading some historians not to look too closely into a set of questions they preferred rather to forget than to exorcize by historical enquiry.

More decisive were institutional factors. The organization of research in France developed along other lines which reflected social pressures, for instance to explore the history of the Vichy regime from 1940 to 1944. A dynamic centre of scholarship, the Institute of Contemporary History (L'institut de l'histoire du temps présent, known as the IHTP), focused and nurtured this research. The Institute of Political Studies fostered political history, traditionally defined, but in ways which were open to new approaches in the emerging field of political science. In this second historiographical configuration, the history of the Great War did not have the benefit of a centre which would have both legitimated and coordinated work in this field, in the way that the Bibliothèque-Musée de la guerre had done before 1940. The opening of the Historial de Péronne in 1992 and the creation three years before of the research centre which had designed it, transformed the situation. But in the 1970s and 1980s, the historians of the Great War were left to their own devices.

In order that the experience of the trenches, an object of innumerable accounts, would become a subject of history in France, sources had to be found. The opening of military archives did not produce much in this regard; military reports on soldiers' morale were not particularly illuminating. Stéphane Audoin-Rouzeau (1986) had the idea of exploring a documentary collection which had been readily accessible for decades but not yet exploited: trench newspapers. Le Canard enchaîné, which still exists today as a satirical weekly, is not one of them, since it was produced in Paris by civilians (Douglas, 2002). But during the war, in sectors and periods of relative calm, there appeared a large body of trench journals written by soldiers for their comrades. Le Crapouillot (The trench mortar) was the best known of these journals, about half of which have been preserved. This means that we have 162 titles for the French front. There is a question of officers' surveillance of these papers, but they had no chance of survival and would not have been read or bought for a cent or two had they reproduced the *bourrage de crâne* or brain-washed prose of the civilian press, which these trench journals denounced.

The analysis of this body of material thus permits a view of daily life in the trenches, of the system of representations which soldiers constructed by and about themselves and about the home front. Soldiers' identities arose out of contrasting who they were with those in the rear. Other work in the 1980s, such as that of Canini (1988), which describes the soldiers' life at Verdun, through a mix of first-person accounts with the archives of the postal control of soldiers' letters and other papers preserved in military archives, further deepened the presence of French scholarship in this field. Time and again, historians returned to the question of eye-witnesses and their accounts, a theme of a conference organized by Canini (1989), who died prematurely.

Towards a history of personal experience

Recent historical work has been marked by a renewal of interest in individual testimony. It would have been unsurprising had the inundation of libraries by Great War narratives in the form of memoirs, novels, essays, and diaries ceased after the Second World War. Too much repetition should have induced a kind of fatigue. But French society was seized at the beginning of the 1970s by an extraordinary passion for life stories. The idea prevailed that all life stories are worth telling: a Breton fisherman, a retired teacher, a weaver from Santerre, a Parisian locksmith: the era of the witness began, and witnessing became a central element in the history of the Second World War.[18] Swept along by this current, historians set off in search of new testimonies, privileging those of working people less well represented in the literature, and interviewing elderly witnesses who were dwindling in number. Among them were veterans, whose families discovered diaries and unpublished letters after their deaths, providing a paradoxical and posthumous flourishing of new witnesses of the war.

Rémi Cazals was without doubt a leader in this kind of research, supported by the Federation of secular works of the Department of the Aude.[19] After the events of 1968, he found a remarkable document which he published in 1978: the diaries of a barrel-maker, Louis Barthas.[20] This work has gone through several editions and has had an immense success, with more than 60,000 copies having been sold. Here is the vision of a socialist and profoundly anti-militarist soldier, whose traits are those found in many other sources. Since Barthas revised his notebooks after the war, his evidence has been called into doubt as a pacifist reconstruction of the interwar years, but the changes he made in the text on his second reading of it were minimal.[21]

Many other similar sources were published, including the diaries of Paul Tuffrau. To refute and neutralize the lies of the civilian press, Tuffrau published his notebooks in serial form in the newspapers during the war. This desire to reestablish the truth gives his writing a particular authenticity. In 1998 Audoin-Rouzeau published the original text,[22] a comparison of which with the published version shows a degree of self-censorship which suggests the weight of pressure resting on the witnesses' shoulders.

The return of the subjective witness opened the historiography of the war to new themes. Sociological and anthropological work in this field focused on more personal questions, on the frontiers of social psychology. It was no longer sufficient to ask how the soldiers lived, but what gave them pleasure and what they disliked. Leed (1979), who worked mainly on German and Austrian sources, posed the question of the soldiers' identity: here we are in the midst of their personal experiences, their representations and emotions. This identity was liminal, located in a kind of personal no-man's-land, where the soldier has left behind who he was before the war without any sense that he could return to his previous self. He was stuck, as it were, between the lines. Social differences persisted, though. Leed notes the incomprehension between German conscripts and volunteers: the former saw the war as work, and deadly work at that, the primary goal of which was to survive in one piece. They could hardly imagine what had come over young men who had volunteered to fight. The community of danger did not obliterate these social distinctions. The volunteers were detested because of their class privileges, and still they were stuck in a cul de sac. Sharing their packages from home with working men in uniform was paternalism; not to do so was egotism. Nor did such contradictions fade at the Armistice. Veterans drew on images of camaraderie and of violence. Some went home and forgot it all; others retained a kind of empty anger, irrational and without an outlet, at least until the Nazis came to show them the way.

This interpretation has greater purchase on the German and Austrian side of the line than on the British and French, though some clear parallels may be traced. In particular Joanna Bourke (1996) has followed Leed's line of enquiry by suggesting that the disorientation of war was most evident in terms of the meaning of masculinity. The dismemberment of male bodies and their rehabilitation were the physical side of the story; but there was a psychological side too with important implications for the way in which former soldiers understood the war and located it within their domestic lives after the conflict was over. The use Leed made of the concept of liminality, borrowed from the anthropologist Victor Turner,[23] has a bearing on the disturbed history of masculinity in the period of the Great War. We shall return to this point later when we consider the history of psychological injury in wartime in terms of the category of 'shell shock', a perennial subject of interest to Anglo-Saxon historians of the war.

Audoin-Rouzeau's study of trench newspapers shows a similar displacement under way in the treatment of mentalities or the mental universe of soldiers taken from these descriptions of trench life. It is evident too in the study of war and faith by Annette Becker (1994). Here the author does not restrict her gaze solely to the question of the faith of the men in uniform, but her study does raise the central question of what we can know of such intimate matters. Perhaps only God knows the mysteries of the soul; in any event caution is unavoidable here. The revival of religious practices in the first months of the conflict was not sustained indefinitely, but for a minority of Catholics the war was experienced in a kind of 'religious and patriotic fervour' (p. 100) akin to a mystical experience.

The German historiography joined this trend. Bröckling (1997) underscored the solidarity of primary groups. Lipp (2003) was interested in soldiers' language from their letters and their trench newspapers. Her work reinforced the view that the stab-in-the-back legend was evident in German trench newspapers well before the Armistice. Reimann (2000) is one of the few historians to compare the language of British and German soldiers. When writing to their families, both described the war in similar ways. Without claiming that the experience was the same for all European soldiers, as Rousseau does (1999), many similarities appeared in the essays collected by Cecil and Liddle (1996).

Over a dozen years or so, two major questions have dominated the historiography of the combatants. They are linked with one another. The first, that of the violence in the war, is common in international historical writing; the second one, that of consent to war, is more prominent in France.

Wartime violence

Wartime violence fascinates. Ironically, many of those very historians who are interested in this subject are the first to have no direct or indirect experience of a single war. This is true, but insufficient. This fascination has two sources. Firstly, our society has continued to raise higher normative obstacles to violence in everyday life, to the point that any physical violence towards the person has become unacceptable. In the 1950s to join a political demonstration in the streets was risky; now it is a carnival, and if someone is injured or killed in a demonstration, now it is a scandal. We

no longer accept life-threatening surgery. Any airline crash is followed by
the immediate provision of psychiatric help for the victims' parents and
their families; such examples can be multiplied.

These changes have made war and wartime violence less and less comprehensible, just as war itself has become much more murderous and
brutal than anyone could imagine in time of peace. This is the second
reason. From 1914 on, the world has gone through such massacres, such
atrocious wars that, in contrast, the Great War seems surprisingly civ-
ilized. Historians now suspect that this was not the case; the war of
1914–18 was a dirty war too. From this questioning has arisen the hypothesis, which also has long precedents, that the two world wars form a
continuum (Audoin-Rouzeau *et al.*, 2002).

Wartime violence hit civilian populations early in the war. Annette
Becker (1998) and Helen McPhail (2001) took up the question of violence in the north of France during the period of German occupation,
the deportation of civilians, as well as the fate of prisoners of war in
Germany. It is perhaps an exaggeration to see in these deportations a
sort of preview or sketch of the deportation which would come in the
Second World War, as Abbal (2001) notes in his study of 600,000 French
POWs. Farcy (1995) underscores the parallel in the use of the term 'concentration camps', invented in 1899 during the Boer war, in which were
interned several thousand aliens and undesirables. It is debatable whether
the treatment of prisoners of war in France or Germany, or on the Eastern Front (Rachamimov, 2002),[24] is at all similar to that in the camps
created either in South Africa around 1900 or throughout Europe in the
1930s and 1940s.

John Horne and Alan Kramer (2001), explore German atrocities committed during the invasion of Belgium and France in August 1914. They
show the reality and the amplitude of this violence – more than 6,500
summary executions in Belgium – as well as debunking the myth of children with severed hands and other barbarous mutilations. In this new
historiographical configuration, however, violence and its denial are not
only social but also cultural phenomena. Horne and Kramer asked what
made these atrocities possible – atrocities which the high command not
only covered up but also instigated. They found that the fear of irregular forces, the *francs tireurs*, haunted the German army after the war
of 1870, and circulated as rumour thereafter. Going further still, they
asked why such incontrovertible evidence, clear since the 1920s, had
been obscured. They show how the excesses of mindless propaganda,
which took on absurd forms in the press in wartime, had discredited
all views which tended to blacken the reputation of the enemy. Thus
by the 1930s, accusations of German barbarism were seen as baseless

propaganda. Bartov (2002) has also reflected on the subject of war crimes and their denial. Here we confront if not the problem of total war, at least the process of the totalization of the war of 1914–18 (Chickering and Förster, 2000).

Wartime violence is above all that which afflicts soldiers' bodies. The history of the body which developed rapidly at the same time as the history of sport, and of private life, found in the Great War exceptionally fertile terrain. Bodies went through a trial of terrifying brutality, as Bourke (1996) shows. Sophie Delaporte (1996) studied the fate of disfigured men, and their surgical and social return to normal life, which was never easy and sometimes impossible. Frédéric Rousseau (1999) included in his study of European combatants a treatment of their suppressed sexuality. Jean-Yves Le Naour, in a larger work, considered how the war changed or modified sexual practices (Le Naour, 2002b); here too he considered the sexual frustration of the soldiers. Following the research of Nouailhat (1977), he showed the different reactions of the French and American command on this point. To the Americans, the battle against venereal disease was a matter of constraint. For the French, persuasion was the way to handle this problem. The Americans placed military police in front of brothels, hoping thereby to reduce the number of their soldiers in the long queues leading to them. American demands for the suppression of prostitution, which was legal in France, led to a conflict at the highest levels; Clemenceau himself intervened. A circular of March 1918 authorized the French army to open military brothels without running them.

Of course, the epicentre of wartime violence was combat itself. The objective of any war is to destroy the adversary, to kill him. Joanna Bourke (1999) addressed the subject of the intimate history of face-to-face killing. Her main sources were first-person accounts written by soldiers, many of the unpublished versions of which are deposited in the Imperial War Museum. In the first chapter of her book, she wrote of the pleasure of killing, then she analysed the discourse of the glorification of the methods, and the ways the army taught people to kill and legitimated the fact of killing, with the support of the churches and the medical profession. She thereby reached a general conclusion: ordinary men take pleasure in bloodshed (p. 364), and the association of the pleasure taken in murder and cruelty is widespread (p. 369). In this study, she covers the war of 1914–18, that of 1939–45, including the war in the Pacific, and the war in Vietnam. She devotes only one page, the penultimate one, to the differences among these wars, without drawing the conclusions which follow from this essential point. Her central argument is that the Great War opened the history of wartime violence in the twentieth century. Bourke's work is a good instance of contemporary approaches, in which the war of 1914–18 is reinterpreted in the light of the history of later wars.

Actually, it is possible to take her evidence and use it to support the view on the contrary that the war of 1914–18 was infinitely less violent on the Western Front than was the war in the Pacific or the Vietnam war, since these later wars brought together soldiers from very different civilizations and cultures, and since hand-to-hand combat was frequent. The war of 1914–18, in contrast, the Great War, was an industrial undertaking of mass destruction in which artillery reigned and where, as many accounts state, face-to-face killing was rare.

Here again we find the question of witnesses. In *Rediscovering the Great War*, Audoin-Rouzeau and Annette Becker (2000) challenged the primacy of soldiers' accounts of the war. On the one hand, the deep vein of post-war pacifism led witnesses to censor themselves, to present themselves as victims of mass killing without killers. On the other hand, to reconstruct a more acceptable self-image, they blurred certain aspects of their experience. 'From the viewpoint of the witnesses, one could easily imagine that most of them wanted to exorcise and reconstruct a different war, in such a way as to permit them to live with the trauma of the experience they had undergone' (p. 58). One could imagine this, but on what basis? Witnesses 'chose not to speak of essential aspects' (p. 53) of the question of violence. Possibly. But on what evidence do historians base their alternative reconstructions? What evidence do they use, and why is it preferable to other sources? What do we do for example with the witnesses' accounts collected by Hardier and Jagielski (2001)? Can we really believe that, for instance, an intellectual can speak in place of all the silent peasants who are supposed to have naturalized violence? The question of the evidence of the eye-witness is circular. The same is true of the question of consent to the war.

Consenting to the war. Why did the soldiers hold out?

This question is not a central one for Anglo-Saxon historians. Conversely, it has become all-consuming in the French debate around 2000. However, the issues were not new. They were already broached in Audoin-Rouzeau's study of trench journals, from which he analysed the growing gap between front and rear. To soldiers the home front was both detested and a subject of fascination. Detested because of its mindless propaganda, its incapacity to understand what war was, its stupid questions, and its easy life. Fascinating, because of the affections, loves, and projects soldiers kept in mind, and because that is where the soldiers sought recognition, which alone could give them solace. Over time the gap widened between soldiers and civilians and endangered national cohesion. The gap between front and rear was bridged by a deep vein of national sentiment. The last chapter of his book was devoted to this subject, treated in a nuanced way.

Later on Audoin-Rouzeau and Becker (2000) presented a more radical interpretation of war culture defined as 'a body of representations of the conflict crystallized in a veritable system giving to the war its profound meaning . . . inseparable from hatred of the enemy' (p. 122). Here was the source of soldiers' consent to the war. War culture is linked to wartime violence in a circular manner: war culture accounts for wartime violence, and wartime violence accounts for war culture. This is a phenomenon with profoundly popular sources, 'pushed up from below' (p. 131). It was not a product of the press and other institutions of the government. It would unify the whole of the nation, front and home front bound together throughout the conflict, thereby assuring Allied victory. This is what gives war culture such a central and pre-eminent place in their interpretation of the conflict.

Other historians, on the contrary, have insisted on the constraints within which the soldiers were trapped: the power of the authorities, the moral force of the home front which it was impossible to betray, the fear of military police and courts martial, which were at times severe. About 500 French soldiers, 383 British soldiers, and approximately 30 German soldiers were executed during the war. On 5 November 1998 the French Prime Minister Lionel Jospin unveiled a monument at Craonne to mutineers shot after courts martial. His gesture was meant to help reintegrate these men, as well as those executed as an example to other soldiers, into the national narrative of the war (Offenstadt, 1999). In this context, patriotism is hardly taken into account. The soldiers held out because they could not do otherwise. They were obligated to fight. This is roughly the thesis of Rousseau (1999) in his *History of European soldiers*: 'What is a soldier, if not a man oppressed, bullied, dehumanized, terrorized, and threatened by death by his own side?' In brief, between what we can term the school of constraint and the school of consent, the exchanges have become highly polemical. This division, however, has not been mirrored in the Anglo-Saxon world. As our aim in this book is more historiographical than historical, we do not here take sides in this debate,[25] the polemical character of which has led both sides unnecessarily to antagonize the other. It is important to note, though, that however they may seem to differ, they both share the same historical paradigm.

One part of this debate echoes earlier historiographical developments. Audoin-Rouzeau and Annette Becker's attempt to escape from the 'tyranny of the witness' is striking, since it means that they set aside the evidence of those cited as representative figures by the school of constraint. After Hayden White and the linguistic turn, after Alain Corbin and Roger Chartier and the history of representations, it is impossible to take eye-witness accounts at their face value without questioning the way they were structured, prefigured by their authors' views. However, this approach in no sense permits the historian to hear in the voice of the witness what he wants to hear.

The resurrection of the work of Norton Cru in the last ten years or so as a major contribution to the cultural history of the soldiers' war, takes on meaning in the context of this debate between consent and constraint. His books are disturbing, and his scepticism about soldiers' accounts is well founded. Better to have a witness who was where and when he said he was, than not. At the same time, Norton Cru's questions are not entirely persuasive, because criticizing those who bear witness about feelings, emotions, personal experiences, is not the same as applying the critical method to a diplomatic document or a military dispatch. Furthermore, there are documents in the middle, which have both an elevated and an intensely personal element, such as the sermons of pastors and priests to the people who heard them, especially during the war.

The accounts of such intense individual and collective experience can never be understood as matters of fact; they need a literary elaboration in order to reach their aim; to move the reader, to make it possible for us to hear his or her voice. This is a point Norton Cru never understood, as many writers noted critically after the publication of his book in 1929 (Rousseau, 2003). In this sense, it would be better to reproach Norton Cru for an insufficiently critical approach to the writing he analysed, rather than for having an excessively critical one, and it is probably better to take account of his books and then to go beyond them, rather than to reject them out of hand. The intimate history of the soldiers of the Great War (or of any war) cannot escape for long from epistemological reflections on the way in which eye-witness testimony itself was produced; only after such a set of reflections can such texts be used as evidence in an historical narrative or account.

Finally, eye-witnesses speak in many different voices. Perhaps it would be useful to revise the presuppositions on which the whole history of the war experience rests. Certainly, all front soldiers were marked by an intense and deep experience, but not at all in the same way. We need to find commonalities which unite the soldiers, but it is dangerous not to take into account individual differences and individual trajectories. The uniform they wore did not abolish the different identities of those who formed what the French term '*the* generation of fire'. The term 'the' which connotes a singularity, after all, may be only a linguistic artefact.

NOTES

1. Jules Isaac, 'La crise européenne et la grande guerre. A l'occasion d'un livre récent', *Revue historique*, 1935, 6, pp. 412–47, citation on p. 420.
2. *Revue historique, bulletins critiques*, 1937, p. 117.
3. Abbé Henri Brémond, *Histoire littéraire du sentiment religieux en France*, Paris, Bloud and Gay, 12 vols., 1916–36.
4. *Guides illustrés Michelin des champs de bataille. La Bataille de Verdun (1914– 1918)*, Clermont-Ferrand, Michelin, 1919, is one of these guides which cover the whole of the battlefield. See below, ch. 7.
5. *L'Anthologie des écrivains morts à la guerre; 1914–1918*, Amiens, A. Malfère, 1924–6, 5 vols., presented by Henry Malherbe, président de l'Association des écrivains combattants, is not an anthology of war narratives, but of the writings about a host of subjects by men who died in the war. In Britain, much later, such books appeared in the form of anthologies of 'Lost voices of the Great War'.
6. Le fonds Péricard, preserved in the Secrétariat d'Etat aux Anciens Combattants, contains 1,200 accounts. Cf. Philippe Glorennec, 'Le fonds Péricard', in Canini, 1989, pp. 313–24.
7. Len Smith discusses his Protestantism in 'Jean Norton Cru, lecteur de livres de guerre', *Annales du Midi*, 112, October–December 2000, pp. 517–28. On Norton Cru, see also Christophe Prochasson, 'Les mots pour le dire: Jean Norton Cru, du témoignage à l'histoire', *Revue d'histoire moderne et contemporaine*, 48, 4, October–December 2001, pp. 160–89, Frédéric and Lefèvre, 2000, and Rousseau, 2003.
8. 'Military history is composed almost entirely of those military facts, and it conveys to the non-combatant this false idea that war is composed of a continuous succession of tactical events: attacks, defence, advances, retreats, seizure of men and material, or, roughly speaking, small victories and small defeats. Aside from this, history written today does not tell us anything. Living at the front taught us something else, and we are no longer superstitious about military facts', Cru, 1929, p. 24, cited by Prochasson, 'Les mots pour le dire', p. 186.
9. *Revue d'histoire de la guerre mondiale*, 1930–1, pp. 77–8.
10. Thus German atrocities in Belgium are attributed to the fear German soldiers had of irregular troops (p. 31). Their discussion of the French mutinies of 1917 is also balanced.
11. Jean-Noël Jeanneney, 'Les archives des commissions de contrôle postal aux armées (1916–1918)', *Revue d'histoire moderne et contemporaine*, 1968, pp. 209–33. In recent years, these sources have been used by younger scholars, including John Horne and Bruno Cabanes.
12. Pierre Renouvin supervised the theses of both Jean-Jacques Becker and Antoine Prost.

13. One of the first articles Becker published on this study may be found in Fridenson (1977). It is entitled 'Here sounds the death knell of our boys', pp. 1–21.

14. Jules Maurin shows as well that young men married and did not go to the cities before their military service. In the conscription district of Mende, the social group from which the 'deserters' are more numerous is that of members of religious orders, who left the country at the beginning of the century, and did not come back to fight Germany.

15. Keegan, 1976, pp. 297–8.

16. Wilhelm Deist, 'The military collapse of the German Empire: the reality behind the stab-in-the-back myth', *War in History*, 3 (1996), pp. 1–18.

17. James C. Scott, *Domination and the arts of resistance: hidden transcripts*, New Haven, Yale University Press, 1990.

18. Annette Wieviorka, *L'ère du témoin*, Paris, Plon, 1998.

19. About a dozen volumes have been published. See Cazals (1983) and Cazals, 'Editer les carnets des combattants', in Caucanas and Cazals, 1997, pp. 31–45.

20. *Les carnets de guerre de Louis Barthas, tonnelier, 1914–1918*, preface by Rémy Cazals, Paris, Maspero, 1978.

21. Pierre Barral, 'Les cahiers de Louis Barthas', in Caucanas and Cazals, 1997, pp. 21–30.

22. Paul Tuffrau, *1914–1918 quatre années sur le front. Carnets d'un combattant*, Paris, Imago, 1998.

23. Victor Turner, 'From liminal to liminoid in play, flow and ritual: an essay in comparative symbology', in Edward Norbeck (ed.), *The anthropological study of human play* (Houston: William Marsh Rice University, 1974), pp. 40–58.

24. Compare the evidence used by Rachamimov (2002) to the well-documented record of the murder of millions of prisoners of war by both German and Russian forces in the Second World War.

25. See Antoine Prost, 'La guerre de 1914 n'est pas perdue', *Le mouvement social*, 199, April–June 2002, pp. 95–102.

5 Businessmen, industrialists, and bankers
How was the economic war waged?

There have been three configurations of historical analysis of the economic history of the 1914–18 conflict. The first focused on economic policies and on the role administrators played in economic affairs during the war. The second phase, evident in the 1960s and 1970s, turned to industrial activity which was analysed in terms of the working alliances between businessmen, experts, civilian officials, and the military. This constituted a broadening of perspective from the analysis of economic policy at the level of the state to what Eisenhower christened as the military–industrial complex. In the third phase, the two approaches were merged in the analysis of war economies, understood as complex systems of production, circulation, and exchange operating on the global level to distribute goods and services among belligerents as between civilian and military claimants.

In these three phases, the work of economic historians showed the unprecedented challenges faced by industry, army, and the state after 1914. With the debatable exception of the American Civil War, there had never been a situation like it. The scale of demands made by industrial warfare after 1914 was hitherto unknown. How officials responded to these challenges, both in the public and the private sectors, forms an important part of any explanation of the defeat of the Central powers and the victory of the Allies, even when experts differ over the weight to accord to economic factors in the equation of defeat and victory.

Military history was much more significant than economic history in the calculus of victory constructed in the first phase of writing on these subjects. But in later decades, economic factors were increasingly chosen as decisive ones. In the 1960s, Germany's defeat was set firmly in the context of an economic failure to provide both for the army and for the home front, without major economic disorder. Inflation, at much higher levels in Germany and Austria than on the Allied side of the lines, was at once a sign and a measure of these economic failings. To be sure, the Allies had a much greater material base of raw materials and manpower on which to draw throughout the war, and draw they did. Even with these advantages, the Allies found victory very hard to attain, and as late as March 1918 the majority of observers were unsure as to which side would win the war. Why the Allies won is a question which remained open in the 1990s and beyond. One school of thought emphasizes the strength of the Allied system of distribution to keep front and home front supplied adequately through these difficult years. Another school has challenged this finding. Nearly a century after the end of hostilities, the economic history of the war remains a subject of fierce debate.

The interwar years: the political economy of war

The Carnegie series: a landmark in the economic history of the Great War

The economic history of the Great War was the subject of a remarkable series of books published in the 1920s and 1930s. They were commissioned by the Carnegie Endowment for International Peace, and came out of a pre-war American initiative, announced at an international conference in Berne in 1911, to explore problems of war and peace as central elements in economic life. The series was guided by a group of scholars from Columbia University in New York, including the economist John Bates Clark and the historian James T. Shotwell. Clark was one of the key figures in the marginal-utility school of neoclassical economics. He believed that once international hostilities broke out, the free market could not operate as the arbiter of the relative prices of goods and services. Thus war was destructive of a liberal social and economic system which he defended on intellectual grounds as well as on political grounds, as providing an alternative to socialism.

This liberal impulse was echoed in the discussion of Norman Angell's book *The great illusion: a study of the relation of military power to national advantage* published in London by W. Heinemann in 1910. That relation, both Angell and Clark believed, was overwhelmingly destructive, a point which imperialist and nationalist elements ignored, thereby imperilling the world order as a whole. After 1914, the need for such an enquiry into 'the extent of the displacement caused by the war in the normal process of civilization' was even more urgent. Works already begun were interrupted, but many studies arose out of experiments in wartime economic controls.

The aim of this series was to provide a kind of semi-official history. Authors were chosen because of their direct experience of aspects of economic and social mobilization. In addition, such people were well placed to take the first step in such a project, which was to provide a survey of the documentary material out of which individual histories would be written. The series was based on this archival review, which incorporated both unpublished and published documents. This aim was reflected in the publication of various bibliographical guides, including Camille Bloch's *Bibliographie méthodique de l'histoire économique et sociale de la France pendant la guerre* (Bloch, 1925). It also explains the invitation to Jean Norton Cru to write a survey of soldiers' accounts of the war. The Carnegie project set its priorities clearly: first came the sources, then the interpretations.

The Carnegie series is not a set of state-sponsored or authorized accounts of wartime administration. Official histories would 'show the achievements of the economic war rather than to indicate its strain'. Like the military histories being compiled by general staffs, official histories intended to 'show the strategy of the work behind the lines; their theme is as much the winning of the war as is that of the narrative of armies in the field. That of the economic and social history was to be the obverse of this conception, namely, the displacement caused in the civilian society by such an economic and social disturbance' (Shotwell, 1924, p. 5). For instance, the official history of the British Ministry of Munitions showed its contribution to the war in terms of output. The Carnegie history, in contrast, 'would deal with such a topic not from the standpoint of the output of shells or guns, but of the effect of such a diversion of energy upon the iron and steel trades and other industries'. Consequently, this scholarly initiative would enable 'the intelligence of future generations to judge of the reach of [war's] destructive power, not merely from the destruction itself but from the very energies which it unloosed – sometimes even creative energies – in the societies whose existence it threatened' (Shotwell, 1924, pp. 5–6).

To write these books, James Shotwell affirmed, the Carnegie Foundation 'has brought into existence a kind of international academy, analysing the effects of war, critically and objectively; and so, from across what were hostile frontiers, both consciously and unconsciously by their common pursuit of similar ends, linking up once more the broken contact of the international mind' (Shotwell, 1924, p. 6). The series was therefore a kind of international colloquium on contemporary history, a scholarly equivalent to the League of Nations.

Most of the authors commissioned to write these histories had held administrative or political positions during the war. Twenty-five of the authors had held cabinet rank. Their privileged knowledge helped give the series its authority. For instance, Alexander Popovics's book revealed dealings he had administered as Governor of the Austro-Hungarian bank, and, Shotwell remarks, his work shows that even had the monarchy not been dismembered 'it would have been ruined financially by the war'.[1]

The French series shows the prominence among authors of professional economists. The editorial board consisted of four men: Charles Gide, then Professor of Political Economy in the Faculty of Law in Paris – some years later he was appointed to the Collège de France; Arthur Fontaine, who had been president of the board of directors of the French railway system during war, and later served as a delegate to the International Labour Office; Henri Hauser, Professor of History at the Sorbonne, who had served in the office of the Ministry of Commerce under Clémentel during the war; and Charles Rist, Professor of Political Economy in the Faculty of Law in Paris. These men commissioned and then vetted volumes produced on forms of war administration, on statistics, and on policies and practices related to virtually every aspect of the social and economic history of the war effort.

Fundamental volumes were contributed by Augé-Laribé (1925) on the land in wartime, and by Arthur Fontaine (1924) on French industry. Gide wrote on the cost of living and on the general economic effects of the war. (Charles Gide and Achille Daudé-Bancel, 1926). The French series, though, has some unusual features, in particular the space and attention given to studies of urban history in wartime. No other national series did the same. Volumes were produced on Paris, Tours, Marseilles, Lyons (by Edouard Herriot), Bourges, by Claude-Joseph Gignoux, another Professor of Political Economy, Bordeaux, and Rouen. In no other national series was such an effort made to isolate and examine critically the multiple facets of the urban history in wartime. As in other national series, some French volumes arose out of the intimate knowledge of ministers of the evolution of wartime policy. Clémentel's volume (1931) on the inter-Allied commissions regulating shipping and the distribution of essential supplies is a case in point.

In total, the Carnegie series numbered 132 volumes. It was probably the largest collective enterprise of its kind in history. While monumental in scope, it still inevitably left large gaps. The German series was subject to official scrutiny, and hence was more akin to official history than that of other nations. The sensitivities of Weimar civil servants about the industrial history of Germany in the war were so marked as to prevent the publication of that volume in the Carnegie series.[2] There were other silences in the project. The history of Russia stops at the Bolshevik revolution. Bulgaria, Czechoslovakia, Greece, and Turkey are treated with one single volume each; Spain is left out, though Italy is included; the Italian series was supervised by Luigi Einaudi, President of Italy after the Second World War. There were several volumes on Japan and on the United States, but the bulk of the series is Northern European in character. Neutrals are surveyed alongside combatants. The distinguished economist Eli Heckscher supervised the Scandinavian series; the Netherlands is treated alongside Belgium, whose series was supervised by the eminent historian Henri Pirenne. In sum, this project was a unique attempt to inform post-war discussions of economic and social policy through a better understanding of the myriad ways the conflict had deflected economic and social trends in motion long before 1914.

In almost every national case, and in an overview, the Carnegie project tried to offer a global cost-accounting as to the material damage inflicted by the war. The direct and indirect costs to Germany were approximately four years of national expenditure; the costs to Austria–Hungary were much higher (Grebler and Winkler, 1940), and these are only the tip of the iceberg of economic damage inflicted by the war (Bogart, 1919). For these calculations ignored the structural shifts in economic power which weakened every European nation after the war. The eclipse of the City of London by Wall Street as the centre of international finance signalled the end of a long period of European mastery, which had provided Britain and other European nations with very substantial invisible income through banking, shipping, and insurance. That supplement to national income was reduced substantially by a war which had shifted the centre of gravity of economic power westward over the Atlantic Ocean (Feis, 1930).

Reparations and the economic blockade

The liberal impulse behind this first generation of writing on war economies was reflected as well in the controversy over John Maynard Keynes's *Economic consequences of the peace* (Keynes, 1919). We have already shown the impact of this indictment of the peace treaty on the debate upon the post-war world. Keynes surveyed the war as an economic disaster, and presented a celebrated analysis of the post-war settlement mainly on economic grounds. Very much in the spirit of Clark and Shotwell, he treated war as a serious and debilitating illness, in the aftermath of which careful convalescence was necessary to nurse the European (and world) economies back to health. In Keynes's view, Versailles made this recovery virtually impossible. This argument, controversial at the time, returned later in the twentieth century as a major theme in the economic history of the conflict.

One particular theme addressed in the Carnegie project had powerful political echoes in the interwar period. It was the question as to the legal character and economic effects of the Allied blockade of Germany and Austria–Hungary. Here we face a second structural element in the economic history of the Great War. The Allies had financial resources and raw material reserves which the Germans painfully lacked. Those advantages were driven home and multiplied by the blockade. Did it strangle the Central powers? Was it a war crime that the blockade extended after the Armistice and was lifted only on 28 June 1919, when the peace treaty was signed? After all, if the German army had ceased hostilities, why were civilians denied essential supplies? The sensitivity of these questions helps account for the fact that the official British history of the blockade was published only in 1961 (Bell, 1961). The book had been completed in 1921, and a limited number of copies were deposited in government ministries. The book was not circulated, though, until well after the Second World War. Ironically, its publication in 1961 was fully twenty years after a German edition had appeared (Bell, 1943), and after an American archive, the Hoover Institution, had published a comprehensive set of documents on the blockade (Bane and Lutz, 1942).

Here is one instance of the distinction between official histories and those written under the aegis of the Carnegie Endowment for International Peace. In 1926, a group of French scholars completed a study of the blockade begun under the lead of the historian Denys Cochin, who had died in 1922 (Cochin *et al.*, 1926). The book saw the blockade as of fundamental importance in the ultimate achievement of victory. This study was paralleled by similar publications in French written by former naval officers as to the tactics and strategy of the blockade (Guichard, 1929).

In the early days of the Second World War, it was apparent that the history of the earlier blockade had strategic significance of the highest order. This present-mindedness helps explain the reticence on the part of the British government to distribute its own official history of the subject in the 1914–18 war. William Beveridge, one of the key figures in the Carnegie project on the social and economic history of the war, made this point in 1939, in a brief essay entitled *Blockade and the civilian population* (Beveridge, 1939). And as the war progressed, the legality of attacking civilians became a subject exploited in the propaganda war. German commentators made much of the Allied war through blockade against German women and children between 1914 and 1919 just as the German army was transforming the notion of war against civilians into a new and more monstrous form. In a series entitled 'The iniquities of the Western democracies during the world war (1914–1918)', published in Brussels,

Werner Schaeffer (1940) indicted the Allies for having waged war against women and children. Given the character of strategic bombing and the debate about its legality in Britain, it is hardly surprising that after 1939 the blockade of Germany in the Great War was a subject to be treated with circumspection.

Both the history of economic blockade and that of the Versailles settlement illustrated the controversial nature of the first generation of discussion of the economic history of the war and its aftermath. International trade was subject to international law, but by the mid-1930s, and certainly after 1939, strategic considerations came before legal distinctions.

The first phase of historical writing on war economies was, therefore, public history. That is to say, it was the account of men of affairs whose intimate knowledge of economic activity in wartime was put at the disposal of future generations. In the 1930s, those lessons were unavoidably part of the build-up to a second world war. Historians were in the minority among these authors, many of whom were economists or public servants. Their outlook was hardly uniform, but the upshot of this enterprise was broadly pacifist. These volumes told what the earthquake of war had done to the economic foundations of the liberal political order. To be sure, the foundations were intact, at least to the west of the Soviet Union, but there were cracks everywhere, and they all had to be repaired. Ingenuity and good management had limited the damage in many cases, but on the whole, the conclusion of the first generation of writing on the war economies and on economic aspects of the war was that the Great War had been a tremendous disaster for winners and losers alike.

The 1960s and after: the corporate economy, and the international order

Civilian and military control of the war economy

After 1945, new approaches to economic history changed the nature of the historiography of the economic effort of the First World War. The post-1945 expansion of the international economy and the project of developing the economies of the 'Third World' helped spawn the emergence of economic history as a thriving discipline in the 1960s. Within this field, the subject of war was relatively marginal, but the intensification of violence in Algeria, Vietnam, the Middle East, and elsewhere, once more drew scholarly attention to the set of problems discussed in the Carnegie project and by other historians before 1939. The 1960s were also a period in which Marxist influences in economic history were palpable, though not dominant.

In this second phase of writing about the economic history of the Great War, a phase lasting from the 1960s to the end of the century, what emerges is what may be termed structural history. That is, the object of study was less factors of production – land, labour, capital – or particular policy initiatives or strategies, and more the emergence of new forms of state capitalism, new forms of corporate management of the economy. One way of understanding this phenomenon was to see it in terms of what the sociologist C. Wright Mills called 'power elites' outside parliament and cabinets. Men of industry, technocrats, experts, scientists, bankers, bureaucrats – these are the people whose hands controlled war economies. Thus from the 1960s scholars explored the political economy of the war, to show how economic interests shaped both war policy in general and economic issues in particular. This kind of history of the emergence of the mixed economy, in which the state and the private sector formed a new and lasting partnership, was not Marxist in character. Indeed, the hand of Keynes may be seen in the way economic historians approached the systematic study of the interaction of private and public interests in the formulation of policies both leading up to the war and adopted during its duration.

We have encountered some of these historical initiatives in the earlier chapters of this book. And inevitably so, since the history of political economy is writ large all over the diplomatic record of the period prior to and during the conflict. The most important intervention in this field was conducted by a non-Marxist historian trained in theology, Fritz Fischer. As we have already noted, his 1961 publication, *Griff nach der Weltmacht: die Kriegszielpolitik des kaiserlichen Deutschland 1914–18*, caused a sensation in Germany. The emphasis on German expansionism and imperial greed was extended in his 1969 publication *Krieg der Illusionen* (Fischer, 1969). Here the power of industrial and other interests in working together with military and naval elements to promote an aggressively expansionist foreign policy was documented thoroughly in the pre-war years. No one could miss the allusion to Norman Angell's book, nor the alarming implications of this study that aspects of the Nazi regime's foreign policy were anticipated before and during the Great War. Echoes of the interwar essays of Eckart Kehr (1965) on the primacy of domestic politics in the formation of foreign policy are evident here as well. Kehr, an economist, had limited, though palpable, influence among later historians like Volker Berghahn, himself a student of Fischer (Berghahn, 1971).

The particular role of big business within the German war economy became the focus of much subsequent study. The pioneering work in this field was Gerald Feldman's *Army, industry and labor in*

Germany, 1914–1918 (Feldman, 1966; Bieber, 1981). This work looked at the power elite that ran the German war effort and reached devastating conclusions about it. Feldman showed clearly and comprehensively the chaos resulting from the dominating partnership of the army and heavy industry in wartime Germany. The outcome was a complete imbalance between the provision of goods and services as between civilian and military claimants. The army took what it needed, supplied by heavy industry, the leaders of which charged the state whatever it wanted to fulfil government contracts. The resulting inflationary crisis was the worst in German history.

This interpretation does not ignore the strengths of the German war effort at the outset of the war. Under the supervision of Walter Rathenau, the director of the powerful electrical firm AEG and the German war raw materials office (KRA), German war production outstripped that of the Allies. In the first two years, Germany, with its powerful science-based industrial capacity, had clear advantages over the Allies in this new kind of war. But from 1916, when the German high command took control of the war economy, the balance between military and civilian authority was totally undermined. The Patriotic Auxiliary Service Law of December 1916 – which was passed just as Hindenburg and Ludendorff took command of the German army – was particularly disastrous. The aim of this measure was to enable the German army to respond to the evident strength of Allied war production, demonstrated in the weight of Allied bombardment during the Battle of the Somme. But instead of making the war economy more efficient, it did precisely the opposite. It wrecked the mechanisms of resource allocation, diminishing the supply of essential provisions to the home front, while not providing the armies with sufficient munitions to shift the strategic balance in the war. Byzantine bureaucratic tangles, bottlenecks at key points, and galloping inflation were the results.

Feldman showed as well that the more precarious the German war economy became, the greater was the appetite of industrialists and their military partners alike for the construction of a vast German economic empire in the east after the war was won. This imperialist dream grew as rapidly as did domestic economic chaos. Feldman traces this history in the last year of the war, as the new patriotic formation, the Fatherland party, and its Allies in the army, like the omnipresent Colonel Bauer, came to the fore. Here is the source of Feldman's overall argument that the history of the German war economy is a classic case of the decomposition and eclipse of 'substantial rationality' (Feldman, 1966, p. 519).

The lethal effects of this kind of military–industrial complex on the German war effort and the regime itself were also the subject of Gerd

Hardach's comprehensive economic history of the war, *Erste Weltkrieg: 1914–1918*, published in 1973. In this book, Hardach examined the economic performance of both sides in the war. He joined other scholars in tracing the strength of the Allied war effort to both supply and distribution. The Allies had imperial resources unavailable to the Central powers, as well as to a more flexible system of war production, whereby governments – and not special interests – determined the destination of scarce resources, and imposed on industry targets and price limits that slowed inflation down to a 'mere' 100 per cent in 1918 compared to 1914. The German figure was probably three to four times as high. The maintenance of political control over the army and industry in France was the subject of John Godfrey's study of the consortium system (Godfrey, 1987). French heavy industry could not imitate its German brethren in making its own determination of what it needed and then getting it. Clémentel's system of consortia was backed up by inter-Allied commissions regulating the supply of essential goods. War industrialists got what raw materials Clémentel decided they deserved, not what they thought they did. The advantage of Allied economic cooperation was clear. In establishing that politicians retained control over what raw materials war industry received and at what prices, this system ensured that, unlike in Germany, the political arm of government ran the war economy. The Allied system rested on the capacity of the Royal Navy to assure lines of international supply and communication, and on the effective operation of inter-Allied commissions, which in some ways prefigure the later development of the European Union fifty years later. The parallel is not hard to make: Jean Monnet, one of the founders of the European community, was a key aide to Clémentel during the Great War. Later on he developed this notion of trans-national structures of production, raw material supply, and trade during the 1939–45 conflict, and later under the Marshall Plan. Here again we see the legacy of the Great War in the subsequent history both of the Second World War and of European unification.

Surveying the British case, Chris Wrigley and others have shown that the way Lloyd George operated as Minister of Munitions was much closer to the French than the German model. Industrialists were subservient to the minister of state responsible for war supplies, and not independent of them (Wrigley, 1976). The politics of manpower was the subject of Keith Grieves's 1988 study, which reinforced Wrigley's interpretation. The question as to whether the Allies won the war because of greater supply or because its political economy was more subject to effective constraints is still an open question. On the supply side, Avner Offer (1989) showed how significant were the Allied material reserves in the

course of an international war of attrition. Studies of the Allied blockade reinforced this point (Siney, 1957; Farrar, 1974; Vincent, 1985). On
the demand side, Winter has suggested that while these material advantages were significant, so was the system of entitlements preserved and
extended in wartime by Britain and France. These entitlements ensured
that the war effort would not be waged at the expense of the well-being
of the civilian population (Wall and Winter, 1988).

Economic war aims and their international consequences

A large part of the literature on the war economies of 1914–18 highlights
the differences between the two sides. But this interpretation was challenged by the publication in 1989 of the thesis of Georges-Henri Soutou.
The strength of his work rested on his command of German, British,
American, and French archival sources. Soutou showed that those in
France or Britain who rest their case on documentation excluding the
holdings of German archives miss a substantial part of their own national
history. Soutou examined Fischer's argument about the aggressive and
imperialist nature of German policy, and he found little continuity
between the pre-1914 and post-1914 stories. He also found many industrialists who had grave doubts about German annexation or expansion in
either Western or Eastern Europe. Soutou challenged those who agreed
with Fischer that the war was an attempt to realize a pre-war plan to
construct a vast German economic empire from the English Channel
to the Ukraine. He saw Bethmann-Hollweg's plan to defend *Mittleuropa*
through the formation of a customs union as less an aggressive policy than
an alternative to the army's annexationist plans. Soutou's innovation is
to present as moderate German wartime thinking about the shape of the
economic world after the war.

The really radical thinking, Soutou held, was on the other side. Here
he presented the inter-Allied economic conference of June 1916, and its
sequelae in 1917 and 1918, as yielding plans to control international raw
materials and world trade in a way Germany never envisaged. Nothing
came of these vast plans in the long term, but studying them enabled
Soutou to show that the Allies, and in particular the French, did accom-
plish much of what they wanted through the Versailles peace settlement
of 1919. His work made it abundantly clear how critical a comparative
perspective is in the analysis of wartime economic history.

One of Soutou's findings, supported by the work of other scholars, is
that in 1915–16 Britain reached the unavoidable conclusion that one of
the costs of the war effort would be the end of her pre-eminent position
in international finance; this price and its consequences were accepted

reluctantly but openly. Part of the change consisted in a new relationship between Britain and the United States, with Britain as the dependent partner. Kathleen Burk showed the way in which these Anglo-American international financial instruments were deployed and realized to pay for the import of goods essential to the Allied war effort (Burk, 1982 and 1985). Here it is evident that the American financial community was in the war on the Allied side long before the American declaration of war in 1917. Germany could not compensate for these financial disadvantages, but her scientists' ingenuity helped compensate for shortages of essential goods.

Science and the corporate world

The history of science in wartime is an important facet of the history of the war economy. As a result of the war, there were substantial technical developments in aircraft engineering, in optics, in chemical production, in medical technology (Hartcup, 1988). Every time we go to the dentist, we benefit from a painkiller – novocaine – developed during the Great War. In addition, it was in military hospitals that the French 1912 Nobel-prize-winning scientist Alexis Carrel tested Dakin, a powerful antiseptic, and proved its effectiveness to his sceptical medical colleagues in uniform.[3] Jean Perrin worked in the acoustics of the underground war, and Paul Langevin devoted his time to submarine detection by ultrasound.[4] These advances proved to many in industry, the army, and government that scientific research was of great strategic significance. Consequently, the funding of such research became a state commitment in a way it had never been before.

Working closely with the army, chemists like Fritz Haber used synthetic means to generate essential supplies denied to them by the Allied blockade (Haber, 1986). Haber was also responsible for the first use of poison gas in the second Battle of Ypres in 1915. His war 'service' was no obstacle to his being awarded the Nobel Prize for chemistry in 1919. In France the chemists Georges Urbain and Charles Moureux also worked on poison gas. The chemist's war in France has been the subject of a thorough monograph by Olivier Lepick (Lepick, 1998). In Britain the mobilization of chemists has also received considerable attention (Richter, 1992).

One particular aspect of this history is worth a few more words, to highlight the ramifications of this kind of warfare. It is the significance of the work of the Manchester chemist Chaim Weizmann in developing a new and more efficient method for synthesizing acetone, essential for explosives. In recognition of this powerful assistance to the Allied war effort, Weizmann received the backing of the British Foreign Secretary, Lord Balfour, for Weizmann's dream – the establishment of a homeland for the Jewish people in Palestine. The chemist's war of 1914–18 had political echoes still audible today.[5]

The scientific war had other effects on economic life which historians have documented systematically. The war made economies of scale so important that it gave a huge impetus to corporate amalgamation. The big producers of munitions, like Brunner, Mond, and Nobel, enjoyed a huge injection of public funding in wartime. They amalgamated into Imperial Chemical Industries shortly after the war. Many other firms followed suit (Reader, 1970). Inflation in wartime Germany, alongside the policies of the high command, favoured the creation of new factories by big business, as opposed to relying on middle- and small-scale firms (Feldman and Homburg, 1977).

Business histories in France similarly showed the powerful effects of the war on particular firms and the way they did business. One important contrast in the history of the war economies emerged in the 1970s, and has remained a constant in the subsequent historiography of the war. In terms of the history of the firm, and its relation to the state, the war was a profoundly important modernizer. As we shall discuss in chapter 6, the war brought Taylorism – a managerial approach to time-and-motion efficiency – and assembly-line production techniques to France and Britain more rapidly than would have been the case without the war, and it gave big firms the impetus and the cash to expand both vertically and horizontally. Powerful figures like Louis Renault and Ernest Mattern at Peugeot stood for the future of corporate history; at times in league with the state, at times independently, these industrialists contributed as powerfully to the war effort as it contributed to the growth of their own personal empires (Fridenson, 1972; Daviet, 1988; Cohen, 2001). In terms of the railways, Caron showed clearly that the war effort had brought about a new relationship between the private sector and the state, a sort of nationalization *avant la lettre* (Caron, 1973). Here too the war provided an impetus for the emergence of powerful alliances of long-term significance to the economic history of the twentieth century. Rationalization was a process with many sources, but the Great War both accelerated its introduction and provided precedents of great importance for industrial strategies in the interwar years and after. The Great War, in sum, was therefore a major stimulus to the emergence of the modern corporate economy (Fridenson, 1972; Caron, 1973; Moutet, 1997; Cohen, 2001).

Given these powerful structural changes in industrial policy and practice introduced in wartime, it is surprising that there is as yet no full economic history of France in the 1914–18 war. The same lacuna exists in other national historiographies. The most succinct commentary we have about these issues in the French case is in Kuisel's survey of French capitalism in the twentieth century (Kuisel, 1981), but here the war was folded into the long term, precluding a more detailed analysis of the war years themselves.

Who won the economic war and why? Alternative explanations

When we turn from micro-economic history to macro-economic analysis, however, the impact of the war appears to be almost entirely negative. The structure of the firm may have been streamlined, and its working relationship with the state revamped, but the economic environment in which entrepreneurs operated after the war was clearly changed for the worse.

Part of the reason is the way the war fuelled inflation. The key work in this field has been done by an economist Holtfericht (1986) and in a host of studies by the historian Gerald Feldman (Feldman and Homburg, 1977 and Feldman, 1993). They have shown how inflation destabilized post-war reconstruction, and distorted labour relations as well as strategies of investment and consumption throughout Europe. For this reason alone, it is hard to avoid the conclusion that the war was an economic disaster for both winners and losers.

In effect, whatever individual firms were able to do in wartime, the decentralization of the international economy, the disruptions traceable to currency disorder, the erection of trade barriers, and chronic indebtedness, made business life in the interwar years a very uncertain affair (Hardach, 1973). What is remarkable is, under these risky conditions, how supple businessmen and their Allies were in retaining their commanding positions within their economies and societies. This 'recasting of bourgeois Europe' is the subject of Charles Maier's important study of France, Germany, and Italy (Maier, 1975).

Had Maier extended his gaze to Britain, his conclusions might have been more negative. The depression began in Britain in May 1920, and did not lift until well after the outbreak of the Second World War. Considering the long-term consequences of the Great War for Britain, Niall Ferguson revisited many of the issues which have dominated the economic history of the war. Ferguson is a revisionist on many different levels. He has returned to Keynes's arguments and to the Fischer thesis, and has found both unpersuasive. The title of the book *The pity of war* (Ferguson, 1999) refers not to the suffering conveyed by the war poets, but to Ferguson's view that the war was worse than a crime; it was an unnecessary mistake. He shifts the blame to the shoulders of the British cabinet, whose decision to go to war was not a reaction to aggressive German plans, but actually precipitated these grandiose notions, inscribed in the September programme of 1914. Germany's appetite for expansion was a response to wartime pressures, and not an outcome of a political programme sponsored by big business and the military. This is just the beginning of Ferguson's revision of received wisdom on the economic history of the war. Germany was very efficient in its war effort; and its investment was more cost-effective than that of the Allies. So much for Feldman, Offer, or Winter. And as for Keynes, Ferguson will have none of his rhetoric either. Ferguson argues that Germany was able to pay reparations, but that Keynes and others were duped into believing that Germany was beggared by Versailles. This conjuring trick was accomplished by the prominent banker and official German delegate to Versailles, Carl Melchior. Incidentally, Melchior was later chairman of the Carnegie editorial board on the economic and social history of Germany during the war.

This broadside on the conventional economic history of the war has not persuaded many scholars, but it has opened up a new set of vigorous controversies on a subject with profound implications for our understanding of the war and of its place in the twentieth century. For what Ferguson is really after are the sources of the decline of Britain to the status of a second-rate power in the twentieth century. These he has found in the commitment of Britain to confront Germany in 1914 and to win at whatever cost. This was the real pity of war; Britain's decision to join the conflict was unprovoked, unnecessary, and led to a monumentally Pyrrhic victory. How near and yet how far we have come from the liberal pacifist assumptions of the Carnegie project. In a more belligerent age, studies of the economic 'audit of war' are conducted in a much different spirit.

It should be apparent, therefore, that discussions of war economies in the 1914–18 conflict are nodal points for much broader interpretations of the sweep of twentieth-century events. Interpretations of the workings of industrial societies at war are therefore likely to remain flashpoints for historical controversy; in this sense, nearly a century after its outbreak, the Great War – the first extended conflict between fully industrialized nations – is still heavily contested terrain.

This argument has a bearing on the structure of debate on the economic history of the war in this third configuration. When Ferguson argues that Germany was at least as efficient as the Allies in waging war, he departs from much of the previous scholarship in this field. But Ferguson shares many of the same assumptions as did his adversaries

Fischer and Feldman: economic history can not be written solely from the vantage point of the state; industrial power is independent, or at least partially so; and the essential task is to work out how the public and private sectors together adapted to economic pressure of exceptional intensity and complexity. Germany was opposed by an alliance which could draw on resources throughout the world. If you follow Ferguson, you can only admire how close Germany came to victory. If you follow Fischer and Feldman, you can only see a growing degree of megalomania or irrationality in German economic thinking and practice the longer the war went on. The argument is phrased somewhat differently by Jay Winter (1988) who claimed that in going to war against the British empire, Germany lost the war on its very first day. Germany fought the war to gain an empire, but she needed an empire to win the war. Soutou is more cautious, but he reinforces the view that the imperial dimension was essential to the economic war aims of the two sides. In this sense, he has applied a corrective to Fischer who held that Germany developed a vast imperial dream before and during the war: it is clear that the story is not as simple as that. Conversely, Soutou showed that at Versailles the Allies imposed an imperialist peace on Germany, forced to reduce its capacity to wage war in the foreseeable future. Ten years later, this policy fell apart, and out of the rubble emerged the explosive mixture which detonated the Second World War in 1939. In a way similar to the thinking of one school of the military history of the war, its economic history is ultimately a study in futility.

The balance sheet of the economic war is still a contested matter. Was it a disaster or in terms of how it was waged an economic miracle? On the one hand, its contours show a degree of adaptation on the part of 'state capitalism' of staggering proportions. In the summer of 1914 Lord Grey, the British Foreign Secretary, had predicted that the abrupt rupture of finance and international trade would create economic chaos and food queues by Christmas. He was mistaken: the partnership formed between labour, capital, and the state was sufficiently supple and robust to enable a relatively smooth transition between peacetime production and the needs of the war economies, and then back the other way in 1919–20. This point needs further elaboration, but it remains clear that the Bolsheviks did not build their 'red bridge' across Europe and that the pillars of capitalism, while shaken during the war, remained on a remarkably stable foundation.

This success had a price to be sure. The inflationary spiral severely damaged the fabric of international finance. The expenditure of capital in the form of explosives throughout Europe was a waste in every sense, only dwarfed by the waste in human life which was larger than in any previous conflict. How can one draw up an economic balance sheet? Nearly a century after the end of the war, that question is still an open one.

NOTES

1. Shotwell, 1924, p. 9; see Alexander Popovics, *Das Geldwesen im Kriege*, Vienna, Hölder-Pichler-Tempsky a.-g. and New Haven, Yale University Press, 1925.
2. James Shotwell, *Autobiography*, Indianapolis, Bobbs-Merrill, 1961, p. 154.
3. Alain Drouard, *Alexis Carrel (1873–1944): de la mémoire à l'histoire*, Paris, L'Harmattan, 1995.
4. Jean-François Picard, *La République des savants. La recherche française et le CNRS*, Paris, Flammarion, 1990, p. 27.
5. See the dossier presented by David Auban and Patrice Brett on this field of research, *14–18. Aujourd'hui. Today. Heute*, 6 (2003), pp. 41–172.

6   Workers
Did war prevent or provoke revolution?

In this book, why do we distinguish the history of workers from that of the home front? The reason is because of the powerful relationship between war and revolution, on which there is a huge historical literature. This body of writing followed the same path as did other kinds of history, from a political to a social approach. In brief, the history of workers has replaced the history of labour movements. In this field, the periodization is a bit different than that we have seen in other chapters. The shift from the first to the second configuration happened later, and without an apparent rupture. The third configuration exists only in a sketchy form.

This particular chronology reflects the importance of the political character of this body of historical writing. As a narrative of secular messianism, the history of the labour movement has been framed as that of the epic of the chosen people marching towards its liberation. To understand how and why the revolution so widely expected happened in Russia, and not in other countries, was a central concern for the whole left, socialist, anarchist, communist, or Trotskyist, with different emphases here and there. In France, the strong influence of the Communist party, from the 1920s to 1968, imposed a division of the labour movement between the good and the bad, the revolutionary and reformists, reflected in a kind of history embedded in value judgments implicit or at times explicit. But when dealing with the labour movement, an object so politically constructed, the majority of historians, including communist ones, respected the rules of the professional game. There were two consequences. First, their conclusions were not trivial; they counted. They wrote history, not propaganda. Secondly, they engaged in professional study which took years to complete, accounting for their relatively late publication. Many of these works were launched just after the Liberation, and were published at the beginning of the 1960s, at a time when social history began to dominate other sectors of the history of the war.

Working-class history, in the full sense of the term, is a subject which takes the existence of the class for granted, as everyone did in the 1960s, and poses questions about the conditions of work and daily life faced by

millions of men and women who work for a living. This history revised
the questions it had received from the preceding generation of historians
by moving away from ideology and politics. It accounted for the failure
or success of revolutionary movements not by reference to the acts of
individuals but through an understanding of objective social forces. The
logic of the situation is more powerful than the intentions of the actors.

Unfortunately, some years later, this kind of working-class history
began to become obsolete. With the fall of the Berlin Wall, the implosion
of popular democracies, the retreat and crisis of the Communist party,
the political context became dominated by the eclipse of the great hopes
born in 1917. At the same time, the social context was characterized
by an economic crisis, unemployment, de-industrialization euphemisti-
cally known as downsizing, or *reconversion* in French, the development of
subcontracting, temporary labour, and casual or part-time white-collar
work. Scholars turned away from a group which no longer carried the
fate of the future and whose existence became problematic. Previously
flourishing, the sociology of labour vanished from the landscape of the
social sciences. The history of workers during the Great War was no less
hard hit by these developments, and the passage towards cultural history
was hardly noticed since the workers disappeared by and large from the
historical and historiographical stage in Europe.[1] This is the reason why
when dealing with the labour history of the Great War it makes sense to
distinguish two rather than three periods of historical writing.

1919–1965: A political history

Modest beginnings

There are several reasons why in the years after the war most historians
did not pay much attention to the war as the source of the revolution.
Firstly, the majority of contemporaries thought that the revolution was an
accident without any future. The Soviet regime would not last long, and
Western governments worked hard to ensure that that would be the case.
Time would have to pass in order that what initially appeared to have tran-
sient consequences began to take on the character of a major upheaval:
the foundation of an empire on the basis of an ideology. The Cold War
definitively gave to the Revolution its status as a foundational event, since
one could seriously envisage Western Europe becoming communist. The
question of the origins of the revolution became much more important
in the 1950s than it had been in the 1920s. Secondly, between the wars,
historians were still too few in number to occupy such a specific field.
The actors played the central roles, but in so far as the labour movement

was at stake, those who had analyses to offer were still involved in policy making. In particular in the Weimar Republic, they occupied posts of responsibility. The coming to power of Hitler forced some of them into exile in the United States. From their recollections and their personal documentation, lacking archives, they wrote histories which are still today of some interest (Sturmthal, 1951; Braunthal, 1961–3). These men were learned amateurs of great ability. The professional study of labour history emerged in part elsewhere and later. In Britain, the influence of the Marxist History Group in the 1940s and the positive echoes of the Labour landslide of 1945 helped create a generation of labour historians. At the same time, in France, the great influence of communism among students stimulated an interest in the history of the communist movement and the working class. From the 1950s, the historiographical landscape changed. The fruits of their work would come later.

As we have seen in earlier chapters, the historiography of labour in the Great War must be traced back to the series sponsored by the Carnegie Foundation on the social and economic history of the war. The books commissioned on labour were not concerned with revolution – the Russian series stopped in 1917 – but rather with the growth of wartime production. Those responsible for manpower in the war effort were well placed to tell this story. Oualid and Picquenard (1928) wrote a well-documented study of wages, strikes and collective agreements in France. Oualid was a professor of law in Paris, an aide to Albert Thomas in the Ministry of Armaments during the war. Picquenard headed the directorate of labour in the Ministry of Labour. They knew what they were talking about. Picard (1928) wrote for the Carnegie series a survey of the French trade-union movement during the war. The formation of the political truce (l'Union sacrée) at the outset of the war is well described, as is the participation of the General Confederation of Labour (CGT) in the Committee of Action which was of great importance in the structuring of a reformist programme during the conflict. Picard also provides essential information on the growth of the workforce, on the social structure of militants and on strikes.

In Britain, alongside Bowley (1921) on wages and prices, there is a series of studies written by G. D. H. Cole (1923a; 1923b; 1923c) on labour in the munitions industry and in coal mining. The Clyde Valley in Scotland was probably the most militant industrial area in Britain, one which has a rich history of strike activity from 1915 to 1919. This region was analysed in the Carnegie series by Scott and Cunnison (1924), more from the point of view of the organization of industry than from that of the labour movement.

However useful these volumes were, their purely national focus meant that they were of relatively little use in examining the problem of war and revolution. That question was addressed head on in all its facets by a pioneer, Elie Halévy, whose point of view was marginal in several respects. Firstly, in the French academic world, he was said to be not an historian but rather a philosopher. Second, he taught at the Ecole libre des sciences politiques, which was not a central institution in the French system of higher education. Thirdly, the analysis he provided was presented in the form of lectures delivered at Oxford and not in France. They were published in English, and only after a decade's delay in French (Halévy, 1930 and 1938). These essays have had a certain cachet in the United States, where they were republished in the 1960s, but not in France. Once again we confront the barriers which separate national historiographies of the war, then and now.

Halévy begins by setting aside the political, military, and diplomatic history of the war, the history of what individuals should have done, on this day or at that hour, to prevent or win the war:

Pills to cure an earthquake! My subject is the earthquake itself! I shall attempt to define the collective forces, the collective feelings and movements of public opinion, which, in the early years of the twentieth century, made for strife. I say purposely 'strife' not 'war', because the world crisis was not only a war – the war of 1914 – but a revolution – the revolution of 1917. (Halévy, 1930, p. 5)

His point of view is emphatically social and international. The first of his three lectures was a panorama of forces which pointed to revolution at the beginning of the century: German social democracy, French syndicalism, Russian social democracy. The second was devoted to those forces leading to war, notably in Austria–Hungary, a state in process of decomposition, on which he puts the principal responsibility for the war. His third and last lecture outlined the unfolding of war and revolution. This global interpretation rests on the choice of the month of August 1914 as the moment from which we can date the 'era of tyrannies', defined in this way:

(a) From an economic point of view, a very broad system of state ownership of the means of production, distribution, and exchange, and on the other hand, a demand of governments to the leaders of labour organizations for their cooperation in this system of state ownership; thereby trade unionism, corporatism as well as state control;
(b) From the intellectual point of view, thought control by the state, this control being two-fold in character: one negative form, leading to the suppression of opinions deemed unfavourable to the national interest; a positive form, in what we will term the organization of enthusiasm. (Halévy, 1938, p. 214)

And to conclude, with a very British ironic flourish, he said that it was a paradox that post-war socialism drew adherents through their hatred of and disgust with war, while at the same time supporting a programme which consisted precisely in the extension of the wartime state into the peacetime world.

Histories of social democracy

Curiously, the link between war and revolution did not emerge in 1917, but in 1914. Historians all too often ignore the Eastern Front. The inaccessibility of Soviet archives, problems of command of languages, ignorance of the administrative and military realities of Czarist Russia, all these dissuaded historians from tackling the history of the revolutions of February and October 1917. They did not ask why the revolution took place in 1917, but why it did not occur in 1914. The question is not whether war produced revolution, but why did revolution not prevent the war?

This history focuses first on what was termed from August 1914 (Haupt, 1965, p. 11) the 'failure' of the Second International, as Lenin put it, or the 'betrayal' of social democracy, and then on the struggle of 'true' socialists to contest the social truce and social patriotism and to construct an authentic revolutionary movement. This history was written by socialists who belonged to the anti-war minority during the war, and who became communists or Trotskyists, later, or sometimes by socialists who had a guilty conscience and who put pre-war social democracy on trial in order to oppose its pro-war stance or to overhaul it.

In the French case, these observers focus on the volte-face of the CGT, much less well integrated into the parliamentary regime than was the Socialist party. How then did it move so abruptly from a position of segregation to one of integration? Above all, the trade-union movement had mass support, which it had very recently pledged to mobilize against war by calling a general strike. The division on the eve of the war was clear: there were the 'good' socialists, in France, Belgium, Germany, Russia, and Austria, who conducted or wanted to conduct revolutionary struggles; and there were the 'bad' socialists, those who did not engage in such struggles. Their 'vocabulary remained inspired by orthodox Marxism', Haupt wrote in 1965 (p. 81), but through their activities and attitudes, they worked 'without an interruption towards reformism'. Finally, this kind of history rested on the implicit assumption that a refusal of the war on the part of French, German, and Austrian socialists could have prevented its outbreak, a point which overestimates the real strength of European socialism in the context of the war crisis of the summer of 1914. Jacques Julliard was very much a lone voice among historians when he remarked that the leaders of the CGT had understood clearly that the workers 'would march' to war, and decided therefore prudently to engage not in a general strike, but in propaganda for one.[2] Jean-Jacques Becker later asked[3] why did the Second International devote so much time to the question of how it could prevent war. He emphasized the gap between the real war and the war imagined by socialists since the beginning of the century, their total underestimation of national realities, to support his view that above all it was the ideology of the International which had been shown to be bankrupt. However, it is important to note that in the first historiographical configuration there were many who worked from within this very ideological position.

The earliest work of this kind is that of Rosmer. His real name was Alfred Griot, and with Pierre Monatte he was against the social truce of the autumn of 1914. He was an authentic *minoritaire*, opposed to the war and a communist of the first generation representing the French Committee which helped form the Third International at Moscow. He was a member of the political bureau of the French Communist party until his expulsion in 1925. Between the wars, he wrote for the journal *La Révolution prolétarienne* and helped form the Communist League, but he was too independent to remain in any particular school. He collected a mass of documents on the wartime conflict between the pro-war majority and the anti-war minority within the French labour movement, beginning with the socialist and syndicalist press, which he systematically searched. His first book on this subject was published in 1936, but he had to flee during the Second World War, when the Nazis seized his papers. Thus the second volume he published appeared only in 1959. The richness of his citations, the precision of his chronology, the personal acquaintance he had with the milieux he studied made his book a classic to which all later scholars refer.

Some parts of the story are well known: the acceptance of the social truce (*l'Union sacrée*) among socialists and trade unionists in France, as in Germany and Austria–Hungary; the assassination of Jaurès in the evening of 31 July; the speech of Léon Jouhaux, the Secretary General of the CGT, at Jaurès's funeral on 4 August: 'we will be the soldiers of liberty'. Rosmer has something to say about the decision of the French government on 1 August not to arrest anti-militarist activists whose names appeared on a police list, the 'Carnet B'; he thought that this matter was resolved between the Minister of the Interior, Malvy, and the CGT through formal and informal contacts. He is very hard on Jouhaux and the way he accepted an official post in a governmental agency, with which he left Paris for Bordeaux in August 1914. Rosmer is particularly useful on the reconstruction of an anti-war revolutionary movement, using as a bridge between his two volumes the important conference of socialists at Zimmerwald in Switzerland in September 1915, a meeting which he himself was unable to attend.

The study of Milorad Drachkovitch (1953) is less politically committed, since he does not treat the period of the war itself. His main aim is not solely to study the position of Social Democrats in France, but in Germany, and in the Second International too. His method is very traditional and deals with texts and debates. Similarly conventional in approach were other works based on the reports and debates of trade-union congresses and the labour press. There are broad studies in which the war is given a prominent place, as in the 1962 book of Georges and Tintant on Jouhaux, for many years an indispensable account of French trade unionism from the pre-war years to the split of 1921. Here we have a classic and non-partisan account of the *Union sacrée*, the development of an anti-war minority, its evolution alongside the majority, the role of different personalities. Georges and Tintant understood well the force and reality of national sentiment, even among the militant pacifists who were imprisoned before the war, and, avoiding Manicheism, they provide a rather sympathetic portrait of Jouhaux.

Among general histories of socialism, most devote considerable space to the conflict between the partisans of *l'Union sacrée* and the minority opposed to the war. These are less studies of the link between war and socialism than histories of socialism during the war. Some were written by German socialists, who fled their country once the Nazis came to power to take up posts in American universities. The approach of these works is broader in the span of time they cover; thus the failure of August 1914 was compounded cruelly by the failure of January 1933. G. D. H. Cole continued his great history of socialist thought in a volume covering the period 1914 to 1931 (Cole, 1965). Similarly framed is the history of socialism edited by Jacques Droz (1974), which appeared later and had a longer sweep. The innovations in this field came from elsewhere.

New departures of the 1960s

In the 1960s new elements entered the historiographical landscape, but the same political approach to the question of war and revolution predominated. This was a period of Marxist history, but paradoxically these Marxist historians were scarcely interested in the economy or in society. To them, the decisive clashes were political and ideological, of which they wrote the history. They were the beneficiaries of the progressive opening of the archives, and in particular, those of the police. Above all, their work was rigorous and professional, and, when appropriate, they integrated in their studies the insights of their politically committed predecessors. Here we have Madeleine Rebérioux's solid and well-documented synthesis on the war in the general history of socialism edited by Droz (1974, II, pp. 585–642). Her political approach turned the war into a searchlight revealing the failings of the Second International, the weakness of its organizational structure, and the frailty of its theoretical reflections on imperialism. The war created the conditions in which twentieth-century socialism emerged, between the long-term decline of anarchism and revolutionary syndicalism on the one hand, and the newly emergent communist movement on the other. But the transformations the war brought about in society, in the working class, and in the role of the state, play only a limited role in this analysis.

Georges Haupt was one such historian. He produced an impressive bibliography on the Second International (1965), alongside a book entitled *Le Congrès manqué*, the Congress that never happened, referring to the international meeting planned by the Second International to take place in Vienna in August 1914, and which naturally was cancelled once the war broke out (Haupt, 1965). Opening with a close discussion of ideological trends, this book is composed of many documents, including the unpublished minutes of the very last meeting of the International Socialist Bureau in Brussels on 29–30 July 1914. Nothing illustrates better the changes in historiography which have occurred since the 1960s than the contrasting successive readings of this document. When Haupt published it, the key problem was to determine precisely the position of each and every member of the executive. Forty years later, this question is no longer important, and we are struck instead by the lack of realism of these socialist leaders, who conduct their discussions as if they have lots of time at their disposal.

The force of communist influence led historians to frame the war years in terms of a progressive shift from social democratic 'betrayal' to revolutionary commitments. This is evident in the work of Badia on Germany, of Ferro on Russia, and of Kriegel on France. Badia's focus is on Marxism in general and on the Spartacists and Rosa Luxemburg in particular (Badia, 1964, 1967, 1975). He edited many of her important theoretical texts, including her analysis of the German revolution of 1918–19 in which she and Liebknecht played central roles. Badia did not hesitate to use these texts in his criticism of their attempt to seize power in January 1919 under unfavourable political and social conditions. In the end, their tragic destiny – they were shot on 15 January 1919 by Freikorps units which had crushed the revolution – made them martyrs to the revolutionary cause. Within this panorama, Badia reconsiders the strike activities of the labour movement, but he was not particularly interested in these matters, which were contextual issues the political leadership had to take into account and which they analysed in different ways. The imposing biography by Peter Nettl (1966) is similar. While he was aware of the integration of the social democratic movement before the war within a society it purported to reject, and therefore highlighted the difference between sociology and ideology, his biography is a powerful political history of socialist ideas and politics, and not a study of war as the driving force of history. The domain of the history of socialist thought and practice was one to which many German historians contributed. Miller and Rürup were among the key scholars who showed the progressive distintegration of a unified social democratic movement into two separate wings, a pro-war party and an anti-war Independent Social Democratic party most (though not all) of whose members ultimately joined the communists (Miller, 1974; Rürup, 1968).

Ferro's research (1967 and 1976) stands out in sharp relief from that of Badia and Nettl. Ferro, who at this time was secretary and then co-director (1970) of the journal *Annales*, was sensitive to economic and social trends, to public opinion, to mentalities, and he was a maverick who prefigured a change in perspective which later would become of major importance. His history of the revolution of 1917 was evidently political *and* social. The difficulties in the condition of the people, strikes, soldiers' protests over the way the high command was waging the war, counted as much as did the mistakes of those in power and the strategies of the various parties.

With respect to French historical writing in this field, Annie Kriegel and her brother Jean-Jacques Becker led the way. Annie Kriegel was an activist of French communism in the Cold War period, and though she broke her ties with the Communist party, she retained her flair for the dialectic and her zest for ideological and political argument. Kriegel and Becker published in 1964 a short book, mostly composed of documents, on the acceptance by the CGT of the *Union sacrée* in August 1914 (Kriegel and J.-J. Becker, 1964), but then their paths parted, leading each in a different direction of research, with a different chronology and set of issues to investigate. The unequal weight they gave to the war led Kriegel to inspire in a generation of students a new historiography of the Communist party, and Becker to do the same with respect to the history of the Great War. Becker, though, never lost sight of the particular place of workers within French society during the conflict (J.-J. and A. Becker, 1988).

We discussed Becker's pathbreaking study of mobilization earlier (p. 90). But in the context of this chapter we should highlight Becker's interpretation of the incident of the 'Carnet B', the list of troublemakers to be arrested by order of the Minister of the Interior in the event of war. The key point is that the minister, Malvy, decided on 1 August 1914 not to make these arrests; how one interpreted this decision had a direct bearing on the overall debate over workers and the war. For the radical right and the military, Malvy had shown weakness, perhaps tainted by complicity with revolutionary groups. On the other hand, pacifists denounced the 'treachery' of the trade union leadership and accused them of selling their freedom by renouncing the call for a general strike, as they had been mandated to do. Malvy's decision not to engage in the preventive arrest of militants, not to treat them as suspects or enemies, had indeed made easier the adherence of workers to the *Union sacrée*. A history of mobilization could not avoid treating this episode, which has its own significance.

After the opening of the archives, Becker (1973) was able to throw much light on this incident. The central committee of the CGT met on 31 July 1914 between 9 p.m. and 10.30 p.m. Jaurès was assassinated the same evening, at 9.40 p.m. Through an informer at the CGT meeting, Malvy knew right away what they had decided: the CGT was not going to call a general strike. Then at 1 a.m., he sent a telegram to every prefect, ordering them not to make the arrests of those listed in the Carnet B. Becker found the note of the informant and the telegram sent to the prefect of the Department of the North, which enabled him to resolve contradictory evidence. The conclusion is illuminating: the CGT did not call off the general strike as the price they needed to pay for the suspension of the Carnet B. What better example is there of the virtues of the practice of historical research into 'mere events'?

Annie Kriegel's enquiry (1964) was on a much larger scale. She explored the origins of the French Communist party. The subject is more centrally political than social, and she focuses more on the profound transformation of the political system after the Armistice than on the war itself. She analysed with subtlety and care the growth of an anti-war movement within the French Socialist party, concentrating in particular on the 1917 to 1920 period. The revolutionary movement sought a political opening in the legislative elections of November 1919, then, after failing to do so, they sought a social opening through the general strike of May 1920. After this double failure, the French Communist party was born at the Congress of Tours the following December.

Twenty-five years later, in 1988, the same author detached from this grand thesis and published as a separate book the section devoted to the 1920 general strike on the railways. Here is a case study wherein we see the two sides: the strikers and their adversaries, who had prepared for this struggle for some considerable time. Publishing this material separately made sense, since this story is the only part of the thesis which took social history as its central concern. The strikes of 1917 and 1918 were barely mentioned, and the crisis of demobilization and the innumerable strikes which it triggered are entirely neglected.

From the point of view of the history of political events, which was that explicitly adopted by Kriegel, the power of her studies derived from their breadth and their precision. Her central conclusion is that communism was a 'graft' onto French socialism, a point which enabled her simultaneously to insist on continuity and rupture. For her the war mattered much less than did the Bolshevik revolution. The decisive period was the immediate post-war years more than the war, and the enduring divisions it precipitated were above all matters of circumstance, both in France and throughout Europe.

The socialist split of December 1920 was thus a matter of circumstances precisely situated between two periods: after it was clear that what had been attained in France was derisory compared to what had happened in Russia; and before the vision of a national revolution as the outcome of the Russian Revolution had faded away. (II, p. 868)

British historians of the 1960s and 1970s posed a similar set of questions. If in France the post-war period was marked by a radically new element in the form of the Communist party, in Britain, the political landscape had been transformed by the fracturing of the Liberal party and the emergence of the Labour party as a national party with an ambitious socialist programme, *Labour and the new social order*. The question arose as to what extent this transformation was attributable to the war. An approach to this question located in intellectual (or more precisely in ideological) history was taken by one of the authors of this book. Winter (1974) studied the four principal socialist thinkers of the pre-war period, the Webbs, G. D. H. Cole, and R. H. Tawney, and focused on the impact of the war on their ideas and their influence within the labour movement. He showed that the Webbs' ideas directly addressed the problems posed by the war, because they were aimed at the institutions of the state. In contrast the Guild socialism of Cole, at home in the industrial world, and the moral socialism of Tawney hardly had any purchase during the conflict. Here is no history of free-floating ideas, though. The critical question is, what were the echoes and the attractions of these positions within the broader political world of labour and within the institutions which mediated the diffusion of these ideas? The study of Sidney Webb led to an analysis of the War Emergency Workers' National Committee (WEWNC) and then of the Labour party, whose programme was in part an extension of Webb's work in that committee. At the same time, the secretary of the Labour party, Arthur Henderson, after a trip to Russia, was prepared to see in Webb's ideas the germ of a left alternative to Bolshevism. A new alliance was born between intellectuals and trade unionists, leading to the mutation of the Labour party in 1918 into a national party with a socialist objective.[4] In this process the war played a decisive though indirect role, a bit in the way a climatic change can permit certain plants to thrive and others to wither. So war presented conditions in which some approaches to socialism grew and others were marginalized. What we see is not the emergence in wartime of new ideas, but the mutation of older ones, some of which are ill-adapted to the new political climate, and others on the contrary germinate and flourish.

This is a conclusion supported by Chris Wrigley (1976), for whom the war forced the WEWNC and other labour organizations to demand that the state control the economy and that it do so in an egalitarian spirit. But these arguments were contested by McKibbin (1974) who believed that political ideas, even contingent ones, mattered much less than the changing structure of the trade union movement and the vote. It was only in 1918 that the working class was fully enfranchised; the electorate rose immediately from 8 to 20 million. Thus the electoral base of the Liberal party in the white-collar sector of society was undermined by an electorate which was more working-class and poorer than ever before. To McKibbin, trade unionists were not socialists; they were opportunists who saw in Clause 4 of the Labour party constitution of 1918, its socialist objective, a good way to bring middle-class voters into the party's ranks. Ideology was a patina, a thin layer of belief which covered a thick layer of trade union bloc votes and interests. To McKibbin, therefore, the later history of the party is not at all one of the failure to live up to the commitment to socialist objectives it undertook in 1918, because the party never made such a commitment in the first place. Written against the backdrop of the Wilson years in Britain, McKibbin's book has a no-nonsense feel about it; from this perspective the Labour party, in 1918 as in 1968, was a trade-union party, no more and no less.

1965–2000: From political history to social history

The labour movement and the state

The passage to social history occurred when historians distanced themselves from the history of parties, ideologies, strategies, and tactics, a history which focused in effect on debates over participation in power, its contestation, or its revolutionary seizure. Political historians of the labour movement spent relatively little time exploring the local level, the level of practice, and the links with the social world of working men and women. The innovation of the last decades of the twentieth century concerned the greater emphasis placed on the encounter the war occasioned between the labour movement and the state, in France, Britain, Germany, and Italy.

John Horne led the way in the work he did in the 1980s, published in book form in 1991. He was resolutely comparative and treated France and Britain with equal authority. In both these contexts, the need for exponential increases in levels of production in war-related industry forced governments to negotiate with trade unions, and their leaders – even the pacifists and revolutionaries among them – turned towards the state. In France, a Committee of Action was formed by trade unionists, socialists, and members of the Cooperative movement. In this body, trade unionists dealt with daily political matters and concrete problems. They thereby discovered, in their dealings with Malvy or Albert Thomas (Shaper, 1959), that the state was not simply the political arm of capital, but that it could play a positive role as arbiter and organizer, one in which labour had to participate. After having reacted to a series of war-related problems – unemployment in 1914, food supply, and so on – and after having participated in a number of initiatives and committees, the CGT came to see the need to frame a reconstruction programme for the post-war years. The Committee of Action launched this effort to envisage the economic reorganization of the state, a programme which was largely approved by the CGT right after the Armistice. Central to it were demands for an economic council and for the nationalization of industries where administration was not solely in the hands of the state, but which was run by a tri-partite administrative council made up of representatives of workers, capitalists, and consumers. British developments were similar, and once again we find that the WEWNC played a leading role. The conclusion is unavoidable: the war yielded a powerful reformist current, one without immediate impact in the post-war years, but 'the legacy of labour reformism in France and Britain would become evident not after the First but after the Second World War' (Horne, 1991, p. 394).

The analysis of German developments undertaken by Feldman (1966) reached similar conclusions. The institutionalization of trade unionism within the state and within industry increased throughout the war, and notably after passage of the Auxiliary Service Law of December 1916, which required the creation of *Betriebsräte*, or consultative committees in all enterprises employing over twenty workers. Elisabeth Domansky even goes so far as to see in the war the culmination of a long struggle by trade unionists to assert their position as spokesmen for the working class and their power to rein in strikers when it was necessary to do so.[5] Here is the context in which to place the well-known Stinnes–Legien accord of 15 November 1918. Under the pressure of revolutionary events, trade unionists accepted participation in joint committees, enforcing collective agreements, the right to join a union, and the eight-hour day. In Italy, the central committee on industrial mobilization was open to trade unionists, as were regional committees dealing with wage demands. Labour representatives on these committees even had the right to visit factories in the region.[6] Everywhere, except in Russia, governments acted, despite the displeasure of employers, to provide the labour movement with considerable concessions so that it would continue to back the war effort. This went on until the sacrifices, human and material, required by the war became unacceptable, by 1917 in most countries, and in Italy, from its entry into the war in 1915.

This collaboration between trade unionists, employers, and the state did not lead in the short term towards a moderate reformism, but on the contrary towards an increase in strike activity. Much work has been done on this strike wave by Leopold Haimson and his colleagues; much of this research is quantitative and international in perspective (Haimson and Tilly, 1989; Haimson and Sapelli, 1992). The results are clear. Italy is an exception here: strikes diminish, notably in Turin after the uprising of August 1917 precipitated by a shortage of bread.[7] Discontent, though, was chronic, and worsened after Caporetto (November 1917). Spies working for the military in war factories forecast an imminent general strike. In Italy, the decision to go to war never commanded a consensus either in parliament or among the people. The conjunction of peasant and worker discontent and bitter military reverses helped build a peace party which aimed at a change of regime (Labanca *et al.*, 1997). In Italy conditions rapidly approached those of Russia in 1917. The regime was saved by Allied reinforcements which stabilized the military situation and which rapidly provided food supplies to the civilian population. But this discontent exploded after the war, and resulted in the factory occupations of 1920 studied by Spriano (1964).

Everywhere else, strike activity largely ceased at the beginning of the war, and returned in 1917–18, spreading when workers no longer feared being sent to the front. The revolution succeeded in Russia in 1917, inspiring everywhere either hope or fear. It broke out in defeated Germany, in Berlin, in Leipzig, in Munich, in the Ruhr. France and Britain were also shaken by major strike movements which took shape in 1917–18, but which in France were minimized by the official statisticians (Robert, 1995, p. 12).

Historians pondered how to account for this powerful and at times violent wave of strikes. They proposed three major lines of interpretation to explain this upheaval. The first was sociological, finding the sources of militancy in the changing structure of the working class. The second was organizational, emphasizing shifts in the structure and rhythms of factory work. The third was cultural, in that militancy arose out of the aspirations and representations workers framed of the world at war in which they lived. These three kinds of interpretation are complementary, and share many similar elements and chronologies.

The sociological interpretation

The war modified the skill composition and the structure of the working class in two respects. Firstly, the labour force was transformed. The growth of war industries required a major increase in manpower, drawn from displaced rural workers, from the female population, from adolescents too young to serve in the army. These new workers, some scholars argued, less habituated to factory discipline, were prominent in the Russian and German revolutions and in the strike wave which hit the Allies in 1917. The social history of the 1980s and 1990s undermined this interpretation. From data derived from the files of the Russian factory inspectorate, Haimson showed that the strikes in St Petersburg which precipitated the revolution of February 1917 were undertaken by urban workers of long standing in the city. The Vyborg district, where the insurrection started, had a high proportion of workers born in the capital, a stable sexual composition of the labour force, and an educational level making it a centre of working-class identity. The women and youths who came to work in the factories were even more urban and working-class in origin than were the adults already there.[8] The sharp growth in the size of the labour force in the big factories did not erode a solid core of workers with well-established identities. The same was true in Germany. In Leipzig, for instance, as Sean Dobson (2001) has shown, the working class was not transformed by the war; on the contrary, it was even more stable than it had been before the war.

In France as well, new workers were not at the heart of the labour movement. The rapid growth in trade-union membership, and its division over the question of joining the Third International, provide data on this point. Were the unions which voted in 1921 against the reformist majority well established before the war or were they the new unions which expanded towards the end of the war and in 1919? This question was put first by Kriegel, and later by Jean-Louis Robert (1980), who employed more rigorous and reliable methods. His conclusion is that the most radical trade unions were those which kept up their protests and militant activity in the last years of the war. Neither the growth of trade-union membership, nor particular political choices are explicable in terms of the sociology of the working class. The essential break 'does not date from 1920, nor from 1919, nor from the pre-war period, but rather to the war years, and in particular to the last years of the conflict' (p. 177). The sole exception is that of Italy (Isnenghi, 1982), where rapid wartime industrialization, on an underdeveloped industrial base, brought into existence a new working class, still very rural in its ties and occupations. This is evident in the sanctions taken against workers who took time off to work in the fields. This is a factor which, according to Giovanna Procacci,[9] helps to account for the strong solidarity between Italian workers and peasants.

If the influx of new workers did not really change the working class, it is for two reasons, emphasized in the major studies of the period. The first is that, in all countries, through different forms of legislation, the governments kept at work in armaments factories workers with essential know-how, developed over a long period of familiarity with patterns of work and with the relevant machinery. These are the workers who led the way at work, and who led the strikes. The second reason is that the new wartime labour force, even in Russia, came from other industrial sectors. This was less true of Italy and of part of France, where immigrant labour was available. The boom in metallurgy and in heavy industry was accomplished at the expense of the older, more traditional, trades. Robert (1989 and 1995) dates from the war itself the moment when the metal worker became the emblematic figure of the worker. Similar developments were studied in the German case by Kocka (1973), and in the case of St Petersburg by Haimson (Haimson and Sapelli 1992); both underscored the huge sectoral mobility of the labour force as well as relativities in wage levels between the war sector, where wages rose rapidly, and the non-war sector, where they did not do so.

In the case of women, those not in the labour force took on paid labour for economic reasons linked to the mobilization of their partners. In every combatant country, the gaps in the industrial labour force created by the call to arms were partially filled in by female labour. Everyone noted this at the time. In France the 'munitionettes' have been studied by Dubesset, Thébaud, and Vincent,[10] and then by Thébaud in a separate work dealing with female labour as a whole during the war (1986). But here too sectoral shifts were of great importance. The emergence of the new woman worker is in part an illusion; most had simply changed factories, quitting textiles or the clothing trades in order to work in war industry, where wages were higher, as Robert showed for France, and which Woollacott (1994) and Thom showed for Britain,[11] Haimson for St Petersburg, Dobson for Leipzig, and Nolan (1981) for Düsseldorf, and so on.

The presence of large numbers of women in war factories poses two questions. The first asks whether the war constitutes within woman's history progress or a parenthesis in the long struggle for female emancipation. We will discuss this matter in greater detail in the next chapter, but for the moment, suffice it to say that the response is largely negative: the advances of the war were followed by a return to the old order. The second question has been less fully treated. It is to learn how, if at all, this strong female presence affected the way the labour movement acted. Jean-Louis Robert showed that strikes of women workers were more spontaneous, shorter, and more likely to succeed than strikes by male workers. Of course, women did not face the risk of being sent to the front if they went on strike; this factor explains why in all countries they played an essential role, notably at the beginning of strike movements. Finally, it is clear that the mobilization of women outraged by food shortages was the trigger for the fateful demonstrations of 23 February 1917 in St Petersburg, but the same was true in Turin and in German cities. These protests would not have turned into strike movements of great significance had female labour been less numerous in the factories, and if sectoral mobility had not created solidarities between factories, as we can see in the case of St Petersburg between cotton factories and metal works.

Through the case of women's work, we come to the second major sociological enquiry: that which is interested in the evolution of the labour process and in particular the progress of Taylorism. If the working class was less transformed by an influx of new workers than was previously thought, then it was transformed from within by the evolution of the production line itself. Undoubtedly, this development can be traced to the pre-war period, and would have emerged had the war never occurred. But at the very least the Great War accelerated this process. Everywhere we see the emergence of new forms of the organization of time and space to maximize output. Assembly-line production is the ultimate form of this process, which began by the division of the productive process into elementary operations undertaken by specialized machinery.

Recourse to female labour in war factories must be set within this framework of the reorganization of production lines. It is not simply the replacement of men by women, but the emergence of new categories of labour. Laura Downs (1995) showed how industrialists created the category of 'female labour', with its particular functions and characteristics, despite the facts which contradicted this naturalization of women's work, and the ways they organized production through this category which survived long after the war. To oversee a labour force so clearly separated into individual units, Downs argued, employers invented the category of factory superintendent, who, in short, reassured management because they were middle-class in origin but presented women workers with a semblance of female solidarity.

The modification of the system of production had other consequences. In France, Taylorization over the long term has been scrutinized by Aimée Moutet (1997) and in the car factories of Renault (Fridenson, 1972) and

Peugeot (Cohen, 2001). This set of developments affected earnings, by substituting piece work for time work. Robert showed that in the Parisian metalworks, 61 per cent of fitters, 73 per cent of turners, and 76 per cent of pressers were paid piece rates (Robert, 1989, I, p. 105). The diminution of the role of skilled and semi-skilled workers did not pose major problems, since workers' control over the labour process was weak.

It was quite different in Britain. Hinton (1973), in his study of shop stewards, emphasizes the struggle over dilution. The most important trade union in the metal trades, and therefore in the armaments industry, the Amalgamated Society of Engineers (ASE), fought hard well before 1914 to defend the interests of the skilled workers it represented. The union had negotiated an agreement whereby their wages would be preserved even if technical change were to diminish the skill attached to their work. In 1914 a large proportion of skilled workers did jobs which did not require significant training. For the ASE, to replace mobilized men who were skilled workers by semi-skilled men or unskilled men was a provocation, leading to the 'dilution' of the skill composition of their trade and to a reduction in the pay they could command. To deal with these objections, the government created through the Munitions Act of 1915 a special category of factories, controlled by the Ministry of Munitions, where trade unions accepted dilution, and the government pledged to restore pre-war trade practices once the war was over. In addition, the government agreed to exempt from conscription union members in these vitally important factories. This privilege lasted from the end of 1916 to the beginning of 1918, and was accompanied by recurrent conflicts between skilled workers and their semi-skilled and unskilled colleagues.

The war helped transform the labour force through the expansion of the semi-skilled sector. Between the still unformed working class of the early nineteenth century and the disaggregated working class of the end of the twentieth century, the war helped re-form the working class into something which resembled a veritable proletariat. In Britain, Waites (1987), paraphrasing the title of the classic book by E. P. Thompson, wrote of 'the remaking of the English working class'. There was little reason to believe that this new working class would be any more revolutionary than the old one, whose militants were still in 1914–18 the vanguard leading strike movements. The sociological paradigm produced important results, but it did not explain why revolution did or did not emerge from the war.

The organizational interpretation

Many historians tend to account for the social explosion at the end of the war and in the immediate post-war period through the analysis of trade-union organization. Everywhere, in effect, trade-union membership soared. In Germany, membership reached 1.5 million in the middle of 1918, close to 3 million at the end of the year, 5 million three months later, and more than 7 million at the end of 1919. In Britain, trade-union membership rose from 4 million to 6.5 million during the war and peaked two years later at 8 million. Even in France, where unionization was traditionally very weak, the CGT, which had only 350,000 members in 1914, reached 1.5 million at the end of 1919, a significant increase, which was matched by an increase in strike activity.

Unionization was but one aspect of the organization of labour. To see what the war brought about, we need to go into the factories themselves. There we would find a local structure, the development of which in Britain or the appearance of which in France is clearly located in the war period. We speak here of the phenomenon of the shop stewards or workshop delegates. Hinton (1973) devoted the first part of his book to the emergence of the shop stewards. At the end of the nineteenth century they were men officially chosen by their union in particular factories to collect dues and to hear grievances. But they slowly became independent and formed local committees which were relatively autonomous with respect to the trade unions to which they belonged. These are the men who led wartime strikes, and not the trade-union officials whose hands were tied by their commitment to the war effort. The first strike in wartime was launched in February 1915 by Glasgow shop stewards, who had been there since 1896. One of the central elements of Hinton's study is the latent conflict, which at times flared up in public, between these shop stewards, elected by workers on the shop floor and therefore holding a mandate to represent them, and trade-union officials who tried to keep control of negotiations in wartime factories.

Hinton's account shows the reciprocal relationship among this binary structure of working-class representation, the new skill composition of the labour force in the factories, and the national politics of armaments and conscription. The shop stewards' strength arises out of the new organization of the factories, and they represent workers not in the ASE. Their position was more intransigent and more radical. The government had to take account of them, Hinton argues, and try to retain control of the situation by negotiating with other unions than the ASE, and by adapting its policy to fit local conditions.

Hinton's interpretation has not gone unchallenged. Keith Burgess explains the final failure of the shop stewards by referring to government action on prices and conditions of life and to the hopes generated by the new programme of the Labour party. Alastair Reid argued that dilution was both less widespread and of less political significance than Hinton suggests. Reid also published evidence to show that the skill differential of wages actually increased in wartime, thus undermining the argument that skilled workers were radicalized by the reduction of the economic distance between these 'aristocrats of labour' and other working men.[12]

In fact, shop stewards were not solely a British phenomenon; they can be found in different places and under different names in most countries. In Germany their role in the factories of Berlin was considerable.[13] In France, workshop delegates were studied by Gilbert Hatry, in the collection of essays published as *l'Autre front*[14] in French and the 'home front' in English, and by Jean-Louis Robert in his thesis. Recognized in 1917 by Albert Thomas, the Minister of Armaments, they acted as intermediaries in war factories between employers and workers; such men were skilled and were seconded to factory work while on active military service. They dealt primarily with wages, but they were trade unionists, and spoke out on wider issues, such as the pacifist demands for the publication of war aims and the right of self-determination. Employers saw them as forming soviets in embryo. Their relationship with their social base was complex, because on occasion the shop stewards led them, but on other occasions the rank and file remained indifferent, for instance when, after the strikes of May 1918, government repression sent these militants, who were soldiers serving in factories, back to the front line. In fact, these shop stewards inaugurated a new form of militancy, centred on the factory. This was not solely a French phenomenon. The politics of industrial mobilization played an analogous role in Italy, where protest was diverted to the local level of the factory.[15] Jean-Louis Robert suggested that one of the key developments within the labour movement in this period was 'the manifest opposition between the factory and Parisian trade unionism' (Robert, 1995, pp. 410–11). With respect to trade unions, and even the most revolutionary among them, it is the encounter with the state which was most significant. Since the unions were taken to be credible interlocutors by the state, they felt obliged to represent the interests of their members, who in turn needed a stable leadership to do so, despite all the difficulties created by the war. If the leadership changed, the state would reconsider its position. Here is the source of the ageing of the leadership, which demographic factors do not explain.

Contrasting with this trade union world was that of the factory and above all of the war factory, with its new and central core of mobilized workers, its new practices of workers' control, of short strikes and of new forms of direct action. Here is a world closed in on itself . . . one in which workers and activists meet in places and at times different from those of trade union custom. This new world of the factory does not manage to express the aspirations of a larger social formation, because it is marked by a very strong local character which weakens every effort at coordination with other workers, as the strikes of 1919 would prove. (Robert, 1995, p. 411)

What emerges from this study is what one could term a 'revolutionary reformism'. This was at times divided, as in the case of the railwaymen, studied by Ribeill (1988), where a reformist leader negotiated a general agreement on the status of railway workers at the same time as his militant adversaries in the union prepared a general revolutionary strike in 1920; at times united, as in the case of many Parisian trade unions in which a set of extreme positions was accompanied by a set of reformist practices. One figure who captures this ambivalence is Emile Hubert, the revolutionary leader of the building workers. Hubert was a pacifist and anti-war activist from the beginning of the war, but he also negotiated in the summer of 1918 with the Prefect of the Seine an agreement whereby workers would be paid directly by the state and not by employers for the work they would do in the Paris fortifications.

We see the same ambivalence in Germany in 1918–19. For Rürup (1968) the revolution ends with its negation. The revolutionaries had for their programme the democratization of Germany, but the constraints under which they operated led them to construct a fundamentally counter-revolutionary regime. In the same vein was Barrington Moore's study of *Injustice* (1978), the focus of which goes outside the chronological limit of the war. His narrative of the 'reformist revolution' of 1918 goes beyond the classic debate which opposes reformists and revolutionaries, by substituting for it the dialectic between the factories and the government. It was no longer of interest to find out who was right among the different factions within social democracy; what mattered was how strike action emerged from the base and how political forces reacted to it.

Moore does not overturn the classic accounts of the events of November 1918 to January 1919: the abdication of the Kaiser and the formation on 9 November of the Provisional Government under Ebert; the meeting the following day of the delegates of workers' and soldiers' councils to form an executive committee to guide or control the Provisional Government. This emergence of dual powers is well known, as is the famous telephone conversation between Ebert and General Groener immediately after this meeting: the army would support the Provisional Government, which in turn would combat bolshevism and support the officers in their restoration of order. Then followed the Congress of workers' and soldiers' deputies in mid-December which insisted upon the election of a constituent assembly, fixed the date for elections, and elected a central council. Finally there was the Spartacist insurrection in January, put down bloodily by the Freikorps, instructed to do so by Noske, Minister of Order.

For Moore, the new government did not opt for revolution for two fundamental reasons. First, the Allies would not have permitted it, and secondly, they believed it was not the will of the people. In fact, Moore argues that there was very little popular support for the minority pacifists, Spartacists and independent socialists, who successively split off from the majority Social Democratic party. The workers who stood behind their factory delegates in the great factories of Berlin were skilled workers, well paid. This avant-garde was much more radical than the reformist masses, whose strategy was not a revolutionary one but focused on industrial action. The majority of workers retained their faith in the Social Democratic party. In the Congress of workers and soldiers' deputies in December 1918, 60 per cent of the delegates were socialists, and the Congress refused to accept as delegates the Spartacist leaders Rosa Luxemburg and Karl Liebknecht. In the elections to the constituent assembly, the Socialist party registered twelve to fifteen times as many votes as did the minority socialists in the working-class cities of Dresden or Chemnitz. The government, under such conditions, tried to consolidate what the workers had gained, but it lacked the power to do so, since its hold was uncertain on the army, on the police, on the bureaucracy, on the press, or on the legal system. Above all, it had to avoid the collapse of the economic system, to assure food supply, and to maintain a minimum of order. The failure of Ebert and Scheidemann arose less from their errors than from the absence of any real revolutionary impulse, from the intact legitimacy of the old forces of order, and from the pressure of events at one of the most difficult points of German history.

Towards a cultural history

The social history of workers during the war seemed at this point to reach an impasse. On the one hand, there was clear evidence of revolutionary aspirations in Germany, in France, in Italy. On the other hand, there was a working class transformed, but with reformist aspirations. In addition the gap between the well paid and the poorly paid diminished, and the social distance between the workers and the white-collar labour force was less than it had been before the war. How can we reconcile these two divergent trends?

It is at this point that historians refer to mentalities (Procacci, 1999) and to culture. There was much to learn about the egalitarian hopes which developed rapidly and incontestably during and because of the war. The reinforcement of national cohesion implied that all social groups participated in a common effort. But such was not the case among profiteers, the well off, and everyone was aware of it. Waites reflects on the paradox that as class differences were diminished by the war, class consciousness in contrast became sharpened through the scandal of profiteering, the vision of capitalists as vultures feeding off the corpses of dead British soldiers (Waites, 1987, p. 68). Kocka (1973) noted that the war deepened both the thirst for equality and the social tensions it produced, largely through the palpable inability of the German government to assure basic supplies to the population. Robert offered abundant citations which show how widespread was the denunciation of the wealthy, those 'fat capitalists [who] for five long years built their fortunes out of the blood shed by the proletariat' (Robert, 1995, p. 310). These are the birds of prey, the millionaires, those stuffed with food, those social parasites who would starve in front of their safes 'if the baker, the farmer, the miner, the butcher, would decide not to exchange their produce for their gold' (Robert, 1995, p. 312).

In this egalitarianism, there is an important element of anti-militarism. Singing the praises of the new Russia, some imagined that there society women swept the streets and officers did household chores. The arrogance of the officer corps appeared to be precisely the kind of authority that no one wanted any more. This is the spirit behind the campaign on the part of the German congress of workers' and soldiers' councils in favour of the election of officers, the rejection of which by Ebert's government signalled that the army and its de facto leader General Groener would rally around the new regime.

But there was more, and Jean-Louis Robert (1989) is without doubt the only scholar to have traversed this ground, in his unpublished thesis. He showed first the ambivalence of the workers' pacifism, which did not exclude an element of patriotism worth defending. This pacifism is first a moral protest, a matter of solidarity with humanity facing the butchery, the massacres built into futile offensives. But the conviction that the war was defensive rested intact in France. Each time the Germans made an advance, in 1918, strikes stopped. The striking workers did not want to be seen as those who bring national disaster in their wake.

After all, it was only workers, and notably workers in war factories, who were labelled as shirkers. However hard they worked, and however hard they protested these conditions, they knew that their hardships were nothing compared to what the soldiers went through. What was at stake was their dignity as men. Robert, who explored the discursive field of the working class through police reports on roughly 18,000 socialist and trade-union meetings during the war, shows this with force. At the heart of the labour movement, we find not a set of social and economic demands, but a cry of protest with a moral, an ethical, core.

The discourse of the militants never ceased to stigmatize the spinelessness of the working class. One of the main activists of the building trades, for instance, Péricat, spoke out in January 1919 at a trade-union meeting of workers in the automotive and aviation industry.

The French working class, the most spineless, the flabbiest on earth, has neither heart nor brains; it only thinks through its stomach, and will revolt only when it is dying of hunger, and then, after everyone else has died. (Robert, 1989, I, p. 179).

The same man was very indignant about material protest: 'How can we erase these debasing words of our wartime trade unionism: wages! wages! wages!' He stigmatized those whose attitude was 'For 10, 15, or 20 francs, I will sell my conscience, abdicate my rights, betray my class' (Robert, 1995, p. 159).[16] The figure of the militant worker is thus, in contrast to the mass of spineless, flabby, and cowardly workers, that of an upright man, courageous, class-conscious, intransigent, educated, a man who pursues a noble ideal. In some respects, the fight against workers' alcoholism during the war shows these elements in relief. An anti-war militant, who rejoined the majority of the CGT at the end of the war but remained a pacifist, Georges Dumoulin, recalls how 'in the trains taking mobilized men to the front, workers cried "to Berlin" at the same time as they were getting drunk on cheap wine'.[17]

The same moral protest which stigmatized the employers and war profiteers did not let trade unionists or the government off the hook. The young militants were opposed to the old frightened men. The majoritarian leaders were seen as terrified, inert, cut off from their base, traitors, bastards, men who have sold out. The register and the invective are sincere. In joining up with the government, these men had compromised both their own dignity and that of the working class.

In terms of this analysis, the social explosion at the end of the war demands a cultural interpretation. Worn out by wartime constraints, humiliated by what they had endured and what was said about them, the workers sought calm and at the same time remained in a state of suppressed anger, which could be directed at times against the militants accused of treason, against the employers, against the government, as in the case of the metal workers in the Parisian suburbs who went on strike in June 1919, demanding that the CGT summon the government to hand over power to the working class. These violent clashes reaffirmed and renewed a working-class culture compromised by the war. The labour movement confronted the state, and thereby modified radically its conceptions about politics. For the reformists, the state became a partner and an arbiter; for the communists, their priority was to seize state power, an idea totally at variance with pre-war anarcho-syndicalism. But the labour movement was also compromised by the war: there was too much submission, too many sacrifices consented to in the name of national solidarity. There was an image – a false image – that workers were privileged men, shirkers, that had to be erased. National solidarity – experienced, practised, and felt – during the war made necessary the reaffirmation of an identity and a sense of dignity among workers, both of which had been compromised. The revolution would no longer appear as the denial of national unity, but as its realization.

NOTES

1. Antoine Prost, 'L'histoire ouvrière en France aujourd'hui', *Historiens et géographes*, 350, October 1995, pp. 201–12; 'Qu'est-il arrivé à la sociologie du travail française?', *Le Mouvement social*, April–June 1995, pp. 79–95.
2. Jacques Julliard, 'La CGT devant la guerre (1900–1914)', *Le Mouvement social*, 49, October–December 1964, pp. 47–62, reprinted in *Autonomie ouvrière. Etudes sur le syndicalisme d'action directe*, Paris, Hautes-Etudes/Gallimard/Le Seuil, 1988, pp. 94–111.
3. 'La guerre imaginée par le mouvement ouvrier international', in Allain, 1995, pp. 41–9.
4. The WEWNC was the subject of a parallel study by Royden Harrison, who reached similar conclusions. See Asa Briggs and John Saville (eds.), *Essays in labour history, 1886–1923*, London, Macmillan, 1971, pp. 211–59. The decline of the Liberal party has an immense literature surrounding it. For elements of it, see Berghoff and Friedeburg (1998).
5. Elisabeth Domansky, 'The rationalization of class struggle: strikes and strikes strategy of the German metalworkers' union, 1891–1922', Haimson and Tilly, 1989, pp. 321–55.
6. See Procacci, 1983 and Tomassini 1997, as well as Luigi Tomassini, 'Industrial mobilization and state intervention in Italy in the First World War: effects on labor unrest', in Haimson and Sapelli, 1992, pp. 179–211.
7. Stefano Musso, 'Political tension and labor union struggle: working-class conflicts in Turin during and after the First World War', Haimson and Sapelli, 1992, pp. 213–43; Tomassini, 'Industrial mobilization'. See also the case study by Morelli and Tomassini, 1976.
8. Leopold H. Haimson and Eric Brian, 'Labor unrest in Imperial Russia during the First World War: a quantitative analysis and interpretation', in Haimson and Sapelli, 1992, pp. 389–451. See also the work of two of Haimson's students, Koenker and Rosenberg, 1989.
9. Giovanna Procacci, 'State coercion and workers solidarity in Italy (1915–1918): the moral and political content of social unrest', in Haimson and Sapelli, 1992, pp. 145–77.
10. Mathilde Dubesset, Françoise Thébaud, and Catherine Vincent, 'Les munitionnettes de la Seine', in Fridenson, 1977, pp. 189–219.
11. Jean-Louis Robert, 'Women and work in France during the First World War', in Wall and Jay Winter, 1988, pp. 251–66; Deborah Thom, 'Women and work in wartime Britain, in *ibid.*, pp. 297–326.
12. Keith Burgess, 'The political economy of British engineering workers during the First World War', Haimson and Tilly, 1989, pp. 289–320; Alastair Reid, 'Dilution, trade unionism and the state in Britain during the First World

War', in Steven Tolliday and Jonathan Zeitlin (eds.), *Shopfloor bargaining and the state*, Cambridge, Cambridge University Press, 1985 and 'The impact of the First World War on British workers', Wall and Winter, 1988, pp. 221–33.

13. Dirk K. Müller, 'Trade unions, workers' committees and workers' councils in Berlin's wartime industry, 1914–1918', Haimson and Sapelli, 1992, pp. 287–301.

14. 'Les délégués d'atelier aux usines Renault', in Fridenson, 1977, pp. 221–35.

15. Luigi Tomassini, 'Industrial mobilization'.

16. There were similar declarations against the 'consumer society' on the part of militant trade unionists during the strikes of May 1968.

17. Georges Dumoulin, *Les Syndicalistes français et la guerre*, Paris, Ed. du comité central des C.S.R., 1921, p. 26.

7   Civilians
How did they make war and survive it?

Introduction

The historiography of civilian life in wartime has developed along three axes over time.

First axis: masses

In the 1920s and 1930s, the masses behind the lines were configured as populations to be mobilized, protected, or coerced into making the sacrifices necessary for the continuation of the war to a successful conclusion. The Carnegie series on the economic and social history of the Great War charted the space of civilian life in terms of social and economic policies and their outcomes. In this period, though, the home front was still seen as the backdrop of, and support for, the battle front.

The focus on the home front in historical writing became significant only in the 1960s. In part this was a reflection of the trend towards labour history and social scientific history, which could handle evidence related to broad populations drawn into war though not in uniform. Here is an excellent example of the return to origins, since the idea behind James Shotwell's 132-volume series (1924) on the economic and social history of the war was to obliterate the distinction between military history on the one hand and 'people's history' on the other.

Second axis: classes

In the 1960s, the study of social movements focused on the contradictory trajectories of labour movements in different countries, both prior to and after the two Russian revolutions. On the one hand, labour opposition to war evaporated rapidly in the midst of the war crisis of 1914. Thereafter, labour organizations joined in the power elites that ran war industry in all combatant countries. On the other hand, the social truce of the first three years of the war was never complete. Shop-floor disputes carried on, and were exacerbated by the rapid and chaotic expansion of war production. Younger workers and women workers transformed the gender and age composition of the labour force in heavy industry, as Barrington Moore showed in the German case (1978). It was only a matter of time until fundamental social conflicts re-emerged. By 1917, that threshold had been passed, and as many historians showed, war-weariness combined with anger over profiteering and inflation to produce an explosive mixture of bitterness and deprivation on the home front. Given the level of casualties already suffered, winning the war became a test of the legitimacy of the political and social order; losing the war precipitated revolutions in the four major empires among the losers – the Russian, the German, the Austro-Hungarian, and the Turkish. Labour historians documented the first three in numerous local and national studies. As we have seen in chapter 6, these trajectories of social conflict and revolutionary impulses, alongside others attending the struggles of pacifist and other dissenters in wartime, dominate the historiography of this second generation of Great War historical literature.

Third axis: war cultures

By the 1980s the problem of consent had begun to displace the problem of conflict and coercion as a key to the history of civil society. The study of modes of comportment and signifying practices drew out facets of the extraordinary social and cultural investment made by groups of men and women in the war effort. Women's history flourished. And by the 1990s, the emergence of war crimes in the former Yugoslavia also helped turn attention back to the question of atrocities in the Great War, from Belgium to Anatolia. What have been termed 'war cultures' were capable of steeling endurance and of accepting a demonized view of the enemy without and within. War crimes leading to genocide were the outcome, and increasingly historians came to address the issue of the deformations of the rules of armed conflict in this, the first total war.

Masses at war: the 1920s and 1930s

Official history and the history of officials in wartime

The series sponsored by the Carnegie Endowment for International Peace provided the key elements of the first phase of the historiography of civilian life during the Great War. As we have already noted, the organizers of the series contacted men who were directly responsible for the organization of the home front in different combatant countries, and persuaded many of them to bring their first-hand experience to the task of documenting how the war was waged at home. The advantages of this approach were evident. Men like William Beveridge, a key British bureaucrat in the development of food policy, were in an ideal position to write the history of that topic (Beveridge, 1928). But official history tends to become the history of officials, and the top-down focus of this work made it difficult either to scrutinize the claims of the author as to the responsible job that he and his colleagues did or to evaluate the effectiveness of the policies discussed on the population they targeted, or the response of these targeted populations to the policies directed at them.

Still, the cumulative effect of the Carnegie series is to show the powerful effects of the war on every facet of civilian life, and in particular on the ways cities were administered. Urban histories of a very high order were produced in the French series. Edouard Herriot wrote about Lyons; Henri Sellier, about Paris. Volumes on Bourges, Rouen, Tours, and Marseilles also appeared in the French series. The problems of housing, food supply, and population and public health were also broached in the French series, as they were in other national series on Italy, Germany, Belgium, and Britain. As we noted in chapter 5, what made the French series distinctive was its contribution to urban history as an entry point into the story of civilian life in wartime.

It is important to note that the notion of urban history developed in these works is very much top down. That is, the populations discussed are passive; they are defined by the basic needs of urban consumption – food, fuel, housing, primary education, traffic, safety. These are masses to be provisioned rather than social formations actively engaged in fashioning their own strategies of survival. The agency of urban masses, and the complexity of their visions and frustrations were not at the heart of this first set of historical enquiries into civilian life in wartime.

The range of these municipal experiments was remarkable. Marseille organized an office of low-cost housing (Masson, 1926). Paris opened 'baraques Vilgrain' (municipal food depots) and popular restaurants to provide essential food supplies to the city's population (Sellier *et al.*, 1926, pp. 26ff.) New schools and tuberculosis clinics were fruits of wartime initiatives in Lyon (Herriot, 1924, pp. 67–70). These forms of municipal collectivism sprang up in every combatant country, a reflection of the ingenuity of administrators working under dizzying pressures and facing bureaucracies of Byzantine density and complexity. The defence of the well-being of civilians is one of the key success stories told in the Carnegie series by the men who organized the effort.

Paradoxically, the heavy emphasis on urban history left in the shadows the majority of the population of all continental combatants who lived on the land. There were studies of agriculture, but few of rural society. Consequently, this array of scholarship left untouched one of the central problems of the war, its effect on the life of peasants and agricultural workers. As we shall see, this omission remains largely unrectified to this day.

Demographic history of the war

In the Carnegie volumes, there was as well the first attempt to establish a demographic account of the war. Estimates were prepared by Huber for France and by Meerwarth and colleagues for Germany, both of which formed the basis of historical discussions of the human costs of the war. Most of these studies were descriptive rather than analytical, and used military sources filled with contradictions. What these studies provided was a global sense of the slaughter, and its effects on family formation and reproductive behaviour. Once the shrinkage of the age cohorts of military age was established, then the demographic distortions of the war became apparent. Studies of the defence of public health were also published under the aegis of the Carnegie project. These provided some insight into the efforts made by public officials at damage limitation, particularly in urban populations facing tremendous war-related pressures. The absence of comparative studies in the Carnegie series made it impossible to see whether one country was better than another at defending the well-being of its civilian population against the ravages of war (Bernard, 1929; Meerwarth et al., 1932). And the long-term demographic consequences of the war remained obscure, in part because insufficient time had passed for a full appreciation of the effect of the war on nuptiality and fertility and because of the absence of the systematic study of migration. The pre-war wave of out-migration of approximately 30 million Europeans came to an end in 1914, and was not resumed after the war. Lacking data on this variable, the Carnegie series offered only a rudimentary, though still indispensable, sketch of some war-related demographic trends.

Propaganda

Another focus of the history of civilian life in wartime written in the interwar years was propaganda. Even before the Nazi seizure of power, the subject of the manipulation of civilian opinion by government became the subject of serious historical enquiry. The origin of this interest lay in accusations that the German army was guilty of atrocities during its move into Belgium and France in 1914, a point to which historians in the third phase of writing on this subject would return. The assumption in much of this literature is that Allied propaganda invented these stories or embroidered them to suit their aim in drawing neutrals like the United States into the war.

How the war fostered engines of disinformation became the focus of scholarly attention in the 1920s. In all combatant countries institutions were formed to help disseminate information and inform public opinion. In this period, such groups were configured as puppeteers, pulling the strings of a passive and pliant population. In *Mein Kampf* Hitler had called the masses 'feminine', needing a strong hand and a strong lead. Propaganda was there to give it to them. Thus the history of propaganda was coterminous in this period with the history of brain-washing.

The pioneer in this work was Harold Lasswell, an American political scientist (Lasswell, 1927). His studies of propaganda presented information flows as lawyers' briefs; filled with valid information doctored to appear to tell the truth about the other side. Lawyers usually do not lie; they merely suppress the awkward facts and highlight or distort points of advantage to their side. What propaganda did was to radicalize lawyers' briefs, to turn advocacy into hatred.

This effort to vilify the enemy tended to turn political rhetoric into racial slander; thus it was the Germanness of German atrocities which defined war crimes, and not the atrocities themselves. Such work seemed to make sense in the period of fascist rule in Germany and Italy, and led historians at the time to under-estimate the core reality behind the accusation of the crimes which had been committed against civilians by the German army in 1914–15 in Belgium and France. The study of propaganda tended to lump these valid claims with all the lies and exaggerations which propagandists had conjured up during the war (Buitenhuis, 1987). Thus it is hardly surprising that in the interwar years the word 'propaganda' came to be interchangeable with the word 'lie'. When reports came out of Washington or London in the 1940s that the Germans were engaged in atrocities on a staggering scale in Poland and Russia, the historical scholarship of the 1920s and 1930s on propaganda in the Great War was there to inform their denial. Lies in one war helped obscure realities in another.

Societies at war: the 1960s and 1970s

Social structure and social conflict

The study of war and society emerged in the 1960s and 1970s, in part as a reflection of contemporary events. The Vietnam war produced heated controversy in many countries, and highlighted the ways the waging of war tended to exacerbate domestic social conflicts. In the 1960s, the notion first suggested by Stanislav Andreski (1954) that war was a searchlight, a probe of the stability conditions of social order, emerged in the work of the British historian Arthur Marwick and a number of other scholars (Marwick, 1967). But in addition to contemporary echoes, there were other sources to this developing historiographical tendency. In Britain, the emergence of the welfare state after the Second World War was directly linked to the way in which social policy – and in particular medical services – were organized during the conflict. Three decades after 1945, the question of the 'audit of war' on the social institutions of different combatant nations was applied to the 1914–18 conflict.

Much of this scholarship stood on the borderline between social and political history, and focused on the way the pre-1914 Liberal party was eclipsed by the Labour party, and how in doing so, Labour adopted a socialist objective. Here three lines of argument diverged, as we noted in chapter 6. The first was structural, and located the demise of the Liberal party in the transformation of the franchise in 1918; this change was a reflection of the fact that a majority of the men who joined the British army were disenfranchised in 1914. It was impossible to ask them to die for their country but to deny them the vote. Of these new voters, a majority were working-class men who, as first time voters, chose 'their' class party on the ballot. The second explanation is ideological. The Liberal party committed 'suicide' by waging total war, and turning the state into the central institution of society, something anathema to liberal thinking. In addition the coercive character of liberal regimes in promoting conscription and in suppressing the revolt in Ireland in 1916 disenchanted many liberals and turned them towards labour. Thirdly, the Russian Revolution created conditions in which the Labour party gained support as a left alternative to Bolshevism. All these tendencies worked for labour, at a time when a personal vendetta broke out between Asquith, Prime Minister from 1914 to 1916, and Lloyd George who first supported and then ousted him from power. The factions around these two men never forgave each other, and preferred to see the party disappear than to work together. A combination of these three wartime trends led to the unmistakable outcome: the displacement of the Liberal party by the Labour party as the non-conservative force in Britain's two-party system (R. McKibbin, 1974; Jay Winter, 1974).

The political focus of the 'audit of war' approach became even more evident in German writing on the Great War. Here the central question concerned the social origins of the German revolution of 1918–19. The key contribution here was Jürgen Kocka's 1973 analysis of the intensification of class conflict, as a reflection of the compression of the class pyramid in Germany. He focused in particular on the deterioration of living conditions and prestige of the lower middle class of employees and civil servants who constituted the *Mittelstand*. This pathbreaking study, partly Weberian and partly Marxist in character, followed much of the social history of the period in reading politics directly out of social structure. Many studies of wartime industrial conflict, as we have remarked in chapter 6, approached the problem of social structure and political commitments from a similarly sophisticated *Marxisant* position. There were numerous studies of social movements on the local level which reiterated this growing historiographical consensus (Mitchell, 1965; Moore, 1978; Nolan, 1981). They all emphasize how food shortages and the black market contributed to the disintegration of German society (Davis, 2000).

The impact of the war on English society was the focus of Bernard Waites's study of *Class society at war, England, 1914–1918*. Though published in 1987, the book reflected the concerns of both Marwick and Kocka, and offered an interesting parallel to the argument Kocka developed that political activism emerged out of an improvement in the social and economic situation of some workers and a deterioration in the position of privileged strata. Full employment and inflation were decisive elements, Waites argued, in the decline of deference in wartime. In essence, Waites and Kocka both argue that the war occasioned a flattening of the class pyramid such that the social and economic distance between social classes diminished. The result was a decline of deference in Britain, and an increase in radicalization in Germany, both on the left, and on the right where a 'proletarianized' *Mittelstand* fought fiercely to defend their status. Anything was better than descent into the working class. Here is the environment in which the National Socialist party found some of its most fervent supporters.

There is no French study of social structure in wartime to parallel those of Kocka and Waites. The only study which dealt with this set of issues is *The French home front* (Fridenson, 1977), which is a collection of essays, not a comprehensive study of the whole subject. This is a surprising omission, which may be related to the greater importance of Weberian sociology in Germany and Britain than in France. Durkheimians pose different questions. On the other hand, the Marxist paradigm was discredited more rapidly in France, where the Communist party had been more powerful, than in countries where communism was weak. Other sources of this contrast may be related to the decline in the comprehensiveness of the French census, which pales in comparison with British census returns and German documentation. Conversely, when French scholars turned to data on public opinion in wartime, through the prefectorial archives, they opened up a field still unexplored in Germany,

Britain, or other combatant countries.[1] Archives still determine the shape of historical enquiry, if not its content.

An early study of civilian life in wartime was published by Perreux in 1966. But the study of the home front in France entered an entirely new and more rigorous phase in 1977, when Jean-Jacques Becker published his thesis on French public opinion in 1914. Drawing on the riches of departmental archives of a kind unavailable in other countries, Becker transformed our understanding of the first months of the war. He showed definitively and rigorously that the notion of 'war enthusiasm' was an entirely misleading guide to public opinion in 1914. While some social groups in the capital did rally around the flag noisily and visibly, the reaction of the rest of the population was more muted and marked by anguish as much as by patriotism. In between blind chauvinism and unalloyed pacifism, the vast majority of the population stood, aware of the awfulness of the task, and prepared stoically to see it through. Becker's study of public opinion in 1914 (1977) was followed by a number of incisive studies of French society at war, which reversed the line of causality from that of Kocka and Waites. Politics was not the destination of Becker's analysis; national sentiment was, and out of this form of *mentalité collective* came the grit that enabled the French nation to hold on through fifty months of war.

Surviving the war: the 1980s and 1990s

The history of the home front during the Great War took on two forms in the last two decades of the twentieth century. The first explored elements of material culture and conditions of survival in wartime. The second explored what is now termed *culture de guerre*, which may be defined as the discursive forms through which contemporaries understood the world at war in which they were living.

Material culture: demography in wartime

The study of the material conditions of everyday life began with the Carnegie project, and continued in the later twentieth century. The complexity of everyday life was evoked by Pourcher for France in a work less systematic than evocative (Pourcher, 1994). Other monographs or personal accounts about life in particular cities or villages provided the same kind of vivid picture of how civilians lived during the war.

There emerged as well a reinterpretation of the demographic history of the war, founded on the rigorous application of the quantitative methods of demography. In 1986 these methods furnished the first authoritative estimate of war losses. These statistics rested on the records of the largest life insurance company in Britain, the Prudential, which enabled Jay Winter to estimate life expectancy and construct life tables for the British population both before and during the war. By extrapolating the pre-war data, Winter engaged in a counter-factual estimate of what mortality levels would have been like had there been no war. The difference between this 'peace estimate' – mortality levels in the absence of war in the years 1914–18 – and a 'war estimate' of registered mortality levels constituted the 'lost generation' whose deaths were attributable to the war. These first data on age-specific mortality due to the war directly show the imprint of social scientific history, developed during the 1960s and 1970s (Winter, in Beckett and Simpson, 1989).

Much of the cultural history written in the following years used qualitative sources alone. But the linkage between qualitative and quantitative evidence is apparent in studies of demographic questions in wartime (Bardet and Dupâquier, 1999). One of the findings of Winter's 1986 study of British public health illustrates this well. At certain age groups, after the age of forty, the counter-factual estimate of what mortality rates would have been without the war produced totals of male deaths *higher* than the estimates derived from wartime data. Astonishingly, this finding implied that at ages beyond those at which men were eligible for military service, men were living longer in wartime than they would have done without the war. This concept of *negative* war-related mortality suggested a hypothesis, tested against other kinds of quantitative and qualitative evidence. It was that a war of unparalleled bloodshed was also the time for an unplanned improvement in the life expectancy of the civilian population. Through studies of infant mortality, the age-structure and cause-structure of mortality, this hypothesis was verified. Why was this so? Because full employment, better social provision, and transfer payments like rent control and rationing improved standards of living, and thereby standards of health. And such gains were registered at a time when over half the population of general practitioners in Britain were away from their practices on military service. Evidence of a material change in the well-being of the population in wartime emerged indirectly out of demographic analysis.

Some critics were unpersuaded. Bryder (1988) showed that tuberculosis mortality among women increased in wartime, a finding which made her sceptical of Jay Winter's claim that civilian health had improved in wartime. In response, Winter proposed a comparative study, using French and German materials to compare with the British data he had already examined. One move was to lower the level of aggregation of the analysis, to enable variations to emerge, variations which may have been smoothed out by using national data. The outcome of this work was an analysis of demographic data, health patterns, and social and economic conditions in Paris, London, and Berlin (Jay Winter and Robert, 1997). Winter's original finding was confirmed through this study, though the data showed a more mixed pattern of ups and downs in trends in civilian health in wartime at the metropolitan level than at the national level. Winter moderated his original hypothesis, but retained its overall thrust: in France and Britain, in contrast to Germany, the war was not waged at the expense of the health of the civilian population.

Here the study of the home front intersected with work on the war economy. Social history and economic history overlap so clearly that it is hard to see where one ends and the other begins. Interjecting cultural history into these discussions simply enriches the conversation. These demographic data showed that while supply questions mattered, demand in wartime mattered too. The theory of capabilities and functionings developed by the Nobel laureate Amartya Sen seemed to account for the fact that a country in which food supply was curtailed was also a country which achieved a better distribution of its resources than in peacetime. The history of the home front was thus a testing ground for hypotheses about the way democracies may have been better at waging total war than a quasi-military dictatorship like Germany. Democracies, even in wartime, are answerable to their populations. The well-being of the home front was never separated from the well-being of the armies in Britain and France. In Germany the balance of power was different, and the result was economic and military catastrophe. The documents published by Wilhelm Deist (1970) constitute probably the best illustration of this kind of disastrous mixture of military power and political and economic failure.

Much more work needs to be done to see whether this hypothesis applies to other combatants and other fronts. A recent study of Vienna (Healy, 2003) helps to fortify this interpretation, but there is all too little available on the history of the home fronts in eastern and southern Europe for us to draw any strong conclusions. But there are moves in the direction of broadening the study of this facet of the war (McAuley, 1991). In particular, German scholars have finally recovered from their allergy in dealing with this set of issues (for a summary, see Herwig, 1997). As we noted in chapter 3 on official histories of the war, the 'stab-in-the-back legend' has cast a giant shadow on the history of the German home front during the war. Confronting these questions means confronting the claims made by Hindenburg and Hitler at the time. Discomfort with doing so is part of the explanation for the imbalance in the historiography of this set of questions, an imbalance that is finally coming to an end.

From social to cultural history

In the 1960s and 1970s, the historical study of the home front was infused with insights drawn from sociological writing, primarily Marxist or Weberian in character. In the third generation of writing about the home front, the shift was two-fold: away from sociology and towards a kind of eclectic anthropology, and away from studies of social conflict towards investigations of the roots of consent.

In both cases the shift of emphasis from social and economic history to social and cultural history was subtle and without much friction. Sometimes it occurred even within the same study as a natural move: for instance, at the end of his quantitative discussion of British demography during the war, Jay Winter (1986) turns to memories of the war and cultural questions. Of course, the general decline of interest in quantitative economic history is evident in studies of the Great War as well, but the framework of social history was porous enough to incorporate elements of economic analysis alongside a close attention to cultural forms. The study of what we now term *culture de guerre* became an eclectic amalgam of all kinds of evidence, some material, some discursive, about the ways social groups and individuals made sense of the war and accommodated their lives and their language to it. After all, mass populations had consented to war at the outset, and with some exceptions, they remained committed to seeing the military struggle through towards victory. Even when millions had died, the pattern of social conflict froze in March 1918 when the last major German offensive threatened to produce the decisive military outcome everyone had feared or anticipated for years. That offensive failed like all the others, and the result was a rapid slide to defeat for the Central powers. But before that outcome was clear, the most striking feature of home front life was the consent of the governed to a war of unparalleled slaughter. In the 1980s and 1990s, historians began to ask systematically how that consent emerged and how it was maintained.

This is the origin of much work on what has been termed 'war culture'. This term means many things, but one of its facets has been located in an anthropology of consent on the home front. Following Becker's lead, his student Stéphane Audoin-Rouzeau and others systematically have explored the way French men and women made sense of the world at war. In doing so, Audoin-Rouzeau and others brought the study of war and society into a new domain. In the 1980s and 1990s, what is called the 'linguistic turn' helped break the link between politics and social history in the historiography of the war. That is, most scholars no longer believed that politics could be 'read' directly out of the social position of a particular group. The focus was less on political conflict than on social consent. The language Audoin-Rouzeau initially examined to shape this field was that of trench newspapers, journals written by soldiers and for soldiers during the war. No chauvinism here; instead, there is ample evidence of stoicism, as well as anger at the civilians whose bellicosity increased in inverse proportion to their proximity to the front. A parallel British study by John Fuller (1990) reached a similar conclusion. In fact much of this work followed the lead offered by Prost's analysis of *anciens combattants* in his 1977 thesis. Veterans' organizations which emerged during the war themselves provided a reservoir of references about the civilian and republican character of the outlook and language of the men who temporarily had put on a uniform to defend their country (Prost, 1977a).

War cultures

What made Audoin-Rouzeau's work influential was its subsequent development from an interpretation of *la culture de guerre* to a global interpretation of societies at war.[2] Stimulated by the work of George Mosse on the brutalizing effects of war on civilians and soldiers alike (Mosse, 1990), Audoin-Rouzeau and Annette Becker, alongside their colleagues at the Historial de Péronne, began to see the ways in which the history of civilian life could be integrated with that of the soldiers. The significance of this move is that it bypassed the earlier and unsatisfactory divide between the history of the front and the history of the home front. War culture, or in a more nuanced way, war cultures within each combatant country, provided the conduit between the men in uniform and the people whose lives they were ostensibly trying to defend. In the design of the Historial de Péronne, completed in 1992 at the site of German headquarters during the Battle of the Somme, the history of civilians is given equal prominence to the history of soldiers. There are no other museums of the Great War (or of the Second World War for that matter) which present the same historical narrative of a cultural commonality among civilians and soldiers alike. For this reason, one way to appreciate the innovative character of the Historial is to see it not as a museum of warfare but as a three-dimensional historical anthropology of war. The work that the organizers produced in *Le Monde* in 1994 (Becker *et al.*, 1994) reflects this reorientation of historical thinking about the war.

This new orientation was clearly in full view in the inaugural conference of the Historial, in July 1992, the contributions to which were published later under the title *War and cultures* (Becker *et al.*, 1994). The book is organized under three subtitles: the war imagined, the war represented, and the war recollected and commemorated. The distinction between those in uniform and those outside the armies was deliberately blurred. The research centre at the Historial continued merging military and cultural history through the yearly journal it launched, *14–18, Aujourd'hui, Today, Heute*. This journal probably gives the best review of publications on the Great War and published sets of articles from interdisciplinary perspectives. Its second issue (1999), for instance, dealt with what archaeological research could teach us about the way the war was waged. The third number (2000) discussed the question of psychiatric diagnosis and healing of those who suffered from shell shock. The sixth number (2003) was centred upon sciences applied to war. In each issue, scholars from different academic disciplines brought authoritative insights to our understanding of the war. Clemenceau said that war was too important to be left to the generals; one could say that the Historial demonstrates that cultural history is too important to be left to historians alone.

'War culture' (*culture de guerre*) is a term alluding to the mental furniture men and women draw on to make sense of their world at war. In a series of studies on childhood, on war atrocities, and on mourning practices, Audoin-Rouzeau (1993, 1995b, 2001) showed the way this *culture de guerre* seeped into every area of domestic life. It is, in many ways, not a pretty picture, since it showed the deformations of civility which war brought about. Here is the cultural history of what George Orwell later termed the moral pollution of war. What Audoin-Rouzeau showed with respect to attitudes to violence and in the signifying practices of mourning, Annette Becker explored in her study of religious fervour in wartime, a point to which we shall return. The sheer pressure of surviving a war and the anguish it brought about the survival of loved-ones intensified a reaching out for signifying practices. Among them were religious forms which moved to the centre of public life. Here the anthropology of survival was informed by a sense of the intense emotionality of war. Part of the power of this interpretation was the way it placed affect at the centre of the narrative of war. In Germany too, at the universities of Düsseldorf, Stuttgart, and Tübingen, there are productive groups of scholars who deal with the history of German soldiers and the home front (Hirschfeld *et al.*, 1993 and 1997); they use the same kind of cultural approaches as do their French and British counterparts. Cultural history has attracted many students to the study of the Great War because it has enabled them to enter into the most intimate facets of political conflict, cultural activities, and domestic, family, and emotional life.

On one level, these developments in what may be termed the cultural anthropology of the war have proved controversial. What is contested is the usage of the singular 'culture' in place of the plural 'cultures of war'.

Important distinctions based on region, social class, and gender have been made in studies of civilian life in wartime. Jean-Louis Robert's thesis on Parisian metal workers (Robert, 1989) demonstrated the need to inflect the notion of *la culture de guerre* by social class, place of residence, and occupation. A collective work, under the direction of Jay Winter and Robert (1997), showed similarly how different approaches to social entitlements in these three capital cities determined the capacity of officials to defend the well-being of civilian populations on the urban level. By and large, the emphasis on civilian rights was maintained in Paris and London and undercut in Berlin. It is as yet unclear whether the findings of historians of capital cities apply to other parts of these nations. A national *culture de guerre* is both evident and insufficient to account for the ways different civilian groups withstood the pressures of war, understood the nature of the conflict and their contribution in it.

The idea of war culture in the singular is primarily urban in character. In order to do justice to societies at war, the majority of whose citizens worked on the land, with the exception of the British case, we must accept the likelihood that there was a different coloration to wartime culture in its rural setting than in its urban setting. Contrasting with urban history, rural history of the war seems weak indeed. As the war was going on, the balance between the fields and the factories radically changed. At the beginning of the war, agricultural production was a matter of concern, for it had to meet the needs of feeding not only civilians, but also soldiers and horses. Industrial warfare made industrial production a major preoccupation for generals, politicians, and officials. Though supplying food to the army and to the home front was critical for the maintenance of morale, agriculture became of lesser concern than the production of guns, ammunition, and other industrial products. Historians have told us little about farm labour. Gender studies show the dialectic between the forces pushing women into jobs in war industry they had not had before the war and the forces impelling them out of the labour force after the war. What they neglect, though, is to take account of the fact that the majority of women workers stayed on the land. Wartime farming entailed back-breaking labour, with fewer hands and animals to help till the soil and take in the harvest. As in so many other domains, the historical literature on the Great War is biased heavily towards urban experience. What happened in the countryside is largely unknown. Exceptions exist. Benjamin Ziemann's study of the Bavarian countryside (1997) is among the few works which break this silence. Robert Moeller (1986) also addressed issues of agrarian society in the Rhineland and Westphalia in the war decade, but his focus was more on politics than on rural society. In the French case, Pierre Barral has highlighted the post-war adjustment of rural society to the loss of life of so many men who had worked the land.[3] Setting aside the case of the battlefields which had to be entirely restored, the main element was inflation, which lessened the weight of peasants' debts. Cash flowed into the countryside, modifying social positions. Hence the balance between owner-occupier and tenant farmers was clearly upset by the war. So were many rural customs, as is suggested in *Le cheval d'orgeuil*, Pierre-Jakez Hélias's memoir of Breton life in the period of the war and after.[4]

Gender and war

The emphasis on affect is in part a function of the intersection of studies of war with studies of gender. On one level, the study of masculinity led to the exploration of a coarsening of gender relations among some German veterans. Klaus Theweleit (1978) explored the sexual fantasies of some veterans turned freebooters, or auxiliary soldiers in the Freikorps. Mary Louise Roberts (1994) showed a less violent though equally troubled landscape of gender roles in wartime and post-war France. Roberts showed how contemporary images of childless or independent women, in popular fiction as well as political discourse, embodied widespread fears about the upheaval of war. Following Joan Scott,[5] Roberts shows how discussions of gender were never limited to what on the surface they seemed to say. They pointed as well to how French society after the war reconstructed its global notions of stability and instability.

Roberts's work is characteristic of much Anglo-Saxon writing in this field. These scholars have departed from women's history as the history of social movements dedicated to women's rights in order to explore the history of gender as a prism through which to study society as a whole. The shift of emphasis from the vote to gender inequality as a whole undermines interpretations of the war as a step towards women's 'emancipation'. After an initial description of women's history during the war (1986), Françoise Thébaud examined the evidence as to whether the war had accelerated the process of female emancipation, and concluded that the war was a parenthesis without a legacy.[6] Other studies developed this interpretation, notably Ute Daniel (1997) for Germany. Both Laura Downs (1995) and Susan Grayzel (1999), used a comparative approach as between Britain and France to analyse the position of women at work and at home. Grayzel took an even more sceptical view of wartime developments than did Roberts. 'The war', she concludes, 'did not shatter gender relations and identities in such ways that they then needed to be reconstructed in the postwar period' (Grayzel, 1999, p. 244). The same inequalities that truncated women's lives in 1914 continued to do so in 1918, only against the backdrop of a harsher political and economic climate.

We can see the same comparative approach in Susan Pedersen's study (1995) of family allowances in France and in Britain. The power of the *patronat* in French social policy survived the war intact; indeed the entire history of family allowances is incomprehensible without reference to their initiatives. However, British and French society considered women's work from very different perspectives; in both countries women were dismissed before male workers lost their jobs when war factories closed, but in Britain it was official policy for married women with children to leave the labour force first, while in France unmarried women did so, because they did not need wages for their families. France created a rather generous system of family allowances after the Great War, while in Britain family allowances dated only from 1945 and were set at much lower levels. Such differences between the two countries are striking indeed. The interaction between what is termed the 'double helix' of gender relations is at the core of the essays in the history of women and war edited by Margaret Higonnet and others (1987). These essays explore the binary character of changes in the distance between the life chances available to men and women of roughly the same social class and age. That is, changes in the position of women are in no sense independent of changes in the position of men. Margaret Darrow (2000) has shown how, even in social roles specifically forged during wartime, such as that of the *marraine de guerre* in France, the traditional definition of femininity could be retained. War valorizes masculinity and produces what Denise Riley terms the 'overfeminization of women' (Higonnet *et al.*, 1987, pp. 260–72), the heightening of the reproductive character of femininity at the expense of the other ways they contribute to society; and this occurred at the very time when circumstances permitted women to occupy more independent positions (Higonnet, 2001). Thus, though gender roles changed, they remained as remote from equality after the war as they had been before 1914.

The same sense of movement and stasis dominates the essays on family, work, and welfare in Wall and Jay Winter (1987). To use a metaphor from physics, two vectors moving in opposite directions can produce a resultant of zero. The war both broke families apart and bonded them more firmly; it brought a wider range of job opportunities for women, and better pay for them, and then returned them to fortify the home after hostilities were over. The strengthening of home life during and after the war made it inevitable that after 1918 domesticity defined even more strikingly the socially sanctioned sphere in which women could operate. And given the harsh climate of wartime industrial work, alongside the onset of unemployment, and the social and political uncertainties of the post-war years, it is evident that most women returned home from war factories to the home with some sense of relief.

Winter (1986) showed in the British case that these dialectical movements, towards fragmentation of family life and its renewal, were evident in marriage patterns. The age structure of marriage changed in such a way that women who would have married much older men on pre-war patterns could not do so, since so many of these men had died in the war. Frenchwomen married men of the same age or younger to avoid remaining celibate.[7] In Britain women tended to marry men of different social or geographical origins. The result was the same; over 2 million men died in the war, and yet celibacy rates remained stable.

Part of the reason for this paradox – a massive blood-letting among potential husbands and a rough pattern of stability in nuptiality – relates to the effect of war on migration. Winter showed that more British men outmigrated in the four years before the outbreak of war than were killed during it. Thus potential marriage partners were 'trapped' in Britain by the war, and they remained there after the war because of the changed international environment. It is a myth, therefore, that the war created a generation of spinsters; women found husbands, perhaps not the ones they would have found on pre-war patterns, but they found husbands nonetheless. Family patterns survived the carnage of war, because men and women were able to change their strategies of family formation in a relatively short period of time (Jay Winter, 1986, ch. 8).

Religion inside and outside the churches

One domain in which the historiography of the home front in wartime has developed rapidly is that of religious history. In the 1960s and 1970s, the institutional history of churches and religious groups such as the Quakers was locked into the question of pacifism and its failure either to prevent war or to shorten it by one day or one hour. But in the 1990s, the subject of study is less churches than religious feelings, and in this respect the balance of study has shifted away from the clergy and towards the communicants (A. Becker, 1994; Landau, 1999). The role of the Papacy in trying to mediate or to broker peace negotiations exposed the conflicts between the national position of Catholics and the ecumenical brotherhood of the faithful on both sides of the conflict (Chaline, 1993; Fontana, 1990). The debates within the Anglican church (Wilkinson, 1978) and the sermons of French Protestant ministers (Gambarotto, 1996) have been scrutinized too. For the first time in history Jewish soldiers in uniform were in a position to kill other Jewish soldiers on the other side of the trenches. This shift towards the nationalization of confessional life (Rozenblit, 2001) did little to undermine older prejudices which informed scepticism as to whether German Catholics or Jews everywhere were fully committed to their motherland. This is evident in particular in terms of the plan to conduct a census of Jewish soldiers in the German army in 1916. The very existence of such a plan clearly implied that the high command wanted data confirming that Jews were shirking military service; this was enough to deepen anti-Semitic hatreds, which flourished both during and after the war. It is important to register the fact that the first encounter of the mass of the German population in uniform with a large population of orthodox Jews was during their occupation of what is now Poland. The encounter was not amicable, though the behaviour of the German army was much less harsh than that of the Czar's troops, who massacred large numbers of Jews in their retreat of 1915 (Liulevicius, 2000).

Societies in mourning

In this third configuration of historical writing, we can see strong evidence of a shift from the history of institutions to the history of sentiments, both among communicants and among the broader population unidentified with different religious groups. At the same time, there has appeared a body of literature which analyses religious and other institutions in terms of their function in mediating bereavement.

The weight of mourning was so pronounced as to throw into doubt the capacity of religious institutions to handle the rites of passage needed by millions of bereaved men and women. Part of the problem was that roughly half of those who died in combat had no known graves.[8] Many of these casualties were first listed as missing in action; it is evident that millions of people waited and waited for some news that their loved-ones were alive, mostly in vain. In his story of the 'still living unknown soldier', Jean-Yves Le Naour (2002a) illustrated this vain hope. Religion tried, sometimes successfully, to provide mourners with a framework for their grief. The pagan perimeters of Christianity have been explored too, to provide evidence of the efflorescence of spiritualistic practices among the populations anxiously awaiting news of their loved-ones in uniform or coming to terms with their deaths (Jay Winter, 1995).

Here is the context in which to place the complex discussions as to where and in what forms to gather the remains of the war dead who were scattered over battlefields throughout Europe and beyond (Winter, 1995; Capdevilla and Voldman, 2002). Here too is the point at which family history and national history coincide in the most powerful manner. The way families fashioned mourning rituals varied enormously; we know only the surface of this subject, the intimacy of which always shields much of it from view. What can be said is that mourning took decades; its rhythms were irregular, and its discursive forms contained some political and nationalistic idioms, and at other times were entirely personal (Jay Winter, 1995; Audoin-Rouzeau, 2001; Trevisan, 2001). The history of mourning has brought women prominently into the cultural history of the war; *stabat mater* became a universal icon after 1914.

From intellectual history to the history of national sentiment

The third generation of writing on the home front has laid low some sacred cows of earlier historiography. One of the significant developments of the period was the full separation of cultural history, dealing with societies, from intellectual history, dealing with elites. Some work on the history of intellectuals offered new insights. Philippe Soulez (1988) edited a collection of essays on philosophers from different countries, himself analysing Bergson's diplomatic role. Wohl (1980) studied the 1914 generation of the main belligerent nations. After publishing a book on intellectuals, socialism, and the war (1993) Prochasson explored with Rasmussen the associative life of scholars and scientists, and showed how new forms of activity, both in conjunction with and outside the state emerged at a time when knowledge was 'nationalized' (Prochasson and Rasmussen, 1996). However, this mobilization of intellectuals (Hanna, 1996) precluded the revival after the war of the pre-1914 culture of international learning.

Scholars' interests shifted towards larger groups of people. They started to look into the world of music hall and popular entertainment which had a much larger audience (Rearick, 1997; Roshwald and Stites, 1999), or into music and theatre (Jahn, 1995). Moving away from the study of intellectuals has helped transform our understanding of public opinion in wartime. In Germany and in Britain, much writing on intellectuals in the 1960s and 1970s had been generalized to an interpretation of massive public support for the decision to go to war in 1914. In the 1990s, that position crumbled. In the German case, Jeff Verhey followed both Becker's study of public opinion and Kocka's work on German social structure in demonstrating the evanescence of *Kriegsbegeisterung* or war enthusiasm in 1914. Here too he distinguished between groups of students on Unter den Linden, photographed in a patriotic fervour, and workers in Spandau a few miles away, who shared none of their outlook nor cared to pose for the camera. War enthusiasm was real enough – for certain groups and for a limited time – but what is more interesting is its standing as a legend, a story used to mobilize populations both later in the war and in the post-war decades (Verhey, 2000). Once again, we are dealing not with one undifferentiated *culture de guerre* but with a number of different, overlapping, and evolving discursive fields.

From atrocity to genocide

One way in which the history of civilian life in the third generation of historical writing has returned to the first generation is in terms of the treatment of the subject of war crimes and atrocities. Partly in light of the recrudescence of war crimes in the Balkans in the 1990s and of the continuing cruelties of the civil war in Ireland, historians began to reassess the vexed question of German atrocities in 1914. The earlier historiography on propaganda had made it difficult to treat such atrocity reports as factual. But in a major study, John Horne and Alan Kramer (2001) found evidence in German army records that crimes against civilians not only happened in 1914, but were known by, tacitly accepted, and even sometimes ordered by elements of the German high command. This was a major breakthrough, since it exploded the notion circulating since 1914 that war crimes committed by the German army in Belgium and France were but a figment of the feverish imagination of Allied propagandists. This is no longer a tenable position. What we need now is a reinterpretation of the degeneration of the limits on extreme violence in wartime in the first phase of the war.

Similarly, research extended to other fronts, though in a less systematic way. The history of Turkish denial of the genocide perpetrated on the Armenian people in 1915–16 parallels that of German denial of atrocities in 1914. Armenian scholars have made an unanswerable case that genocide did occur, and that it was ordered by the wartime leadership of Turkey. But like most of the historiography of the Great War, the study of civilian life and conflict on the Eastern Front is much less well developed than the study of the Western Front. There are exceptions. Vejus Liulevicius has examined the German occupation of Oberost, what is now Poland and the Baltic states, and the *mission civilisatrice* Germans organized among populations they saw as exotic and primitive. It is chastening to think of this story as the prelude to later and more sombre developments (Liulevicius, 2000). This work helps us to see as well how much a war of occupation in the east of Europe was a cultural war, a way of bringing 'Western' forms of thinking and organization to bear on what the occupiers saw as 'primitive' populations. What Christophe Charle terms 'the crisis of imperial societies' is vividly apparent in the imperialist character of the German occupation of the east. Ostpolitik was 'racial' politics long before the Nazis came to power.

Liulevicius's study is important in another way. It shows how much is still to be done in shifting the emphasis in First World War scholarship away from the west and towards the east and south of Europe. Indeed it points the way towards taking seriously the global character of the war, in bringing together racial and national groups in such a way as permanently to transform their troubled intersection. Trans-national history is now a partner with national history in slowly developing our understanding of the complex process of 'living and surviving in time of war'.

In sum, the three generations of writing on the home front approached the question of 'total war' from different angles. The first dealt with social mobilization as a problem of state policy; the second with social structures and social conflict; the third with material culture, with social consent and cultural mobilization. These bodies of historical literature overlap and inform each other. What they do not allow is any form of segregation of the history of soldiers from that of the societies for which they went to war. In the spirit of Bloch and Febvre, those who write the history of civilian life affirm that total war deserves nothing less than total history.

NOTES

1. For instance, P. J. Flood (1990) for the Isère département, or Alain Jacobzone (1988) for the region of Anjou, gave interesting accounts of the living conditions of the rural population.
2. Audoin-Rouzeau and A. Becker (2000). A shorter presentation of this thesis can be found in Stéphane Audoin-Rouzeau, 'Historiographie et histoire culturelle du premier conflit mondial. Une nouvelle approche par la culture de guerre', in Maurin and Jauffret, 2002, pp. 323–37, and Stéphane Audoin-Rouzeau and Annette Becker, 'Violence et consentement: la "culture de guerre" du premier conflit mondial', in Jean-Pierre Rioux and Jean-François Sirinelli (eds.), *Pour une histoire culturelle*, Paris, Seuil, 1996.
3. Pierre Barral, *Les Agrariens français de Méline à Pisani*, Paris, A. Colin, 1968.
4. Pierre-Jakez Hélias, *Le Cheval d'orgueil*, Paris, Plon, 1975.
5. Joan W. Scott, *Gender and the politics of history*, New York, Columbia University Press, 1988.
6. Françoise Thébaud, 'La Grande Guerre, le triomphe de la division sexuelle' in Françoise Thébaud (ed.), *Histoire des femmes en Occident*, vol. V: *Le XXe siècle*, Paris, Plon, 1992: 31–74.
7. Louis Henry, 'Perturbations de la nuptialité résultant de la guerre 1914–1918', *Population*, 21, April–June 1966, pp. 272–332.
8. British fallen soldiers remained buried in France. Stéphane Audoin-Rouzeau indicates that less than one-half of French fallen soldiers, only 700,000, were identified, and 240,000 corpses given back to their families. 'Trois exemples de deuils de guerre', *Annales*, 2000, 1, pp. 47–71.

8   Agents of memory

How did people live between remembrance
and forgetting?

In April 1920, the casket of the French unknown soldier was chosen
at Verdun. Twelve years later, the ossuary of Douaumont, containing
the mixed remains of French and German soldiers who died there, was
inaugurated in the presence of the President of the Republic in 1932.
The practice and discourse of remembrance unfolded without reference
to historians or their activities. In the interwar years, the language of
commemorative practices was formed and used by others: by political
leaders, always ready to conjure up the spectre of those who died for 'us';
by *anciens combattants*, and their varied organizations, by the nationalist
Stahlhelm and the socialist Reichsbanner in Germany, by the conservative
American Legion and British Legion, and by a host of French associations
which adopted a moral discourse in preference to a party political one.

In September 1984, the President of the Republic François Mitterrand
and the German Chancellor Helmut Kohl came together to Verdun.
There they joined hands to affirm the future of an integrated Europe,
built over the ruins of the disintegrated Europe which perished at Verdun
and a dozen other sites of carnage during the 1914–18 war. The commemorative practices carried on, but now the language of remembrance
was both a social practice, shared by millions of ordinary people, and an
object of scholarly activity. What historians began to do was to historicize
a ritual which combined elements of the sacred with lessons in citizenship directed in particular at the young. The German historian Reinhard
Koselleck was among the first to explore this field,[1] and he was joined
by colleagues throughout the world. What these historians did was to
take what was *visible* and turn it into what is *legible* within an historical
narrative. War memorials were there throughout the twentieth century,
but only in the 1980s and 1990s were they decoded to yield important
messages about the way communities of people remembered the Great
War.

In this chapter, we survey the historical literature produced in two
broad periods, from 1918 until 1970, and in the last three decades of
the twentieth century. In the first period, the survivors and their families

dominated the public (and private) conversations about the war. In the second period, with the progressive dwindling of the population of those with direct experience of the war and its immediate aftermath, the subject of remembrance took on a new form. Commemoration continued, fixed in the calendar, and attracted new adherents, but now it was both subject and object, both a matter of participation and of contemplation.

The authority of direct experience: 1918–1970

The first conversation in the discursive field of remembrance was between and among combatants. It proudly asserted the authority of direct experience, and spoke to a public with a seemingly unquenchable thirst for accounts of 'what the war was really like'. These witnesses of warfare were overwhelmingly male, and deeply committed to a privileged insight into the events of the recent past. Witnesses distinguished sharply between what they knew – which we term 'memory' and what others thought they knew about the war – which we term history. They did not use these terms, since their memories *were* history, because they spoke the truth, and history was a matter for non-combatants, always open to the suspicion that they spoke of what they did not know.

The authority of those in power

In this first period, there was an avalanche of publications written by those who were in positions of power, both political and military, during the war. As in earlier chapters, we can see in the field of 'memory' that the professional historian is but one of many commentators, and always in a minority. Publishers benefited substantially from a flow of books in the interwar years from former officials, who aimed at a magisterial survey of 'their' war. Winston Churchill's *The Great War* (1933–4) was one such attempt to justify and contextualize the personal contribution of one of the war's central statesmen and strategists. The leaders of every major combatant nation followed suit, and published memoirs of varying degrees of interest, though few matched the rhetorical grandeur of Churchill's narrative. Poincaré, Clemenceau (1930), Lloyd George, Ludendorff were among the many prominent figures whose memoirs formed part of the ongoing public conversation in the 1920s and 1930s about what the war had meant. Before the full archival record of the war was made public in the 1960s and beyond, these individuals had privileged access to records and to events which were of vital interest to a very large reading public.

In another respect, Churchill's *Great War* was characteristic of the memoirs of those in power during the war.[2] He adopted an Olympian tone in his writing, which enabled him to convey the drama of the war as if it were part of a Greek epic or tragedy. It is hard to blame Hector or Oedipus for bringing catastrophe down on his head. Churchill's prose, later made famous by his wartime speeches in the Second World War, placed his own war in a gigantic panorama of great dramatic power. In his view the Allied attack on Gallipoli was a 'military tragedy' (Churchill, 1934, vol. III, p. 1599), and who can be blamed for a tragedy? Not Churchill, the politician responsible for the invasion of the Turkish peninsula in 1915. The fates were to blame.

'The story of the human race is War', intoned Churchill, but after 1914, war was 'stripped of glitter and glamour'. Henceforth its destructive powers were exposed to all, full of the menace of mass destruction on an unprecedented scale. Only the study of history, Churchill suggests, would enable men to avoid a terrible fate. In chronicling the war he knew from the inside, Churchill was exposing a real and present danger. 'Death stands at attention', he wrote, 'obedient, expectant, ready to serve, ready to shear away peoples *en masse*; ready, if called on to pulverize, without hope of repair, what is left of civilization. He awaits only the word of command. He awaits it from a frail, bewildered being, long his victim, now – for one occasion only – his Master' (Churchill, 1933–4, III, p. 1605).

In his hands, memoirs encapsulated and deepened a wider 'repulsion from the horrors of war' (Churchill, 1934, vol. III, p. 1608). In the hands of those on the losing side, the business of remembering looked different. Memoirs diminished individual culpability, but they generally retained a sense of the nobility of the profession of arms and of the sacrifices made by all those who fought to defend their country (Prior, 1983).

Voices from the rank and file

Memoirs were political weapons in other more direct ways as well. We have already discussed in chapter 4 the way Henri Barbusse's novel *Under fire*, published in 1916 yielded sufficient income to help finance the veterans' organization Association Républicaine des anciens combatants (ARAC). On the other side of the political spectrum, memoirs fortified the German nationalist movements. Ernst Jünger wrote *In Stahlgewittern* (1920) in part as a diary, in part as a polemic synchronized and revised to fit the outlook of the *Stahlhelm* and other nationalistic elements of the German veterans' movement. And then there is Hitler's *Mein Kampf*, a melange of war memoir, political sermon, and apologia, which he wrote in prison after the failure of the Munich putsch in 1923, linking his war service with his politics of revenge.

Hitler's memoir, and even more so Céline's vicious satire on all war memoirs, *Voyage au bout de la nuit*, raises one of the key issues of the first generation of remembrance. The truth value of these documents is very difficult to establish. Soldiers distrusted those who were not there, or who were there and cleaned up the world of war in their accounts of it. This need to sweep away the phoney in order to see the true vision of war is at the heart of the two remarkable books by Norton Cru we have already cited. Both *Témoins* (*Witnesses*) and *Du Témoignage* (*On witnessing*) are archives of memory, or rather archives of 300 published memoirs produced by French veterans of the war. For Norton Cru facts speak for themselves, and when unvarnished, they lead us to the 'real' war. Those who coat the truth with a patina of rhetoric inevitably lie about the war. Cru's certainty about who was a truth-teller and who was not led to judgments of a disputable, and even of an actionable, nature. James Shotwell of the Carnegie Endowment, and the French editorial committee of the national series it funded, were sufficiently alarmed by Cru's language to decline to publish his work as part of the project. They did help him find a Parisian publisher, who brought out the work in 1928, and then in abbreviated form in 1929.

It may be easier to tell those who are lying about the war than to recognize who are telling the truth. And whose truth is it anyway? Among French veterans, Norton Cru's books were well received and his judgments generally accepted, with some reservations about particularly popular books on which he was especially severe. Among these men there was a sort of eye-witness consensus about true and false memory. But at the same time, the notion that the writings of eye-witnesses were likely to be a misleading guide to the war was widely circulated. The Nazis could not stomach Remarque's vision of combat or of the pointlessness of German sacrifices in the war, and when the film *All quiet on the Western Front* was shown in Thuringia, they let mice out in cinemas, creating both pandemonium and an excuse for public officials to ban the film from public showings. Milestone's film was shown in Germany only after the Second World War (Eksteins, 1989).

The transmission of war narratives

The transmission of narratives about the war took place in other social contexts. *Manuels scolaires* (high-school textbooks) reached a very wide audience, and provided a structure of knowledge and interpretation of a very high order. As we have already noted, Jules Isaac, a war veteran himself, helped shape the way the younger generation understood the war and its effect on their lives in the interwar period. History taught may not always be history remembered, but no account of the historiography of the war would be complete without reference to the role school texts had in passing on a particular vision of the war.

In the textbooks of Malet–Isaac (1930), the patriotic touch of earlier treatments published in the immediate wake of the war had gone; instead there was a balanced account of the causes of the war, its conduct on various fronts was illustrated by various maps. But trench warfare was treated very soberly, and as Isaac put it, since 'no text can convey fully the idea of what the infantry went through, we are content here to present some soldiers' accounts of the war, chosen among the most accurate and the most moving' (Malet–Isaac, 1930, p. 702). Here Isaac shows a sensitivity to the limits of historical representation, and because literature is a more powerful stimulus to the imagination, he refers to war writing in order to do justice to the history of the men who fought the war. For this reason, he included in his textbooks sections drawn from the accounts of eye-witnesses, such as Genevoix, Pézard, Delvert, Meyer, Lemercier, P.-M. Masson, and Duhamel. In addition, the industrial war and the problem of supply, the blockade and its consequences were also narrated. The war indeed ended with the Allied victory, but the last illustration in the textbook is that of collective mourning: a photograph of a military cemetery.[3]

Publications for pilgrims and tourists constituted another important layer of commemorative historical literature about the war. Since 1919, the Michelin tyre company has published well-documented guides for visitors to the main battlefields.[4] Gabriel Hanotaux took time off from his work for the League of Nations to pen *Circuits des champs de bataille de France. Histoire et Itinéraires de la Grande Guerre*, a work produced under the aegis of the Comité France-Amérique. This is triumphal history *tout court*. It ends with the 'triumphal return' to liberated Flanders of the King and Queen of Belgium, during which passage 'an enthusiastic population greeted with acclaim the victorious King Albert who was returning in a cloud of glory' (Hanotaux, 1920, p. 482).

Witnesses of war left many different kinds of testimony. Memories of war are embedded in painting and photography. Artists like Georges Rouault devoted part of their work to the war. The German artillery-man and painter Otto Dix wrote that the business of the artist is not to instruct, but to bear witness. And he did so in a series of paintings drawing from the German Renaissance figuration of the Apocalypse. Other artists drew upon different national tropes – Raoul Dufy borrowed from *Imagerie d'Epinal*, Paul Klee converted aerial images into angels, and Paul Nash and C. E. W. Nevinson constructed a different kind of English landscape art, one which hinted at the devastation of the war on the Western Front.

Dix's great cycle *Der Krieg* was derived not from his wartime sketches but from photographs. And in this medium many soldiers found a ready-made and inexpensive way to trigger war remembrance. Louis Barthas created a scrapbook for his family about his war – including comments, postcards, and photographs.

Letter-writing was one of the key signifying practices of the war. Hundreds of millions of letters and cards circulated between front and home front during the war (Baconnier *et al.*, 1985), and these letters frequently found their way into family collections, and then into print. Some of these collections were memorial acts: consider the numerous editions of *War letters of fallen German students*, collected by Philip Witkop from the parents of these men, and first published in 1916. Witkop (1928) put this edition together himself, and eliminated those elements of letters which did not accord with his own views. He also reorganized the selection to reinforce the heroic image of German students captured in the legend of the 'victory of Langemarck', exposed as a legend by Unruh (1986). This collection was re-edited and reissued six times in the next three decades, including a Nazi edition, minus the letters of fallen Jewish soldiers. Here we see an editorial practice familiar among German publishers, who intended to offer a politically correct view of the war, concerned as they were for the need of the military to present the story as 'a time of grandeur' (Natter, 1999).

National differences mark the framing of participants' memory. War poetry mattered much more in Britain than in other European combatant countries. Perhaps the music of the King James Version of the Bible was in the minds of the millions of readers of the poetry of Wilfred Owen, a Welsh poet killed a mere week before the Armistice in 1918. Poetry as memory distilled is deep in the English romantic tradition, and for this reason the doomed voices of Great War poets became part of the canon of remembrance in Britain in a way few poets' voices did elsewhere.

We have emphasized the domination of the discourse of commemoration by those who had direct experience of the war. In the 1960s and 1970s, the public conversation about the Great War took on new inflections, inspired in part by the passing of the veterans in increasing numbers, and in part by significant anniversaries. The fiftieth anniversary of the outbreak of war in 1914, or the marking of fifty years since the landing of Australian and New Zealand troops at Gallipoli, stimulated much reflection on the war in Britain and the Dominions. This commemorative phenomenon was less marked in France and Germany. In France, the shadow of both the Algerian war, just concluded, and the Second World War, made remembering the Great War more complex and filled with dissonant echoes. In Germany remembering the veterans of the Great War meant remembering Hitler, and the failed revolution of 1918. What Freud termed screen memories largely eclipsed the Great War in German historiography. But in the Anglo-Saxon world, and to some extent in France in the 1960s, there occurred a sea change in the study of the memory of war.

That change rested on the opening of archives, and the publication of collections of memoirs and recollections of a broad range of men and women who had survived the war. As we have already noted in chapter 1, in Britain, following the broadcast of the television series of 1964, more veterans came forward to record and publish their memoirs. A televised history of the Great War in France had similar, though perhaps more limited, repercussions. In effect, by the end of the first period the gap between memory and history began to be bridged. These two categories – never really distinct – overlapped more and more. Remembering in print and in interview became a commemorative industry, with a wide audience and a mode of institutionalization through the schools and universities, where the study of the poetry and memoirs of the Great War became part of the state secondary school curriculum in Britain and in the Commonwealth. In France, as we have noted in chapter 1, the turning point is marked by the publication as early as 1959 of Ducasse, Meyer, and Perreux's important study *Vie et mort des français, 1914–1918*. This work was testimony to the passage from one generation to another, and to the inclusion of memory in the historical narrative.

The authority of historical narratives

The opening of the archives

The arrival of historians in this field dates from the 1960s and 1970s, the period of the greatest growth of the academy as a whole, and the historical profession within it in this century. There were simply more historians around and more students interested in studying history at the tertiary level than ever before.

The materials available for such a history were also more voluminous than ever before. After a fifty-year pause, war archives entered the public domain, enabling new kinds of scholarship to emerge. Collections which had been started during the war itself now drew scholars from many parts of the world, and constructed *lieux de mémoire* understood as repositories of the traces of those who fought in the war. The BDIC in Paris, the Imperial War Museum in London, the Australian War Memorial in Canberra all provided the materials out of which a new and richer form of war remembrance emerged. Bill Gammage's history of the Anzac expedition to Gallipoli and Europe (1974) was the first systematic exploitation by a non-veteran of the rich archives collected by C. E. W. Bean, the official war historian. Gammage's work marked a break from the period when the survivors of the expedition themselves told the story. Now historians were able to speak with authority, comparing different archives and published records to create their own narratives of the war.

Pedagogical institutions emerged in the 1960s to preserve the traces of the war on the site of the great battles. In 1951 a committee for the remembrance of Verdun was established, and by 1961, it launched a local museum, a Mémorial de Verdun, opened in 1967 on the site of the village of Fleury, which had been obliterated during the battle fifty-one years before. These groups helped draw out of private homes and attics materials which supplemented the great national collections. Private archives now joined public ones in offering material for historical analysis. Undoubtedly the history of the war thereby could be based on a much wider range of materials.

The shadow of 1933

A different impulse brought many historians to the study of the remembrance of the 1914–18 war. Among German historians, 1933 was always and already embedded in 1914. Thus 'the myth of the war experience', a phrase first coined by Mario Isnenghi (1970) and then developed by George Mosse (Mosse, 1990), was a sanitized narrative, which helped the Nazis and other fascists mobilize public opinion around the cult of the fallen soldiers of the Great War. As we have noted in chapter 7, the psychoanalytically inclined historian Klaus Theweleit explored the fantasies of a cohort of First World War soldiers who stayed in uniform after the war. The pathway between their thoughts of blood lust and Nazi crimes is all too evident (Bartov, 2000).

French historians have been heavily influenced by Mosse's work. The notion of brutalization has been used, in particular by Audoin-Rouzeau, to describe less the descent into thuggery of individual soldiers than the acceptance by particular social groups or society as a whole of norms of behaviour which were unacceptable prior to the war. Thus the real meaning of 'brutalization' is to be seen in the way war rendered brutal the norms of social life both during and after the conclusion of hostilities. Another way of putting the point is to see war as lowering the threshold to the recourse to violence in domestic social and political life, as well as in international affairs. Violence, because of the Great War, became more the *prima ratio* and less the *ultima ratio* of politics.

Here we confront a broader set of historical questions, related to the location of the 1914–18 war within a framework of a Thirty Years War of the twentieth century. We shall return to this point in the conclusion. What matters in this context is how it relates to historical narratives of commemoration. In Mosse's hands, remembering the fallen was part of the cultural preparation for the second round. Prost's study of French veterans (1977a) and Jay Winter's analysis of war memorials (1995) present an alternative view. It is clear that veterans of the 1914–18 war took very different positions on the meaning of commemorative activity. The stakes of this argument are high: for if we see the 'brutalization' of the Great War as a pathway leading from Verdun to Auschwitz, we ignore the thousands of veterans who fervently commemorated war in order not to inflict it on their children. The historical jury is still out on this particular matter, which is of central importance to the history of the first half of the twentieth century.

The shadow of Vietnam

Historians never work in a vacuum. The harsh international climate of the late 1960s and 1970s helped animate this broad conversation among scholars about memories of the Great War. This was especially true in the United States and Britain. In the aftermath of the Vietnam war, two scholars of English literature, working independently, made memory into the centrepiece of the cultural history of the war in the Anglo-Saxon world, though they had no immediate influence in France or elsewhere.

The first of these scholars, Paul Fussell, produced a seminal study in 1975, entitled *The Great War and modern memory*. It is dedicated to the sergeant in his infantry unit with whom Fussell served in the latter part of the Second World War. The sergeant was killed, but Fussell survived. That arbitrary event – the absurdity of survival – is at the heart of this study of irony as the iconic language which emerged from the war. Irony here means many things: the contrast between anticipation and outcome, the shifting sands of judgment about the moral justification of war among soldiers themselves – what could be more ironic than to see war writers as soldier pacifists? – the impossibility of saying anything directly about an event as uncanny and weird as industrial warfare. But Fussell goes further. He sees irony as a language which emerged out of the war, since pre-war language could not accommodate the sense experience of the trenches. Instead those who wrote during and after the conflict wrested language to new uses, and created a vocabulary which helped frame our sense of the later catastrophes of the twentieth century. Thus 'modern memory', emerging out of the Great War, is the syntax and grammar of our understanding of the violent world in which we live. The war produced a language which is right at the heart of our own signifying practices about collective violence, its oddities, its cruelties, its enormities.

Samuel Hynes too was a veteran of the Second World War, but his autobiography is less directly evident in his writing on war than is Fussell's. In two important books *The war imagined* and *The soldiers' tale*, Hynes explored what he calls the way the war created 'myths'. By this term he means the narratives which give life histories meaning. These life histories can be individual or collective, and together, repeated among families and in other ways, they create the 'war-in-the-head', our sense of what the Great War was like and the damage it did to the world. Hynes believes that here we move from memory – which only those who were at the front had – to representation, and in this shift the 'soldiers' tale' plays a significant part. Note the singular in this term – if you added up all the stories told by soldiers about modern war, you would, Hynes believes, get one master narrative – one tale about the uncanny, the weird, the other-worldliness of war. That tale has been told many times, usually in a laconic, no-nonsense style, and at its core is what Tolstoy termed 'the actual killing', the cutting edge of combat.

The modern and the traditional

The position developed by Fussell and Hynes has been enormously attractive to several cohorts of students, who have found in their work a way of marrying cultural history and military history. It also announced the fact that historical work is not done solely by those working in departments of history in universities; we live with the neighbours in this field in close and fruitful collaboration as never before. On one level, what Fussell and Hynes have done is to suggest that no one interested in the cultural history of the twentieth century as a whole can ignore the Great War. This position is shared by those who have taken issue with the particular interpretation these literary historians have fashioned. This is the central point of Jay Winter's *Sites of memory, sites of mourning. The Great War in European cultural history* (1995). Winter acknowledges that Fussell and Hynes have much to teach us about how contemporaries understood the Great War. But there was an equally powerful and very different trajectory in the signifying practices of wartime and its aftermath. That trajectory was framed in traditional language, understood as commonly shared images and ideas derived from classical, romantic, and Christian sources. Why the turn back to the familiar? Because in these traditions contemporaries found the languages in which they could mourn. 'Modern memory' could shock, or stimulate, or delight, but most of the time, it could not heal.

And healing was the order of the day in the aftermath of the carnage of the war.

Taking a diametrically opposite point of view, the Canadian scholar Modris Eksteins, a student of Mosse, sees the war as the harbinger of modernism. Its destructiveness was foreshadowed by iconoclasts like Stravinsky, whose *Rite of spring* – adapted by Eksteins as the title of his book – turned into shocking ballet by Diaghilev, announced the opening of a terrifying era in human affairs. The war validated the modernist moment in the arts, Eksteins argues, and provided a mountain of reasons to see 1914 as an irreversible caesura in European and world history.

These moves in the understanding of representations of war are not contradictory. Something as vast as the Great War was bound to set in motion many different cultural trends. But what these different interpretations have in common is the sense that the Great War was a moment when earlier representations of war began to fracture and ultimately to decompose. What has taken the place of the vocabulary with which contemporaries went to war in 1914 is a much more sombre vision, one in which death dominates the story of war in such a way as to make heroic or romantic notation take on the taste of ashes.

The proliferation of studies of war memorials on the local and national levels shows how widespread this historiographical tendency has become. Prost's 1984 studies of French war memorials and of Verdun as a site of memory, complement the findings of his thesis (Prost, 1977) on the character of the veterans' movement.[5] Both commemorative forms and the veterans who made their pilgrimages to them each 11 November reaffirmed their hatred of war and their commitment to a kind of Republican pacifism. In the two decades which have followed, there have been dozens of learned works concerned with commemorative forms in every combatant country of the Great War, with the exception of Russia (Tippett, 1984; Vance, 1997; Gaffney, 1998; A. King, 1998). Perhaps the most exhaustive of these works is Ken Inglis's account of every single war memorial in Australia (Inglis, 1998), but we have many learned works which touch on memorials within the South African, Canadian, American, New Zealand, as well as European traditions. Irish, Welsh, Italian, Austrian, and more recently German historians have contributed to this historical conversation about war memorials. For France, several well-illustrated studies have been published on war memorials (A. Becker, 1988; Rivé, 1991; Bouillon and Petzold, 1999) and inventories by French departments have been compiled, though it is impossible here to provide a complete list of their coverage. A glance at the bibliography of Inglis's book will show how varied and rich is this literature, and since his book was published much additional work has appeared. Since there are thousands of such memorials, and only some have been studied, it is likely that this wave of cultural historical investigation will continue to grow.

In Britain the Imperial War Museum has established an inventory of all the war memorials in the country. This data base has helped scholars delve far and wide into the local history of Great War commemoration. The creation of an archive in the Commonwealth War Graves Commission has also helped extend this work into the field of pilgrimage (Lloyd, 1998). Connelly (2002) studied commemorative practices in London, while Gregory provided an insightful history of the practice of the two-minute silence, observed between 1919 and 1938 at the eleventh hour of the eleventh day of November, and thereafter at the same time on the nearest Sunday to 11 November (Gregory, 1994). That Sunday is now termed 'Remembrance Sunday'. Gregory's book is the only such study to our knowledge which has silence as its subject. For more vocal and musical commemorative forms Glenn Watkins's recent study of music and the Great War offers insights which complement Gregory's work (Watkins, 2003).

Our understanding of the impact of violence on the scale of the Great War has been formulated in other ways too. What the German historian Reinhard Koselleck termed *Begriffsgeschichte*, or the history of semantics, understood as the history of popular terms in their social and semantic context, has been very influential in historical circles. Here are striking parallels to the work done in France by Audoin-Rouzeau and Becker, among others, on the notion of 'war culture' as a semantics of consent among soldiers and civilians alike. In the Anglo-Saxon countries, the semantics of 'modernism' or 'modernity' were traced in various artistic movements, such as surrealism, or in abstract painting. A return to order is one way that these historians (Silver, 1989; Dagen, 1996) described the renewal of the figurative in painting and sculpture in the war years and their immediate aftermath. Whether as a caesura or a counter-revolutionary upheaval, the war became a critical moment in the history of artistic representations as a whole.

War and madness

Another facet of contemporary history helped inform writing about the cultural history of the Great War. In 1980, in the aftermath of the Vietnam war, the American medical profession accepted the category of 'post-traumatic stress disorder' as a medical syndrome, with recognized origins and treatment. In subsequent years, historians have traced this condition back to what was named 'shell shock' by British army physicians in the First World War. The term itself has no direct equivalent in any other

European language; its economy and allusive character helps explain why the term 'shell shock' has entered the vernacular of the English language. Anglo-Saxon historians have studied this phenomenon in three overlapping yet distinctive ways.

A first group of scholars saw the term as connoting male hysteria, a kind of psychological emasculation derived from the stark features of immobility and the stalemate on the Western Front (Leed, 1979; Showalter, 1985). A second group located the condition in the militarization of medical service. Army physicians were confronted by huge numbers of cases of men whose disabilities were not primarily physical. How to separate the shirkers from the 'real' casualties was an extremely difficult task. The army needed men; the doctors were therefore trapped between their medical duty to the patient and their military duty to the army. The outcome was different in different countries; the German case was the most heavily geared to quick 'cures'; the British case had room for convalescence over time and for the use of electric shock treatment by those determined to replenish the lines as quickly as possible (Binneveld, 1998; Shepherd, 2000; Micale and Lerner, 2001; Leese, 2002; Lerner, 2003).

A third approach was adopted by Winter and Baggett (1996), who explored the frontier between psychological disorder and mutiny. The poet Siegfried Sassoon was a man who won military honours and who then wrote a letter to *The* [London] *Times* refusing to go back to the front, on the grounds that the war he had joined to fight was continuing only because no one had the brains or the courage to end it. He was sent for psychiatric examination to Craiglockhart Hospital in Scotland, where he met Wilfred Owen, a shell-shocked officer and poet, who died just before the end of the war. The difference between men who had what Sassoon's doctor W. H. R. Rivers called an 'anti-war complex' and men who had shell shock was not at all clear. The political overtones of mental breakdown, Jay Winter and Baggett suggest, made it very difficult for the army to recognize. In this sense, shell shock was a kind of 'mutiny', a way of dealing with a war which pushed individual soldiers beyond the limits of human endurance (Babington, 1983).

In all three of these approaches, we can see how historians have incorporated in the cultural history of the conflict what may be termed 'embodied memory' – the traces of the war in the faces and minds of the men who survived it, and whose stories have become important parts of the cultural legacy of the conflict. Their words and their presence in post-war societies gave a visceral meaning to the notion of 'representation', for in their infirmities both contemporaries and to this day historians have seen war re-presented, re-enacted, re-lived. Here on the frontier between medical history and military history, cultural historians have found some very fertile ground on which to work.

In this area of research, national differences in the way cultural history is done are particularly evident. French scholars have only recently begun to study *choc traumatique* (Crocq, 1999), and the only rigorous account of conflict between French army physicians and their psychiatric patients has been written by an American scholar at the University of California at Berkeley.[6] The Anglo-Saxon fascination with shell shock has no equivalent in the historical literature on Continental countries in wartime, though important work has been done by German and Italian historians of psychiatry during the Great War (Gibelli, 1991; Eckart and Gradmann, 1996; Bianchi, 2001).

Visions of war: museums, novels, films

There is another dimension to the dissemination of representations of war in the 1980s and 1990s. Here we refer to war museums. The demand for what in the United States is termed 'public history' – history for the population outside the academy – has grown substantially, and one source of this growth is an increasing interest in the Great War. In London, the Imperial War Museum, set in what had been the Bedlam lunatic asylum, started in 1917, but expanded to cover the other conflicts of the twentieth century. It is a major tourist attraction, second to none in its appeal to all ages. In Britain, popular images of the 1914–18 conflict which have dominated public opinion throughout the twentieth century reflect the collections and displays of this museum, a national monument to the war. The same is true of the Australian War Memorial in Canberra, a museum of great distinction.

In France, representations of the Great War have been offered to the public in Les Invalides, in occasional exhibitions in the BDIC, and at Verdun. In Belgium, a new museum of the Great War was opened in the year 2000 at Ypres. It is adjacent to one of the central sites of British remembrance, the Menin gate, through which tens of thousands of British soldiers marched to their deaths in the Third Battle of Ypres, popularly known as Passchendaele. The organization and presentation of objects are not far from those developed in the Imperial War Museum.

In contrast a different approach emerged in 1992, with the opening of the first international museum of the Great War, the Historial de la Grande Guerre at Péronne. We have already underscored the importance of this museum in the shift from social to cultural history. What we would emphasize now is the originality of the representation of war it provides. What made the Historial de Péronne different was its self-conscious presentation of the war from both sides. It is a tri-national European museum. All exhibits are trilingual, in French, English, and German. It opened in the year that the Maastricht Treaty, strengthening the European Union, came into effect. The guest of honour at its inauguration was the German writer Ernst Jünger, who had fought on the Somme seventy-six years earlier.

The fundamental premise of the museum's architecture is that the war is built into the landscape of Western Europe; thus the building, made of concrete like so many blockhouses of the 1914–18 war, rises out of the ground. The hidden, though powerful, archeological existence of war is further emphasized by the location of the building behind a medieval castle; you need to penetrate conventional history to get to the Great War. Inside the building, visitors are given a vision of the war of a very unusual kind. The axis of display is horizontal. In each of the museum's rooms, the visitor's gaze is directed downward. In the first room, the visitor looks down towards maps of points of conflict before 1914; thereafter to shallow rectangles or *fosses*, in which objects soldiers carried are arrayed in a clean and stylized manner. The similarity between the nature of trench warfare known to German infantrymen and their British and French adversaries is evident. So too are the similarities in the war civilians knew, portrayed in showcases on the walls and on forty video screens scattered throughout the museum. Through these images, visitors integrate the soldiers' war with the war on the home front. The same point is evident in the Hall of Portraits, where floor-to-ceiling panels of photographs of pre-war normality occlude a horizontal presentation of the series of horrifying lithographs produced by Otto Dix who had fought on the Somme.

In a host of ways, the design of the Historial avoids triumphalism. This point is emphasized in particular by the horizontality of its spatial organization. Verticality is the language of hope, horizontality that of mourning. The discourse presented by the museum is one of a common catastrophe. The other striking innovation in the museum is its interrogation of the very possibility of representing battle. The building is on the site of the German headquarters during the Battle of the Somme, but nowhere is there a representation of the battle. Visitors are asked to ponder how is it possible – if at all – to represent war. The otherness of the experience of combat, its strange, uncanny character, is highlighted in this way. The museum thus represents a flight from pseudo-realism, from the first generation of memoirs of the Great War purporting to tell readers or viewers what war 'was really like'.

This form of reflexive history, engaging visitors in a conversation as to how we imagine war, is strikingly different from the approach offered in other war museums. There is no doubt whatsoever that the Imperial

War Museum in London has had a powerful effect on the ways in which generations of British and Dominions visitors have imagined the war. It is after all the *imperial* war museum. There are naval cannons outside the entrance; there are tanks and airplanes from the Great War in well-designed displays; in many other ways the history of the war is brought to life in a straightforward representational manner, which is quite characteristic of the first and second generations of historical writing. In the Imperial War Museum there is an exhibit entitled 'the trench experience'. Visitors see plastic rats, and hear the noise of bombardment. Not so in the Historial, where there is no sound at all. The voices of the survivors are heard separately, in a film presenting the image of one British infantryman who fought on the Somme, and who never really left it, even though he survived in Northumberland for seventy years. The story of this man, Harry Fellowes, is set to the music of Benjamin Britten's *War Requiem*, thus reinforcing the elegiac character of the museum's historical message.

In a sense, though it is couched in the language of cultural history as the history of representations, the Historial has gone back to the 1920s, in creating a reflective space parallel to that of the war cemeteries which surround Péronne and many other places in France, Flanders, and beyond. These cemeteries were constructed in the first decade after the Armistice. A glance at the visitors' books will be sufficient to show that those who come tend to bring a personal agenda to their reflection on history in these places. Here memory and pilgrimage have not lost their affinity. Indeed one reason for the 'memory boom' of recent years – the tendency for historians to turn to the subject of memory – is the conflation of the familial and the national or global in historical narratives of the 1914–18 conflict. The Great War was the time when family history and world history collided; the national cemeteries, orderly, regular, though with different national inflections, make this point in a visceral way. A visit to one of the Commonwealth War Graves Commission cemeteries can suffice to tell people what the 'lost generation' of the Great War was. Whether in English country garden forms, or French Republican uniformity, or in German 'heroes' forests', *Heldenheine*, these war cemeteries re-present the war in evocative and enduring ways.

Another dimension to the efflorescence of interest in representations of the Great War is the appearance of novels and films in the 1980s and 1990s which have robustly revived the genre of 'war literature'. The reasons for the success of these books are multiple. The Great War is now iconic, a symbol of the catastrophic character of the twentieth century as a whole. The authors marry family history and national history in powerful ways. Some writers heard of the war when they were young from their grandparents, and see it as a foundational myth, a story of great power and appeal, in part because it is imbricated in family history. Sebastian Japrisot's *Un long dimanche de fiançailles* (Paris, Denoel, 1991), Jean Rouaud's *Champs d'honneur* (Paris, Editions de Minuit, 1990), and Marc Dugain's *Chambre des officiers* (Paris, Edition J. C. Lattes, 1998) have found a market in the French publishing world for Great War narratives. So have Sebastian Faulk, in *Birdsong* (London, Hutchinson, 1993) and Pat Barker in the *Regeneration* trilogy (London, Viking, 1996) in Britain and North America.

It is impossible to take account of the circulation of images of the Great War at the end of the twentieth century without discussing film. The history of the cinema of the war paralleled the history of war literature, as much in the 1920s and 1930s as in more recent times. While some early films offered a pacifist message, the majority of the filmic representations of war conveyed an epic or romantic story and sidestepped any pacifist messages. Abel Gance, in his two versions of the film *J'Accuse* in 1919 and in 1937 portrayed the soldiers' point of view through the apocalyptic landscape drawn by Barbusse and other war writers. The film directed in 1930 by Milestone of Remarque's *All quiet on the Western Front*, published the previous year, presented war as a monumental waste. *La Grande illusion* of Renoir (1937), had an entirely different tone, that of the promise of Franco-German reconciliation. However, the majority of war films in the 1920s and 1930s were lucrative adventure films, celebrating camaraderie, love, and heroism. From the 1950s, war films took on a more complex coloration, more ironic, in the spirit of war literature. Stanley Kubrick's *Paths of glory* (1957, but distributed much later in France), Joseph Losey's *King and country* (1964, distributed in France later), and Richard Attenborough's *Oh! What a lovely war!* (1969) managed to show both the sentimentality and the brutality of ordinary soldiers. Kubrick's film portrayed the French high command at the Chemin des Dames as both immoral and incompetent. It is hardly surprising that it was not shown commercially in France before the 1980s. The Australian film by Peter Weir, *Gallipoli* (1981), turned battle into the destruction of noble lives. *Life and nothing but* (1988) and *Capitaine Conan* (1997), both by Tavernier, show as well the sombre side of the war and its aftermath. In the first of these films, Tavernier shows the process whereby the French army chose its 'unknown soldier' for interment under the Arc de Triomphe, and in the second, the brutal conduct of the war on the Eastern Front. In 1999, Pat Barker's *Regeneration* was released as a film about shell shock and its treatment, a theme also treated through the story of Septimus Smith, in the 1999 film of Virginia Woolf's novel *Mrs Dalloway*, which was published in 1925.

For the most part, at the end of the twentieth century, filmic representations of the war have helped turn it into an icon of futility. In a much lighter vein, British television played with this history. *Blackadder* (1989) ends with an attack of British soldiers (presumably) on the Somme. The comic tone of this film vanishes at its end, when the company prepares to advance over the parapet of the trenches. The show ends with all the actors frozen at the moment of their attack, with only silence to accompany their passage into history (and eternity). These images of the Great War as tragedy or futility circulated widely at the turn of the century. Those who read – or write – history do so with such images at the back of their minds. Novelists, museographers, artists, directors, shape representations of the 1914–18 conflict. Once again, we see how historians are but minor actors in a much larger set of cultural productions. We profit from these trends, but in no way create or control them. Now, as in the twentieth century, the history of the Great War remains everybody's business.

Conclusions

In this field, as in all the others surveyed in this book, national differences are pronounced. In France, the centralization of educational provision creates a space for historians to contribute directly and systematically to a national pedagogical project. Here the study of the Great War is an integral part of the preparation of pupils for active citizenship. In Britain, the role of historians is less salient, in part because there is no effective national curriculum, and in part because there is little sense of the Great War as having been a British victory. It was, in the words of the late Poet Laureate Ted Hughes, a defeat around whose neck someone stuck a victory medal. Poets and novelists have been much more important than historians in shaping the British discursive field of remembrance of the Great War. In Germany the study of the remembrance of the Great War has mushroomed in recent years, but it is still in its early phases.

What these scholars share, though, is an interest in the subject of representations. Since the 1970s 'memory' has been configured in a host of ways, but among them, the word connotes stories, myths, and legends ordinary people tell about the past, usually their past, but sometimes about the abstract national past. Thus the 'memory of the Great War' is the sum total of stories told about it. Now those tales are told by those without direct experience of the war or even contact with the survivors. The stories have become iconic. Verdun, the Somme, Passchendaele: these words carry baggage with them, and at times that baggage has been fashioned by historians. But only at times. Mostly we historians are fellow travellers in the broader conversations about the languages – written, oral, visual, material – in which we collectively inscribe the 'meaning' of the Great War. This book *The Great War in history: debates and controversies, 1914 to the present* is one such effort to contribute to the ongoing conversation about what it means to recollect, to acknowledge, the Great War as present in our lives.

NOTES

1. Reinhard Koselleck, 'War memorials: identity formations of the survivors', in Koselleck, *The practice of conceptual history. Timing history, spacing concepts*, trans. T. S. Presner, Stanford, Stanford University Press, 2002, pp. 285–326.
2. Robin Prior (1983) has reached similar conclusions.
3. On this point, see Hubert Tison, 'La mémoire de la guerre 14–18 dans les manuels scolaires français d'histoire (1920–1990)', in J.-J. Becker *et al.*, 1994, pp. 294–314, 'L'image du "poilu" dans les manuels d'histoire', in Allain, 1995, pp. 505–20, and 'La mémoire de Verdun dans les manuels scolaires', in Canini, 1989, pp. 325–40.
4. Antoine Champeaux, 'Les guides illustrés des champs de bataille, 1914–1918', in Canini, 1989, pp. 341–54.
5. Prost, 'War memorials of the Great War: monuments to the fallen', pp. 11–43 and 'Verdun: the life of a site of memory', pp. 45–71 in *Republican identities in war and peace: representations of France in the 19ᵗʰ and 20ᵗʰ centuries*, Oxford, Berg, 2002. These essays were first published in Pierre Nora, *Les lieux de mémoire* in 1984 and 1986.
6. Marc Roudebush, 'Un patient se défend', *14–18, Aujourd'hui, Today, Heute*, 3, 2000, pp. 57–68.

9   The Great War in history

Historical writing about the Great War forms a tableau of a rich and varied kind. Virtually all of those who lived through the war have passed away. But the further the event fades into the past, the more interest in it seems to grow. Today we have thousands of books, well-stocked journals, fascinating and heated debates at colloquia, museums, films. A large multi-disciplinary community of scholarship exists, including alongside historians, literary scholars, art historians, sociologists, anthropologists, jurists. It took generations to create this scholarly milieu.

The achievements have been considerable. Part of them is due to the explosion of the university sector itself. In all countries, despite national differences, the academic profession has grown in a manner and at a pace which their predecessors could not have imagined. The student body has grown exponentially too; they now number in the millions, and those who study history in the tens of thousands. This difference in scale has led to changes in kind. Where there once was a small number of individuals, there is now an entire scholarly community.

For historians, the gains have been made possible by the accumulation of evidence, by the opening of archives, by the enlargement of the repertoire of potential sources: monuments, commemorative plaques, postcards, objects of all kinds, buried remains and objects discovered on battlefields, and so on. To construct a history of the Great War is first and foremost to treat critically this immense and growing body of material.

But the task of the historian of the war is more than the application of a critical method to the sources, or even the organization of a collection of verified facts through a chronological narrative. The narrative has to say something; it has to make sense, convey meaning. To write history is to construct an intelligible object through a series of questions and concerns – what the French term a *problématique* – and to build arguments which provide some kind of response to these questions. It is striking, though, that the historians and writers whose work we have surveyed rarely imagine the war in the same way. They do not speak of the same reality. The history of the war is profoundly fragmented.

Is it possible to go beyond national boundaries of interpretation?

Towards a European history of the war?

In most respects, the war has been constructed in discrete national terms. The first rule that seems to govern this historiography is that every nation has its own Great War.

Firstly, the global perspective is absent. The war mobilized men all over the world: nearly a million Indians were under arms; perhaps half a million French colonial troops also served. The peace conference at Versailles elicited huge hopes and equally powerful disappointments, with far-reaching consequences, as in the case of China and Japan (Macmillan, 2001). These nations were treated as secondary or marginal to the major discussions of the day. Most of the time they were simply ignored.

A nascent European perspective on the war is beginning to emerge nearly a century after its outbreak. The opening of the Historial de Péronne was a step – but only a step – in that direction. The need to Europeanize the discussion of the war is frequently affirmed, but rarely practised. There are some exceptions. Firstly, there are books which bring together national studies on similar themes, such as the treatment of women's work in Wall and Winter (1988) or the essays on military themes in Cecil and Liddle (1996). Then there are studies which compare aspects of the war in two countries, with respect to a single theme, for example Pedersen's study of family allowances in France and Britain (1995). Much rarer are fully comparative studies where the different national materials are examined by a group of historians working together, adopting a single conceptual framework and firm methodology, and reporting collective conclusions. Haimson has produced such a study of strikes in wartime (Haimson and Tilly, 1989; Haimson and Sapelli, 1992), and Jay Winter and Robert (1997) have followed a similar path, together with a large working group investigating first the social and economic history of Paris, London, and Berlin in wartime, and then the cultural history of these three metropolitan centres. But we must add that these research groups were made up of both new researchers and more experienced ones who knew each other and who benefited from the solid logistical support of centres of research and from financial assistance over many years. These indispensable conditions for collective work are very hard to ensure, and remain exceptional.

We can see the outlines of a real European or even global history of the war in other kinds of historical publications, though. The first are textbooks for higher education. Their specifications are well known: they have to present the important facts, with their dates, their ins and outs, according to a didactic plan which will help students to absorb the material. They have to provide a bibliography with some commentary to help guide the reader. A good example of this genre which takes on a European perspective is that of Jean-Jacques Becker (1996). The second is a history more accessible to the general public and whose narrative is less didactic, such as that of Keegan (1998), or the collection of essays edited by Hew Strachan in Britain (1998), or de la Gorce (1991) in France. Jay Winter's *The Experience of World War I* (1988) illustrates this format, in providing a matrix of four themes – the politicians' war, the generals' war, the soldiers' war, and the peoples' war – each followed in four periods – the outbreak of the war, the stalemate, the great battles of 1916–17 and the return of social conflict, and finally the road to Allied victory. As a counterpoint to the text, there are many illustrations used, with captions linking them to the text. Thirdly, through a relatively formal framework and approach, and with a single *problématique*, it seems possible to treat the war in comparative terms. This is the case in the work of Christophe Charle, *La crise des sociétés impériales* (2001). Since this work is not a history of the war, the author is freed from the obligation to cover the whole of the subject and can focus on his central *problématique* of imperialism and social conflict, on both the domestic and the international level.

The power of the national framework

The entirely exceptional character of trans-national historical work within this immense literature is both obvious and should give us pause. One reason is the challenge to any historian who wants to command huge bodies of comparable documentation on any two countries. But there is more to it than that. Comparative history is really what may be termed 'relational' history. The key framework is national, and so is the *problématique*. The enemy, from ordinary citizens to the high command, constitutes one pole, and the Allies, another pole. Bringing them together is a way of deepening national history by measuring the relation between the central national case and the others. Other countries at war are configured in terms of the national case with which historians start and in which they are primarily interested. Our understanding of the war effort unfolds, therefore, from the interplay of these similarities and these differences. The historian considers other countries, but he sees them in the mirror of his own.

This domination of national perspectives has several sources. The first, and perhaps the most fundamental, is inherent in the subject: war is imbricated in the history of the nation; war is even its affirmation. Raymond

Aron defined the nation state as an autonomous subject in international law by its indivisible right to be the sole judge of its vital interests and to go to war to defend them. The tie between war and the nation is strong, fundamental, constitutive. In this sense, we can follow Jaurès in saying that a nation carries war in its flanks the way a cloud carries a storm. War is the destructive apotheosis of the nation. From this perspective, the very idea of a war which would not be national is something of a paradox, or rather a sign that times have changed and that the era of nation states has passed. Recent developments, in which armies confront partisan groups or even faceless bands of armed men, have arrived after what Charles Maier has termed 'the era of territoriality'.[1] These troubling events have made historians of the last twenty years even more sensitive than were their predecessors in the first two configurations to the significance of the national framework.

The second source of the power of the national perspective arises out of the fact that all history is written from a particular point of view, of which historians may not be fully aware. Why? Because we are formed by the very evidence we are trying to understand. It may be useful at this point to refer to James Joll's phrase and to speak of the unspoken assumptions on which rests the construction of historical writing. In the last two decades, the linguistic turn in historical study has habituated us to the exploration of those pre-suppositions which pre-form and pre-structure historical narratives. The point is, though, that these assumptions differ in each country.

Any professor who began a course of lectures in France on this subject with the statement that the war of 1914–18 was not a victory would stun many of his students. In France, the assumption that she won the war comes from within. The 'obvious' question to pose is why did she win the war and lose the peace? Over the last few years, and during a period when the very existence of the nation state in Europe has been contested and its authority blunted by the development of the European Union and European citizenship, this assumption is less self-evident. It was even possible to hear the President of the French Republic state that 3 million French and German soldiers had died during that war for nothing,[2] an affirmation unthinkable a generation earlier. But not for the British. On the other side of the English Channel, the national interest was less directly challenged in the war; the national territory had not been amputated or invaded. The sense that all these dead men who fell in the war had died for nothing, that the war had been futile, informed soldiers' accounts even before structuring historical enquiry. The Italian and German cases are different as well, given the elision between war and fascism, a point to which we shall return. But it is evident that we cannot treat in a comparative perspective a war which is at one and the same time deemed a victory and an absurdity. Or perhaps it is necessary to make these assumptions explicit and turn them into the subject of historical enquiry, in the manner we have attempted in this book.

In addition, each national culture has developed narrative models through which they characterize their national history and in particular their history of the Great War. British irony, that sense of a cultivated distance between one's self and the world developed systematically in the boarding schools, the finishing schools of the dominant social class, the internalized practices of understatement, pre-form British narratives of the war. This sense of irony as a way of life is also deeply ingrained in a number of American anglophiles, like Paul Fussell, whose vision of the Great War is profoundly strange to French students of the subject (Field, 1991). Perhaps this is one reason why the pioneering work of Fussell on 'modern memory' has never been translated into French. His definition of the war as ironic makes little sense to many French readers, who would be equally scandalized by A. J. P. Taylor's *Illustrated history of the First World War*. In this book, both text and captions offer a withering and – from a French perspective – shocking irony, like jokes at the bedside of a dying man. And yet Taylor's paperback edition of this book was a best-seller; it is still in print and going strong. The extreme contrast between anticipation and outcome, the tendency not to take anything too seriously, created this ironic distance among soldier writers. Just consider the titles of two of them: *Goodbye to all that* and *Journey's end*. The war is the example *par excellence* of an event set in motion by leaders who had no idea what they were doing. From this assumption, it is easy to see why so many British historians refer to the war as the quintessence of futility; the French do not even have a word to describe this mixture of the useless and the absurd.

In France, no one jokes about the Great War. It was experienced intensely as a drama in which the stakes were the survival of the national collectivity. This is remote from the way British soldiers saw it, and this initial perception has durably marked British approaches to the war ever since. French education valorizes a positivist, or rather a scientific, approach to problems – which foreigners all too quickly attribute to the Cartesian tradition – an approach in which it is difficult to think about results without thinking about causes. What happened had to have its causes. British observers of the Great War, then as now, had their doubts. Thus the Franco-British dialogue on the war has not been an easy one.

German historiography has developed much later than the other two bodies of historical writing on the war. The gap is palpable. Gerd Krumeich noted that the great German historians of the 1920s kept their distance from historical writing on the war.[3] It was a professional soldier, von Wegerer, who took on the mantle of the specialist, but the dominant characteristic of his history is not its objectivity. In fact, it would take generations before German scholars would write the history of this lost war. The very disputed character of the defeat is part of the reason for the delay, since for many Germans 1918 was not a defeat. The Armistice intervened before combat had reached German soil; the army had indeed been beaten in the field, but they still stood on enemy soil on 11 November, and certainly did not know defeat the way the French army did in 1940. They marched home and paraded in military order before the families and friends they had left behind years before, as if they had been victorious. And there was more. In general, after a defeat, the losers seek to learn something from the winners. This is what happened in Prussia after Jena, in France after 1871, but nothing of the kind happened in Germany in 1918. The defeat was not accepted; it was denied. The stab-in-the-back legend let them escape from reality.[4] To write history, it was necessary to restore it. It would take time before this would become possible.

Hitler's rise to power not only set back this task, but it created new obstacles. For to interrogate the war is to interrogate the history of Nazism. The intellectual tradition of Max Weber helped launch the first attempt to historicize the war, through Ritter's construction of the ideal type of militarism. But Fritz Fischer desacralized the army by turning it into a social formation like all the others and, in the midst of the debate over German rearmament, he set off a veritable earthquake in the historical world by insisting that his colleagues face the history of the army and its role in twentieth-century German history as a whole.

To think historically about the war, finally, is to integrate it into a relevant chronological structure. The problem is that different national historical schools adopt different periodizations in which to set the war. The French chronology starts in 1871 and unfolds around the pivotal years of 1914–18, 1939–40, and 1944. The German chronology terminates not in 1918 but in 1933 or 1945. The Russian and American chronologies accept the year 1917 as a turning point. These different forms of periodization have meant that each national school stands alone; their encounter in the same war did not eliminate the differences in these national chronologies. History can never escape from its context.

We have noted that the very act of imagining the war varies in different countries due to the power of different national assumptions and frameworks. These arose because the collective experience of the war was historically very different: a defeat denied in Germany; a painful victory in France; a mixture of futility and victory in Britain. But these variations also reflect different cultural traditions: British irony, French

Cartesianism, Weberian sociology do not go together easily. History is always pre-formed by assumptions and pre-suppositions which define possible interpretations. It is evident that assumptions underlying historical accounts of the Great War are defined in national terms. It is not possible to imagine the Great War as a European war if one starts from so clearly nationally structured frameworks.

Ebb and flow

There are other sources of these national differences, though perhaps not of the same order of significance. These concern what comes before and after the construction of historical narratives: archival work and publication.

Historical work begins in the archive, as Paul Ricoeur has justly noted.[5] From this point of view, the differences among the belligerents are marked. The first difference is in the losses of Great War archives due to bombardment during the Second World War. The destruction of large parts of the archives of the German army in the Great War is an obstacle very difficult to overcome. Fortunately, copies of correspondence existed in other archives, and given the federal nature of the Kaiserreich, material on particular armies has been preserved, for instance in Stuttgart or Munich. But differences arise too out of different administrative structures and archival practices. The riches of departmental archives in France, and the role played by prefects in linking Paris and the provinces facilitated local studies of broad interest to general scholars. The older European states, with long diplomatic traditions, have public archives, though in both the United States and Britain, private archives are of great importance. The analysis of these national differences should not be neglected, since they pre-condition what history can be written.

But history which is effectively written must be that which finds a publisher. The role of publishers is of the first order in any treatment of historiography. German and French historiography has suffered from a smaller market for their works in the original language, compared to the market available to Anglo-Saxon writers. This handicap is reduced among German historians by their mastery of English, in which some of them write in the first instance, and by their fuller integration into Anglo-Saxon debates.

To be sure there are markets of different sizes in different countries for writing about the Great War. But publishers approach these markets in ways which have real importance for our understanding of the historiographical field as a whole. One of the leitmotifs of our book is that the war is not the property of historians. It is of real and enduring interest to the public at large. There is a robust market for books on the war; a national market not particularly interested in what happens elsewhere. French books on the war have to show a recognizably French soldier on the jacket; and British books need a Tommy to serve the same iconic role. This tendency to nationalize the war makes it very hard to go beyond national historiographies. Publishers believe there is no market for comparative works on the war, but then again, they have hardly produced books that might appeal to such an interest, if it were there. Publishers with an eye on the general reading public rarely invest in learned books. And translation is expensive, a point which has a direct bearing on the intermingling of different national interpretations. In our bibliography, the names of several publishers recur. The work of the Carnegie Endowment was published by Yale University Press in the United States, by Oxford in Britain, and by the Presses Universitaires de France. Closely linked to the work of these distinguished publishing houses is the capacity of the authors who published in them to receive subventions for their books. That is what the Carnegie Endowment assured, even for the work of Norton Cru which they rejected. Malraux was among the first to say that cinema is an industry; the same may be said, on a much more modest level, for history.

There are other publishers who make it possible for the latest research to appear in print. Agnès Viénot, for example, publishes some of the works of the Historial. In the Anglo-Saxon world, Berg and Cambridge University Press are active: each sponsors a series on the Great War, in which both original works and translations of works in French and German appear side by side.[6]

It is evident that the national character of Great War historiography is very difficult to overcome. We have many books on nations at war. We do not have a history of the war on a global level. Or more precisely, we have successive visions of the war, which hardly overlap at all.

Confronting the Great War: three generations of historians

While historiographical schools are strongly national in character, they share certain common questions, which they develop in their own ways. Throughout the period under review, three questions keep coming back, as if they had never received a satisfactory answer and therefore each generation had to try to answer them anew. None has ever solicited uniform answers, but the same questions recur. Why and how did the war break out? How was it conducted; how was it won and lost? What were its consequences?

It is in no sense a matter of concern that these three questions remain open, for the meaning different nations ascribe to the war, the content of the simple word 'meaning', differs both over time and space. As time passes, new events refract the image we have of the war: the superimposition of revolution on war radicalizes the discourse surrounding the conflict; to understand the rejection by the Nazis of the Treaty of Versailles we need a longer time frame than that of the war itself. Finally, it is worth posing the question as to whether the revival of interest in the Great War in the last years of the twentieth century might be related to the progress of the European project and the putting into question of the future of the nation state. All nations respond to real historical rhythms, but never in the same way. The weight of revolution is less evident in Britain than in France; that of the Nazis is a crushing burden for German historiography. But temporal differences inexorably reflect national distinctions as well.

To situate the differences between successive generations of historians better, we highlight three successive dates: 1935, 1965, and 1992. 1935: the year of the first public encounter of French and German historians of the war; 1965: a date which straddles both the fiftieth anniversary of the outbreak of war in 1914 and the fiftieth anniversary of the Russian revolution of 1917 and of the Armistice of 1918; 1992: after the fall of the Berlin Wall, the year of the opening of the Historial de Péronne. Three useful points of reference, to which we should not ascribe too much importance.

The generation of 1935

The first generation configured war in Clausewitzian terms. War is politics by other means. Renouvin's synthesis of 1934 embodies this historiography, the epistemology of which Raymond Aron analysed in his *Introduction à la philosophie de l'histoire* (1938).[7] For Aron, the example he cites in his reflections on causality in history is a declaration of war: the Ems Dispatch. Did it cause the war of 1870, he asked, or was it only an accident which triggered the conflict? The historians of the generation of 1935 remain in a framework inherited from the nineteenth century, and they used a long periodization which extended from 1870 to 1918. In this setting, their view was that the Great War reversed the outcome of 1870.

This approach made of the nation the central factor in history. The Great War was configured as an historical event which ended and fulfilled the century of nationalism and of national unification. It was the last nineteenth-century war. The identification of the nation as embodying history was such that historians could act like diplomats, discussing cordially, nation to nation, in order to find points of rapprochement in their points of view, as happened among German and French scholars in 1935 and 1951.

The historical project thus defined shaped inclusions and exclusions. It included evidently diplomats, the Quai d'Orsay, Wilhelmstrasse, the Kaiser, heads of state, governments, parliaments, administrations. Armies occupied a central place, but they were conceived of in nineteenth-century terms. They were unities of considerable size, seen through the eyes of the general staffs, with their hierarchical chain of command and their generals. Outside this field of historical vision were industry, banks, the ports. There is not a hint of the powerful echo of factories straining to provide cannons, machine guns, and munitions for the front. Their histories are not those in which concrete collective populations live; those men and women whose hustle and bustle drive forward the work of the rear and the front: workers, peasants, wives, children, the elderly, and above all, the ordinary soldiers. This kind of history is one in which the sea breeze does not blow, as Lucien Febvre put it. We do not see convoys converging on Britain from all the corners of the world, bringing the Allies meat, wheat, primary products of all kinds, but also soldiers and workers. The European powers conducted the war as a kind of domestic matter, drawing into Europe assets from everywhere, while forgetting what they owed to the colonies and to the rest of the world.

The historians of this generation engaged in dialogue with privileged partners: politicians, civil servants, writers, officials. And with their students. But at this time the study of history concerned only a small number of people who were destined for careers in teaching at the secondary-school level, then restricted to a tiny elite, or in administration or politics. For this minority, to be interested in the history of the war was part of a wider interest in politics, since, on the grand scale, it depended on war and peace. Politics here was understood as the business of wise and educated men, who had nothing in common with popular emotions or revolutionary upheavals. But they had a sense of politics in which the stakes were very high, because of the indelible memory they carried of the inhuman sacrifices of the war. Peace – always commanding a capital P – was one of the central objectives of politics, one of the three great words through which the Popular Front defined itself. Pacifism was even stronger, since it was built into a war the very prolonging of which made permanent peace its meaning and its objective; the war to end war. At no other period had pacifism as much political force as it had in interwar Britain and France

(Ceadel, 1980; Ingram, 1991). The German case is different, but peace was no less the principal political problem confronting governments and public opinion.

The second generation: fifty years on

One generation later, the context had changed entirely. Commemorations brought out the passage of time: fifty years already since the outbreak of the war. A second war had taken place, one which had drained the Great War of its image, its meaning as the war to end war. In terms of killing and massacre, the Second World War outshone the first, whose costs appeared in a somewhat different light. Above all, a radical change in the nature of war had intervened. War was no longer defined in terms of the clash of armies on the battlefields; it was no longer solely a professional affair; civilians were just as much participants and targets in war as were soldiers. This evolution had begun between 1914 and 1918, but still the rupture of 1939–45 was stunning. From Dresden to Hiroshima, women, children, and the old died by the tens of thousands, and one night of bombardment, indeed one atomic bomb, destroyed the lives of more people than a month of combat at Verdun or Passchendaele. With nuclear deterrence, peace rested henceforth on the menace of the instantaneous destruction of entire cities, and the balance of terror put into question the existence of entire populations.

The second change was political. From the perspective of the 1950s, the image of the war of 1914 was not only distanced and blurred; in a sense it had contracted. In comparison, it seemed more European than global. The advent of the two great power blocs made nations less sovereign. Neither the outcome of a war, nor even its outbreak were in the hands of the states which had declared war in 1914. Paradoxically, since the stakes were much higher than prior to 1940, war ceased to be at the centre of political debate in the former combatant states of Europe. Peace did not disappear from the political agenda, but it was not of pre-eminent importance. Now the focus was first on decolonization, and then on the problems of economic development and growth, on the 'take off', as well as on the competition between international communism and economic liberalism in Africa, in Asia, and in Latin America.

If war was no longer a central political problem, that of 1914–18 was no longer of great interest to the political world. There was a change therefore in the audience for whom historians wrote, in their target population, their interlocutors, those whose works historians read and those whom they hoped would read their histories. The conversation was no longer primarily between historians and men in power, who served as trustees or advisors to the French Foundation of Political Sciences or to Chatham House, the Royal Institute of International Affairs, or who became heads of house in Oxford or Cambridge. Historians went public; they addressed their work to a different public, more diffuse but much larger, among whom the veterans of the Great War, who had reached the age of retirement, were particularly significant. Historians were both joined by and were in competition with journalists converted to history, alongside some historians converted to journalism, and television and radio historians; gone was the partnership of historians of the Great War and wartime political leaders with whom they were familiar.

In truth, even the idea of power was displaced. For the earlier generation, power was easy to identify; it belonged to particular men and to particular sites, and the war unfolded in these places, among these people. For the generation that had gone through the Resistance and the wars of decolonization, who confronted the problems of growth and development, power was evidently in the hands of different groups with different social characteristics. Indeed power was located in society itself.

The historians of this second generation configured the war therefore as a tragedy played out by powerful collective actors: soldiers, workers, civilians. The army was still at the heart of the story, but it was no longer configured through the eyes of the general staffs. It was henceforth a collective of soldiers, thousands of men who formed army corps, who resisted or mutinied eventually, according to their internal cohesion and solidarities, like all other social groups. The historical object shaped by historians of the Great War now included revolution as an essential phenomenon, a prism through which were refracted the tensions provoked by the war. Hence this second historiographical generation drew a different circle around people at war. In the main, women and the extra-European world were still excluded; only marginal treatment if at all, was given to legislatures, generals, churches, political elites. When they appeared, it was in a reduced role, as representatives of particular social groups. On the other hand, very material social groups entered onto the scene as collectives: employers and workers, Tommies and *poilus*; revolutionaries and mutineers, militants and intellectuals. Now the war was one of masses on the move, and of mass movements.

The generation of 1992

The third generation is our own. We adopt the date of 1992 because of its historiographical significance: in that year the Historial de la grande guerre opened at Péronne, and marked its inauguration by an important international conference on 'war and cultures'. But there was a much broader context in which we need to set the emergence of a new kind of history of the Great War.

The first element of the story is institutional: the explosion of universities since the 1960s had created an academic milieu of a kind and on a scale hitherto unknown. This affected all domains of the humanities and social sciences, not just the history of the Great War. In 1968 for example, the history of education was in France a vast wasteland, and no more than a few months were needed to read everything published over decades on the subject with respect to the nineteenth and twentieth centuries. Today books abound; a specialist journal, founded fifteen years ago, devoted each year a double issue to the annual bibliography of this field, including works by historians, sociologists, specialists on science or sport. The same is the case for the history of the Great War. The growth of universities drew many scholars to this subject as to the others. New journals appeared; older institutions devoted to the study of the war, such as the BDIC or the Imperial War Museum, or the Australian War Memorial, or the Canadian War Memorial, launched their own reviews and publications. If some historians who submitted their theses in the 1960s thought that they would be the last people to be interested in this war, they were profoundly mistaken. Theses, conferences, workshops, meetings, events proliferated and so did the audience for what they had to say. The statistics we cited in chapter 1 on the evidence of this explosion in historical publications on the war supports this claim. In brief, the key interlocutors in this third generation were historians, speaking to others in their own countries or in neighbouring ones. These meetings were facilitated by cheapening transport, but more importantly by a greater sense of the need to make the conversation fully international, despite some French tendencies to the contrary.

There were other causes of these developments. After the fall of the Berlin Wall and the Treaty of Maastricht, a new Europe emerged. Revolution was no longer a hope nor was it a menace. The national idea was in crisis, and a new term appeared to describe those who have tried to rescue it: 'sovereignists'. The link between war and nation, so fundamental for Raymond Aron, was severed, and henceforth the Great War appeared as a European civil war. This term was adopted in French high schools.[8] Wars certainly did not disappear, but they were not seen as confrontations of sovereign nation states, with their military and diplomatic corps at their heads. Now wars were the province of guerillas, led by groups demanding national independence, or who turned to violence in order to impose their will on a polity. Then came the 'war against terrorism', which confronted recognized states, with their armed forces, however sophisticated, against small groups, made of men and women in the shadows, acting outside the boundaries of state politics and at times for unattainable or incoherent objectives. From the former Yugoslavia to black Africa, from Colombia to Chechenya, not to mention Cambodia, the Middle East among other places, violence has escaped from any kind of law or norm.

At the same time, unlimited violence became a central subject of public debate. Through a renewal and elaboration of forms of remembrance, the Nazi genocide played a much more important and more central place in representations of the war of 1939–45 than in the preceding generation. The Armenian genocide was rediscovered as well, and in many countries was officially recognized, over vociferous and persistent Turkish objections. Our sense of history was invaded at the end of the twentieth century by a catalogue of bloody abominations and massacres arrayed throughout the century. Contemporary pacifism was born out of a rejection of these crimes. It is as deep as that of the interwar years or of the period of anti-nuclear protest, but it is no longer a political force of the same kind since it no longer challenges the idea of the national interest.

Our sense of what war is, a set of ideas which historians have helped shape in this context, now includes other collective agents. Now the spotlight is on survivors, writers, artists, victims, the wounded, crippled, mutilated veterans, as well as their families, their widows, their orphans. Representations of armies have fragmented too. They are no longer seen as units which manoeuvre or solid collectives, but as sites where men suffer, know hardship or despair, and kill in the heat of battle. In a sense, the army has become hidden behind the individual and collective image of the soldier, a man broken by an instrument of suffering and death, which cannot be resisted. The individual case study is central in this kind of historical writing, because micro-history promises through its careful and sensitive examination of the small-scale to clarify large-scale historical issues invisible, as it were, from above. And in a society of rampant individualism, historians are fascinated by the singularity of individual cultural forms and destinies, most of which, though not all, are European. On the other hand, institutions and organizations quit the scene: trade unions, political parties, organic intellectuals fade away, brushed aside as the apparatchiks of states guilty of the brutalization of societies. Power certainly exists in this set of representations, but it no longer resides in institutions or in great collectives; it is diffused in the atmosphere Foucault termed 'discourse', and it hides behind the term 'public opinion', which takes on new importance.

Three notions of the same war

We have seen how, as contexts changed, historians constructed different histories of the war. The historical object 'the war of 1914–18' cannot be defined in any one way, and deservedly has received a plurality of interpretations. The war has been configured and constructed in a number of ways. And if the national and generational affinities are strong, they do not rule out common assumptions and particularities tied to the way historians represent the world. In this ecumenical spirit, we take the risk of identifying three overarching conceptions of this war.

Nations at war: the last war of the nineteenth century or the second Thirty Years War

The first of these three organizing visions of historical writing configures the war fundamentally as a clash of nations. Seen from this angle, the Great War marked the end of the nineteenth century or, if you prefer, its culmination. The progressive recognition of national aspirations, the realization of Italian and German unification, the conflict of nationalities in the Dual Monarchy, colonial rivalries, all led to this final explosion. It marked the recognition of the impasse of this system of international relations, and the attempt, through the League of Nations, to open a new period. Bloodied Europe saw the establishment of American power without managing to crush the Bolshevik revolution. The culmination of the nineteenth century is at its end: something is over.

This notion is preponderant in the first generation of historians. What gives it force is the way it makes nations the central characters of the story, and this choice leads to the construction of the historical object 'the war', of which we see the outline and from which flow key interpretations. This history of the war is a narrative in which decisions are explained through the analysis of the intentions of those in charge of the interests of each nation and empire, since these nations at the apogee of their power were at the head of extended empires. There are modulations and different inflections in this narrative, to be sure. In France, 1914 is set in perspective by reference to 1870, as the two acts of the same play, the second of which tells the story of 'revenge' for the first. It could also take an ironic turn, as in British historiography, when the intentions of the main actors are compared to the outcome of their decisions. Inversely, the story could take on an epic or a tragic tone, if the historian magnified or dramatized it. It could also take on a biographical form. But in all cases, the fundamental interpretive core remains the same.

In the presentation of these narratives, we can distinguish three variants which reflect different world views or different political philosophies. These notions are not linked to particular political programmes, but they colour the interpretation proferred in the history. The most frequent, in this first configuration, is liberal, in the sense it has of the importance of particular agents. But there were two other perspectives, which we may call the *Marxisant* or lightly Marxist, and the humanist. The *Marxisant* variant is more determinist in character and places great weight on the conditions under which these agents acted and had to act. The third variant, which we term the humanist one, for lack of a better phrase, is marked by a central concern with and sympathy for individual men and women, ordinary people caught up in a history in which they were used in a way as puppets.

In the following generations, these notions did not vanish. They retained an explicative force which offered a first line of analysis, in secondary or university textbooks, as in books written for the general reading public. The most important shift came after the Second World War, when the link between it and the post-1918 settlement became evident. The periodization of a new Thirty Years War had already been suggested in the 1930s, when the fear of another war of revenge to reverse the previous war of revenge informed the pacifist movement. The parallelism between the two wars was striking: in the two cases, a limited war became global; in the two cases, war began like the preceding one, and finished in an entirely different way, on battlefields utterly transformed from the first war; each time, the United States entered the lists two years after everyone else and its intervention was a decisive factor in both conflicts; and finally, the war that happened was utterly different from the one imagined before it had broken out. The links between the wars are there if one looks at the principal actors: Churchill, Eden, Attlee, Pétain, de Gaulle, Mussolini, Hitler all fought in the war of 1914–18, and some played significant roles in both. And the parallelism of the issues at stake is also striking. The key question in both wars was what role in Europe would Germany play? Would she through force of arms and the power of industry come to dominate Northwest Europe or even the whole Continent? In the aftermath of the Second World War, Jean Monnet (another participant in the Great War) and others constructed a European entity first in the form of a joint Franco-German and then European consortium on iron and steel and coal, all three essential to the waging of war and economic power.

The location of the Great War in a longer periodization, as the first part of a second Thirty Years War, does not contradict the notion that war is essentially about nations. The League of Nations did not fundamentally challenge national sovereignty, which the interwar economic crisis reinforced and which reached its end point in the war of 1939–45. But the Second World War was not only a war of nations. The resistance to the Nazis took place within a set of civil wars, more or less officially declared, between locals who supported the Nazis and those who opposed them. The rules of war which had more or less been applied and respected during the First World War were torn up during the Second World War, which merged with genocide. The boundaries between civilian and military populations had been breached during the First World War, but they still were there and retained a clear moral and legal standing; such limits disappeared during the Second World War, during which civilian targets and populations were specifically sought out. Here we enter a field in which the paradigm of war as a matter of nations does not fit; such is not the case with respect to the First World War, but this contrast does highlight the heavy constraints, notably economic in character, with which they struggled. In this context, the *Marxisant* variant of this paradigm took on greater importance.

Societies at war: the revolutionary moment

The second interpretation of the war consists of its configuration as a clash of societies, themselves composed of social groups or classes, defined by different material interests and moral outlooks, and represented in different associations and organizations. From this perspective, the boundaries of the object, 'the war of 1914–18', expanded. If we need to seek the causes of success or failure in the resistance of societies, we must analyse the economic substructure of the war effort, production, manpower, food, wages. Other people come to the fore: employers, financiers, trade unionists. The dangerous mixture of national war turned into civil war, a melange which often evoked fear, sometimes exploded. Consequently, interpretive approaches shifted. The narrative of this kind of Great War history continued in part to articulate decisions in terms of the intentions of the major figures, while putting greater emphasis on collectives: workers, civilians, soldiers. But these studies unfolded above all as narratives of the limits and determinants of war policies. The logic of the situation took precedence over the intentions of the actors. We are in the grip of forces which develop autonomously, and of which the major figures are either the spokesmen or the puppets, and not the masters. Political and military leaders do what they can and not what they want to do.

This mode of configuring the history of the Great War is both more universal and more deterministic. More universal, because it forces us to take into account the ebb and flow of the war in order to understand how the war changed the respective positions of different social groups and the amplitude and duration of the transformations it brought about. This form of analysis leads to painstaking statistical analysis, which at times can lead to surprises, such as when a study of demographic data yielded the hypothesis that the life expectancy and standards of health of the British population lucky enough not to be in the army actually rose in wartime, despite food restrictions and the mobilization of half the medical profession. More determinist, since these narratives demonstrate the law of unintended consequences which arise out of the force of things. There is but little irony here, since there is no contrast between constraints and their results, only between what the leaders thought were the constraints within which they were acting and the real material world in which they were encased. The danger here remains, though, that determinism can become mechanical or functional, and reduce the complexity of the situation to a simple linear equation.

The paradigm of the war of societies is more salient during the second generation of historical writing about the Great War than during the first generation. But it is there early on, for example in the Carnegie series. Some of these interpretations have Marxist shadings – what we call here *Marxisant* – for instance in the 1929 lectures of Elie Halévy, undoubtedly a liberal in his political outlook, but a man more sensitive to the social force of nationalism than were most of his contemporaries. This kind of interpretation was probably under-represented in British historiography and over-represented in the German literature. It continued to thrive in some places in the third historiographical period, notably in Italy. The work of Christophe Charle (2001) shows a similar inclination.

People at war: the matrix of a tragic century

The third configuration of war is marked by the horror of the Holocaust and the Gulag and by the persistence of barbaric violence throughout the world. This is the reason why, as we have already suggested, the sense of tragedy is more important in this third historiographical configuration than in the first two. To be sure, earlier studies of warfare, and in particular of civil wars, in which violence was almost always particularly intense, pointed towards these crimes. The question remained, though, did the Great War unleash what was to come? Did war give birth to Soviet, fascist, and Nazi totalitarianism? Was Auschwitz thinkable without Verdun or the Somme? Here are huge questions, especially in Germany and Italy, questions leading to dead ends, for instance in the work of Nolte on the supposed identity of Bolshevism and fascism. But these questions approach the Great War from another point of view: that of the victims and tormentors. They require us to contemplate mass death and murder in order to try to make sense of them.

This paradigm configures a tragic war in which the principal figures are the victims, who do not act, but suffer. Here we see ordinary people, in their anonymous individuality, outside social groups and public institutions; people, as they live, love, endure pain, because they are trapped in an exceptional situation which they are unable to change and which at any moment threatens to crush them.

Here the emotional dimension is essential, and leads us to consider the entire array of symbolic practices: artistic, religious, literary, commemorative, or those linked to mourning. The framework of this interpretation has shifted in such a way as to put institutions outside its perimeter; the state enters only in its protective and repressive function. Its impotence to control the industrial machinery of death which the state itself launched is one of the tragic facets of the war. Also excluded from this interpretive framework are social groups and economic interests, except when they can explain how individuals differ, for this history does not consider people in constituted groups, but as a collection of individuals. Each individual is legitimate; each life counts, and every single one has to be taken into account. This humanist vision fits this history of individuals better than does the liberal or the Marxist ones. In the context of the history of the soldiers' war, both the school of constraint, as much as the school of consent, though entirely at odds, share the same fundamental attitude.

The paradigm of people at war leads to different patterns of interpretation. We are no longer in the mode of narrative explanation nor of objective structural analysis. Now the challenge is to identify meanings, to reconfigure the symbolic universe of the time. Approaches borrowed from various forms of psychology, semiology, and ethnology provide historians with a way to deal with this kind of history with imagination and empathy.

This approach to history is not entirely new. In the interwar years, this was what the veterans had wanted. It emerged in a number of studies about trench life. But it was only during the last twenty years of the century that it became prominent, through histories of brutalization, mourning, suffering, violence, and hope.

This history poses the question of its own limits. It is impossible to represent some realities, such as combat. We can imagine it, but we cannot represent it. The Historial de la grande guerre precisely chose to remain silent on this point, contrary to the position adopted by other museums, which exhibit stereotypes, with sound effects of multiple explosions. This pseudo-realism is more than mistaken; it transforms the spectator into a voyeur. The historian must accept his limitations, which are those of the historical narrative itself. There are some thresholds that should not be crossed; some silences that should not be broken. Alongside and beyond what an historian can say, there remains unlimited space for poetry and meditation.

How to configure the war?

Among these three configurations, which one should we choose? Which is the best? To this question, we provide no answer at all, for two reasons.

Firstly, we do not want to do so. By definition an historiographical project cannot be normative. Our aim is to understand how successive generations of historians have configured the war and bring to the surface the logic which underlies their work and structures it. This book bears the traces of historiographical gaps, such as the taboo which prevented Soviet historians from dealing with the history of the war prior to 1917. No one has given us the mandate to tell our historical colleagues what should be their research agenda. Let us leave such instructions to those who wish to found historical schools, if such people still exist.

Secondly, it is impossible to answer this question; it is one without an answer, and its only meaning is rhetorical. The whole of our enquiry leads to the conclusion that there are several ways of configuring the war. We have identified three main paradigms, each of which has several variants. They constitute three ways of constructing the historical object 'war' and three patterns of interpretation, drawn from an emphasis on three kinds of historical sources. All three of these configurations of the war are historically legitimate and well founded. All three respond to critical questions; all three produce conclusions which can be verified or falsified. It would be absurd simply to repudiate one or the other through rash judgment, and through the pejorative labelling suggested by words such as outdated, obsolete, Marxist, liberal, military, and so on. These polemical characterizations are useful to mark academic boundaries, but they are not worth refutation.

The claim of total or totalizing history, which aims at a synthesis of these different narratives of the Great War, is obviously impossible to reach for practical reasons. The object is too large to be embraced. Is such an embrace logically or epistemologically possible? Can one conceive of a history which does not remain content with the juxtaposition of different histories, but would be able to structure them in a global form in which each would find its place? We have doubts, and we do not believe that this undertaking is possible, or even if possible, meaningful. It may be possible to configure some kind of global history about particular subjects or issues, for example, this or that battle, the suffering of the soldiers, the medical care of the wounded, public opinion, and so on. On limited issues like those, it is possible to construct a history which allows for the convergence of different approaches in a single narrative. But these histories are not histories of the war itself, as a global phenomenon. Each conception of the history of the Great War is a response to the questions of the here and now, of a particular milieu and a particular time; no one ever hears the response to a question no one poses.

The principal lesson of this historiographical survey is an invitation to appreciate and to accept the irreducible plurality of histories. There is no total history, composed brick by brick like some grand edifice, but rather there are several ways of framing the same history according to different logic, different questions, and different sources, which lead to different narratives and different conclusions. Each narrative of the Great War is no less true or less real than the others. We must critically accept them all and view them as complementary, even when they appear strange or radically different from each other. We subscribe to a kind of historical pluralism which, however, does not imply that all claims are equally true. Truths emerge from narratives constructed from different perspectives, each of which has to be understood in its own terms. On the other hand, different historical accounts are not intrinsically true or false, but their truth or falsity must be judged in terms of the evidence they marshal and the coherence of their arguments.

This is the reason why it is neither contradictory nor out of place to end this book by reminding the reader of the nature of the historian's duty, which is no less demanding when dealing with the war of 1914–18 than with any other subject. Historians aim to create order out of the disorder of the world, at the very least to offer explanations for both. We must throw light on an historical plot always complex and in which multiple passions are always at work. Historians have to make reason and intelligence triumph over feelings and emotions which like everyone else they never escape, especially when dealing with war. This is no recipe for impersonal or insensitive writing, but a plea for accuracy and truth.

And it is entirely appropriate, in conclusion, to evoke the figure of Pierre Renouvin, to whose memory this book is dedicated. We know perfectly well the limits of his historiography, and we did not hide them. They are those of his generation. But by his rigour, his high-mindedness, his openness to objections, his care not to assert anything which he could not prove, he remains a model for us to follow. When a man who had fought in the war and had paid such a high personal price is able to take the critical distance needed to write the very history of that war, when he feels sufficiently secure in his own conclusions to discuss them with his military adversaries of yesterday, we are in the presence of historical thinking of the highest order. To read him, one feels a bit more intelligent, a bit more tolerant. Is there a better ambition for an historian?

NOTES

1. Charles Maier, 'Consigning the twentieth century to history: alternative narratives for the modern era', *American Historical Review*, 105 (3), June 2000, pp. 807–31.
2. Press conference of Federal Press Office, 27 June 2000.

3. Gerd Krumeich, '80 ans de recherche allemande sur la guerre de 14–18', in Maurin and Jauffret, 2002, p. 27.

4. Gerd Krumeich, 'La place de la guerre de 1914–1918 dans l'histoire culturelle de l'Allemagne', in Becker *et al.*, 1994, pp. 36–45.

5. Paul Ricoeur, *La mémoire, l'histoire, l'oubli*, Paris, Seuil, 2000, pp. 209ff.

6. We could cite Fridenson, J.-J. Becker, A. Becker, Audoin-Rouzeau, and Prost as French scholars whose works have been published in English, and Kocka and Daniel as German.

7. Raymond Aron, *Introduction à la philosophie de l'histoire*, Paris, Gallimard, 1938, p. 164.

8. For the term in the French context, see the historical programme of classes L and ES, terminal classes, under the subtitle: 'Europe and the West in construction until the end of the 1980s: The building of Europe requires several factors: an ideal which associated the rejection until the end of the 1980s of European "civil wars".' Thanks are due to Patrick Garcia for having given us this information.

Bibliography 1914–2003

This bibliography does not cover publications on general historiographical or methodological issues. We limit our citations to those works on the Great War which we discuss in the text. We do not pretend in the least to cite all the important works on the war; that is beyond us. Initially we thought that it would be sufficient to limit this survey to 500 titles, but could not hold the line. Other scholars would no doubt have made a different selection of scholarly works. We accept the responsibility for presenting a simple sketch of the avalanche of publications on the Great War.

Every day, it seems, new books on this subject appear. For a guide to this literature, including references beyond those we have included here, there are now two substantial encyclopedias of the Great War at our disposal. The German encyclopedia of the Great War, edited by Gerhard Hirschfeld, Gerd Krumeich, and Irina Rens, is a pathbreaking compilation, showing the full flowering of German and other European research in recent years. The full reference is: G. Hirschfeld, K. Krumeich, and I. Rens (eds.), *Enzyklopädie Erster Weltkrieg* (Pederborn, Schöningh, 2002). Similarly valuable is the new French encyclopedia of the war, edited by Stéphane Audoin-Rouzeau and Jean-Jacques Becker, *Encyclopédie de la grande guerre. 1914–1918. Histoire et culture* (Paris, Bayard, 2004), a book with wide reference and an unsurprising emphasis, given the editors' expertise, on French cultural history.

In order to help the reader consult the texts to which we refer, we list them in simple alphabetical order. The names of the authors are followed by the date of first publication. When the reference comes from a later edition or from a translation, we provide the full reference to the book we quote but nevertheless register the book under the date of its first publication. If the original title is very different from that of its translation, for instance in the case of Fischer, 1961, we indicate this variance, though not when the title is directly translated.

We would like to emphasize the unconventional character of this bibliography. It is not a guide to the sources used in the arguments developed chapter by chapter, but rather an incomplete survey of the historical literature dealing with the Great War published between 1914 and 2003. It does not cover the period between the publication of the French version of this book and 2005. This bibliography is incomplete in a second sense too. We do not cite books which have sections or chapters on the war; to do so would be to include virtually every single text on twentieth-century history. Thirdly, we have not cited articles in scholarly journals, except in the form of footnotes to the text. We admit that much innovative work appears first and sometimes only in the form of articles, but the huge dimensions of the historiography of this field would be entirely unmanageable if we were to decide to include hundreds, indeed thousands, of scholarly articles here. For such omissions, we ask the reader's indulgence. Once again, without the slightest pretence of being exhaustive, we offer here a list of journals in which readers can find up-to-date accounts of current scholarly research.

14–18, Aujourd'hui, Today, Heute (1998–)
American Historical Review (1914–)
Annales (1929–)
Genèses (1990–)
Geschichte und Gesellschaft (1975–)
Guerre mondiale et conflits contemporains (1987–)
Historische Zeitschrift (1914–)
Imperial War Museum Review (1986–)
Journal of the Australian War Memorial (1982–)
Journal of Contemporary History (1966–)
Journal of Modern History (1928–)
Le Mouvement social (1952–)
Matériaux pour l'histoire de notre temps (1985–)
Quaderni storici (1966–)
Revue européenne d'histoire (1994–)
Revue d'histoire de la Guerre Mondiale (1923–39)
Revue historique (1914–)
Revue de synthèse (1914–)
Vingtième siècle, revue d'histoire (1984–)
War and Society (1983–)
War in History (1994–)

1914, les psychoses de guerre? Actes du colloque du 26 au 29 septembre 1979, 1985. Mont-Saint-Aignan, CRDP.

Abbal, Odon, 2001. *Soldats oubliés: les prisonniers de guerre français*, Betz-et-Esparon, Etudes et Communication éditions.

Afflerbach, Holger, 1994. *Falkenhayn: politisches Denken und Handeln im Kaiserreich*, Munich, Oldenbourg.

Albertini, Luigi, 1942–3. *Le origini della guerra del 1914*, Milan, Fratelli Bocca, 3 vols.

Allain, Jean-Claude (ed.), 1995. *Des étoiles et des croix: mélanges offerts à Guy Pedroncini*, Paris, Economica.

Andreski, Stanislav, 1954. *Military organization and society*, London, Routledge & Paul.

L'année 1917, 1968. Actes du colloque organisé par la Société d'histoire moderne, 7–9 octobre 1967, numéro spécial de la *Revue d'histoire moderne et contemporaine*, tome XV, janvier–mars.

Appuhn, Charles, 1926. *La Politique allemande pendant la guerre*, Paris, A. Costes.

Artaud, Denise, 1978. *La Question des dettes interalliées et la reconstruction de l'Europe*, Lille, Service de reproduction des thèses, 2 vols.

Ashworth, Tony, 1980. *Trench warfare, 1914–1918: the live and let live system*, New York, Holmes and Meyer.

Association des écrivains combattants, 1924–7. *Anthologie des écrivains morts à la guerre 1914–1918*, Amiens, Edgar Malfère, 5 vols.

Association nationale du souvenir de la bataille de Verdun, Université de Nancy II, 1976. *Verdun 1916, Actes du colloque international sur la bataille de Verdun, 6–7–8 juin 1975*, Verdun.

Audoin-Rouzeau, Stéphane, 1986. *14–18, les combattants des tranchées*, Paris, A. Colin.

1993. *La Guerre des enfants 1914–1918, essai d'histoire culturelle*, Paris, A. Colin.

1995a. *Combattre*, Amiens, CRDP.

1995b. *L'enfant de l'ennemi 1914–1918*, Paris, Aubier.

2001. *Cinq deuils de guerre*, Paris, Noêsis.

Audoin-Rouzeau, Stéphane and Becker, Annette, 2000. *14–18, retrouver la guerre*, Paris, Gallimard.

Audoin-Rouzeau, Stéphane, Becker, Annette, Ingrao, Christian, and Rousso, Henry (eds.), 2002. *La Violence de guerre, 1914–1945: approches comparées des deux conflits mondiaux*, Brussels, Complexe.

Augé-Laribé, Michel, 1925. *L'agriculture pendant la guerre*, Paris, PUF [Publication of the Carnegie Endowment for International Peace].

Aulard, Alphonse, Bouvier, E., and Ganem, A., 1924. *1914–1918, Histoire politique de la Grande Guerre*, Paris, A. Quillet.

Babington, Anthony, 1983. *For the sake of example. Capital courts-martial 1914–1920*, London, Lee Cooper.

Baconnier, Gérard, Minet, André, and Soler, Louis, 1985. *La Plume au fusil: les poilus du Midi à travers leur correspondance*, Toulouse, Privat.

Badia, Gilbert, 1964. *Les Spartakistes: 1918, l'Allemagne en révolution*, Paris, Julliard (Archives).

1967. *Le Spartakisme. Les dernières années de Rosa Luxemburg et de Karl Liebknecht*, Paris, L'Arche.

1975. *Rosa Luxemburg: journaliste, polémiste, révolutionnaire*, Paris, Ed. sociales.

Bainville, Jacques, 1920. *Les Conséquences politiques de la paix*, Paris, Gallimard, 2002 [1st edn, Paris, Nouvelle librairie nationale].

Bane, Suda Lorena and Lutz, Ralph Haswell (eds.), 1942. *The blockade of Germany after the armistice, 1918–1919; selected documents of the Supreme Economic Council, Superior Blockade Council, American Relief Administration, and other wartime organizations*, Stanford, Stanford University Press and London, H. Milford, Oxford University Press.

Bardet, Jean Pierre and Dupâquier, Jacques (eds.), 1999. *Histoire des populations de l'Europe*, vol. III: *Les Temps incertains 1914–1988*, Paris, Fayard.

Bariéty, Jacques, 1977. *Les Relations franco-allemandes après la Première Guerre mondiale, 10 novembre 1918–10 janvier 1925, de l'exécution à la négociation*, Paris, Pedone/Publ. de la Sorbonne.

Barnes, Harry Elmer, 1929. *The genesis of the world war: an introduction to the problem of war guilt*, New York, A. A. Knopf [Fr. trans. as *La Genèse de la Guerre mondiale*, Paris, M. Rivière, 1931].

Barnett, Corelli, 1963. *The swordbearers. Supreme command in the First World War*, New York, Signet Books.

Bartov, Omer, 2000. *Mirrors of destruction. War, genocide, and modern identity*, Oxford, Oxford University Press.

Bartov, Omer (ed.), 2002. *Crimes of war: guilt and denial in the XXth century*, New York, The New Press.

Bean, Charles E. W., 1934. *The Story of Anzac*, Sydney, Angus and Robertson.

Becker, Annette, 1988. *Les Monuments aux morts: patrimoine et mémoire de la Grande Guerre*, Paris, Errances.

1994. *La Guerre et la foi, de la mort à la mémoire, 1914–1930*, Paris, A. Colin.

1998. *Oubliés de la Grande Guerre. Humanitaire et culture de guerre*, Paris, Noêsis.

Becker, Jean-Jacques, 1973. *Le Carnet B: les pouvoirs publics et l'antimilitarisme avant la guerre de 1914*, Paris, Klincksieck.

1977. *1914: Comment les Français sont entrés dans la guerre, contribution à l'étude de l'opinion publique printemps–été 1914*, Paris, Presses de la FNSP.

1980. *The Great War and the French people*, Leamington Spa, Berg.

1996. *L'Europe dans la Grande Guerre*, Paris, Belin.

1997. *1917 en Europe. L'année impossible*, Bruxelles, Complexe.

2002. *Le Traité de Versailles*, Paris, PUF [coll. 'Que sais-je?'].

Becker, Jean-Jacques and Audoin-Rouzeau, Stéphane (eds.), 1990. *Les sociétés européennes et la guerre de 1914–1918*, Actes du colloque organisé à Nanterre et à Amiens du 8 au 11 décembre 1988, Nanterre, Université de Paris X.

Becker, Jean-Jacques, with Becker, Annette, 1988. *La France en guerre (1914–1918). La grande mutation*, Brussels, Complexe.

Becker, Jean-Jacques, Becker, Annette, Audoin-Rouzeau, Stéphane *et al.* (eds.), 1994. *Guerre et cultures 1914–1918*, Paris, A. Colin.

Beckett, Ian F. W., 2001. *The Great War 1914–1918*, New York, Longman.

Beckett, Ian F. W. and Simpson, Keith (eds.), 1985. *A nation in arms. A social study of the British army in the First World War*, Manchester, Manchester University Press.

Bell, Archibald C., 1961. *A history of the blockade of Germany and of the countries associated with her in the Great War, Austria-Hungary, Bulgaria and Turkey, 1914–1918*, London, H. M. Stationery Office. [German trans., Bell, Archibald C., 1943, *Die englische Hungerblockade im Weltkrieg 1914–15, nach der amtlichen englischen Durstellung der Hungerblockade*, Essen, Essener Verlagsanstalt.]

Bendick, Rainer, 1999. *Kriegserwartung und Kriegserfahrung: der Erste Weltkrieg in deutschen und französischen Schulgeschichtsbüchern (1900–1939/45)*, Pfaffenweiler, Centaurus-Verlagsgesellschaft.

Berghahn, Volker Rolf, 1971. *Der Tirpitz-Plan: Genesis und Verfall einer innenpolitischen Krisenstrategie unter Wilhelm II*, Düsseldorf, Droste.

1973. *Germany and the approach of war in 1914*, London, Macmillan.

Berghoff, Hartmut and Friedeburg, Robert von (eds.), 1998. *Change and inertia. Britain under the impact of the First World War*, Bodenheim, Philo Cop.

Bernard, Léon, 1929. *La Guerre et la santé publique. La défense de la santé publique pendant la guerre*, Paris, PUF [Publication of the Carnegie Endowment for International Peace].

Bernard, Philippe, 1975. *La Fin d'un monde 1914–1929*, Paris, Seuil [Nouvelle histoire de la France contemporaine, vol. XII].

Bessel, Richard, 1993. *Germany after the First World War*, Oxford, Clarendon Press.

Beveridge, Sir William, 1928. *British food control*, New Haven, Yale University Press [Publication of the Carnegie Endowment for International Peace].

1939. *Blockade and the civilian population*, Oxford, Clarendon Press.

Bianchi, Bruna, 2001. *La follia e la fuga. Nevrosi di guerra, diserzione e disobbedienza nell'esercito italiano (1915–1918)*, Rome, Bulzoni.

Bidou, Henri, 1936. *Histoire de la Grande Guerre*, Paris, Gallimard.

Bidou, Henri, Gauvain, André and Seignobos, Charles, 1922. *La Grande Guerre*, vol. IX de Lavisse, Ernest (ed.), *Histoire de la France contemporaine depuis la Révolution jusqu'à la paix de 1919*, Paris, Hachette.

Bieber, Hans Joachim, 1981. *Gewerkschaften in Krieg und Revolution. Arbeiterbewegung, Industrie, Staat und Militär in Deutschland 1914–1920*, Hamburg, Hans Christians.

Binneveld, Hans, 1998. *From shell shock to combat stress. A comparative history of military psychiatry*, Ann Arbor, University of Michigan Press.

Birdsall, Paul, 1941. *Versailles twenty years after*, New York, Reynal and Hitchcock.

Bloch, Camille, 1925. *Bibliographie méthodique de l'histoire économique et sociale de la France pendant la guerre*, Paris, PUF [Publication of the Carnegie Endowment for International Peace].

1933. *Les Causes de la guerre mondiale. Précis historique*, Paris, Paul Hartmann.

Bock, Fabienne, 2002. *Un parlementarisme de guerre 1914–1919*, Paris, Belin.

Boemeke, Manfred (ed.), 1998. *The Treaty of Versailles: a reassessment after 75 years*, Cambridge, Cambridge University Press.

Bogart, Ernest L., 1919. *Direct and indirect costs of the Great War*, New York, Oxford University Press [Publication of the Carnegie Endowment for International Peace].

Bond, Brian, 2002. *The unquiet front: Britain's role in literature and history*, Cambridge, Cambridge University Press.

Bond, Brian (ed.), 1991. *The First World War and British military history*, Oxford, Oxford University Press.

Bond, Brian and Cave, Nigel (eds.), 1999. *Haig: a reappraisal seventy years on*, Barnsley, Pen and Sword.

Bonnefous, Georges, 1957. *Histoire politique de la Troisième République*, vol. II: *La Grande Guerre (1914–1918)*, Paris, PUF, 1967.

Bouillon, Jacques and Petzold, Michel, 1999. *Mémoire figée, mémoire vivante. Les monuments aux morts*, Paris, Citédis.

Bourget, J.-M., 1932. *Petite histoire de la Grande guerre mondiale*, Paris, Rieder.

Bourke, Joanna, 1996. *Dismembering the male. Men's bodies, Britain and the Great War*, London, Reaktions Book.

1999. *An intimate history of killing. Face-to-face killing in twentieth-century warfare*, London, Granta.

Bourne, John M., 1989. *Britain and the Great War 1914–1918*, London, Arnold.

Boutefeu, Roger, 1966. *Les Camarades. Soldats français et allemands au combat 1914–1918*, Paris, Fayard.

Bowley, Arthur L., 1921. *Prices and wages in the United Kingdom, 1914–1920*, New Haven, Yale University Press [Publication of the Carnegie Foundation for International Peace].

Bracco, Rosa Maria, 1993. *Merchants of hope. British middlebrow writers and the First World War, 1919–1939*, Providence/Oxford, Berg.

Braunthal, Julius, 1961–3. *History of the International 1864–1943*, London/ Edinburgh, Nelson, 1966–7, 2 vols. [1st edn, Hanover, Dietz Nachf, 3 vols.].

Bröckling, Ulrich, 1997. *Disziplin. Soziologie und Geschichte militärischer Gehorsamproduktion*, Munich, Wilhelm Fink Verlag.

Bröckling, Ulrich and Sikora, Michael, 1998. *Armeen und ihre Deserteure, Vernachlässigte Kapitel einer Militärgeschichte der Neuzeit*, Göttingen, Vandehoeck and Ruprecht.

Bryder, Linda, 1988. *Below the magic mountain: a social history of tuberculosis in twentieth century Britain*, Oxford, Clarendon Press.

Bucholz, Arden, 1991. *Moltke, Schlieffen, and Prussian war planning*, Providence/ Oxford, Berg.

Buitenhuis, Peter, 1987. *The Great War of words. British, American and Canadian propaganda and fiction, 1914–1933*, Vancouver, University of British Columbia Press.

Burk, Kathleen, 1985. *Britain, America and the sinews of war, 1914–1918*, London: Allen and Unwin.

Burk, Kathleen (ed.), 1982. *War and the state. The transformation of British government, 1914–1919*, London, Allen and Unwin.

Canini, Gérard, 1988. *Combattre à Verdun. Vie et souffrance quotidienne du soldat 1916–1917*, Nancy, Presses Universitaires de Nancy.

Canini, Gérard (ed.), 1989. *Mémoire de la grande guerre. Témoins et témoignages*, Nancy, Presses Universitaires de Nancy.

Capdevila, Luc and Voldman, Danièle, 2002. *Nos Morts. Les sociétés occidentales face aux tués de la guerre*, Paris, Payot.

Cardinal, Agnès, Goldman, Dorothy and Hattaway, Judith (eds.) 1999. *Women's writing on the First World War*, Oxford, Oxford University Press.

Carlier, Claude and Pedroncini, Guy (eds.), 1997a. *Les Etats-Unis dans la première Guerre Mondiale: 1917–1918*. Actes du colloque international, à Paris, Assemblée Nationale, les 22 et 23 Septembre 1987, organisé par l'Institut d'histoire des conflits contemporains, Paris, Economica.

Carlier, Claude and Pedroncini, Guy (eds.), 1997b. *Les troupes coloniales dans la Grande guerre*. Actes du colloque organisé à Verdun le 27 novembre 1996, Vincennes, IHCC, Verdun, CNSV, Paris, Economica.

Caron, François, 1973. *Histoire de l'exploitation d'un grand réseau. La Compagnie du Chemin de Fer du Nord 1846–1937*, Paris, Mouton.

Caucanas, Sylvie and Rémy, Cazals (eds.), 1997. *Traces de 14–18*, Carcassonne, Les Audois.

Cazals, Rémy, 1983. *Années cruelles, 1914–1918*, témoignages recueillis par Rémy Cazals, Claude Marquié, René Piniès, Carcassonne, Fédération audoise des œuvres laïques.

Cazals, Rémy and Rousseau, Frédéric, 2001. *14–18, Le Cri d'une génération*, Toulouse, Privat.

Ceadel, Martin, 1980. *Pacifism in Britain, 1914–1945: the defining of a faith*, Oxford, Clarendon Press.

Cecil, Hugh and Liddle, Peter (eds.), 1996. *Facing Armageddon: the First World War experienced*, London, Cooper.

Centre de recherche de l'Historial de Péronne, 1994. *14–18, la très grande guerre*, Paris, Le Monde-éditions (series published daily in *Le Monde* in the summer of 1994).

Chaline, Nadine-Josette (ed.), 1993. *Chrétiens dans la Première Guerre mondiale*, Paris, Cerf.

Charle, Christophe, 2001. *La Crise des sociétés impériales: Allemagne, France, Grande-Bretagne: 1900–1940: essai d'histoire sociale comparée*, Paris, Seuil.

Chickering, Roger, 1998. *Imperial Germany and the Great War*, Cambridge, Cambridge University Press.

Chickering, Roger and Förster, Stig (eds.), 2000. *Great War, total war. Combat and mobilization on the Western Front 1914–1918*, Cambridge, Cambridge University Press.

2003. *The shadows of total war*, Cambridge, Cambridge University Press.

Churchill, Winston, 1933–4. *The Great War*, London, G. Newnes, 3 vols.

Clemenceau, Georges, 1930. *Grandeurs et misères d'une victoire*, Paris, Plon.

Clémentel, Etienne, 1931. *La guerre et le commerce. La France et la politique économique interalliée*, Paris, PUF [Publication of the Carnegie Endowment for International Peace].

Cochin, Denys, Gout, Jean and Fouques-Duparc, Francis *et al.*, 1926. *Les Organisations de blocus en France pendant la guerre: 1914–1918*, Paris, Plon.

Coetzee, Frans and Shevin-Coetzee, Marilyn (eds.), 1995. *Authority, identity and the social history of the Great War*, Providence, Berghahn Books.

Coffman, Edward M., 1968. *The war to end all wars. The American military experience in World War I*, New York, Oxford University Press.

Cohen, Yves, 2001. *Organiser à l'aube du taylorisme: la pratique d'Ernest Mattern chez Peugeot*, Besançon, Presses universitaires franc-comtoises.

Cole, George Douglas Howard, 1923a. *Workshop organization*, New Haven, Yale University Press [Publication of the Carnegie Endowment for International Peace].

1923b. *Trade unionism and munitions*, New Haven, Yale University Press [Publication of the Carnegie Endowment for International Peace].

1923c. *Labour in the coal-mining industries*, New Haven, Yale University Press [Publication of the Carnegie Endowment for International Peace].

1965. *A history of socialist thought. IV, Communism and social democracy, 1914–1931*, London, Macmillan and New York, St Martin's Press, 2 vols.

Collinet, Paul and Stahl, Paul, 1928. *Le ravitaillement de la France occupée*, Paris, PUF [Publication of the Carnegie Endowment for International Peace].

Connelly, Mark, 2002. *The Great War, memory and ritual. Commemoration in the City and East London, 1916–1939*, Woodbridge, Royal Historical Society and Rochester, Boydell Press.

Constantine, Stephen, Kirby, Maurice W., and Rose, Mary B. (eds.) 1995. *The First World War in British history*, London, Arnold.

Contamine, Henry, 1970. *La Victoire de la Marne, 9 septembre 1914*, Paris, Gallimard [series 'Trente journées qui ont fait la France'].

Cork, Richard, 1994. *A bitter truth. Avant-garde art and the Great War*, New Haven, Yale University Press.

Cornwall, Mark, 1990. *The last years of Austria-Hungary: essays in political and military history 1908–1918*, Exeter, Exeter University Press.

Creveld, Martin van, 1985. *Command in war*, Cambridge (Mass.), Harvard University Press.

Crocq, Louis, 1999. *Les traumatismes psychiatriques de guerre*, Paris, Odile Jacob.

Crosby, Gerda Richards, 1957. *Disarmament and peace in British politics, 1914–1919*, Cambridge, Mass., Harvard University Press.

Cru, Jean Norton, 1929. *Témoins*, Paris, Les Etincelles [repr. Nancy, Presses Universitaires de Nancy, 1993].

1930. *Du témoignage*, Paris, NRF [repr. Paris, Allia, 1989].

Crutwell, C. R. M. F., 1934. *A history of the great war, 1914–1918*, Oxford, Clarendon Press.

Dagen, Philippe, 1996. *Le Silence des peintres. Les artistes face à la Grande Guerre*, Paris, Fayard.

Dallas, Golden and Gill, Douglas, 1985. *The unknown army*, London, Verso.

Daniel, Ute, 1997. *The war from within: German working-class women in the First World War*, Oxford, Berg.

Darrow, Margaret H., 2000. *French women and the First World War: war stories of the home front*, Oxford/New York, Berg.

Dauzet, Pierre, 1915. *Guerre de 1914: De Liége à la Marne*, with preface by Gabriel Hanotaux, Paris, Charles-Lavauzelle.

Daviet, Jean-Pierre, 1988. *Un destin international: la Compagnie de Saint-Gobain de 1830 à 1939*, Paris, Ed. des Archives contemporaines.

Davis, Belinda J., 2000. *Home fires burning: food, politics and everyday life in Berlin*, Chapel Hill, University of North Carolina Press.

Debeney, Général Marie-Eugène, 1937. *La guerre et les hommes. Réflexions d'après-guerre*, Paris, Plon.

Dedijer, Vladimir, 1967. *The road to Sarajevo*, London, MacGibbon and Kee [French trans. Paris, Gallimard, 1969].

Degroot, Gerard G., 1996. *Blighty. British society in the era of the Great War*, London, Longman.

Deist, Wilhelm, 1976. *Flottenpolitik und Flottenpropaganda: das Nachrichtenbureau des Reichsmarineamtes 1897–1914*, Stuttgart, Deutsche Verlagsanstalt.

(ed.), 1970. *Militär und Innenpolitik im Weltkrieg 1914–1918*, Düsseldorf, Droste.

(ed.), 1985. *The German military in the age of total war*, Leamington Spa, Berg.

Delaporte, Sophie, 1996. *Les Gueules cassées. Les blessés de la face de la Grande Guerre*, Paris, Noêsis.

Delbrück, Hans, 1929. *Die Friede von Versailles, Gedenkrede, geplant zu der vom Ministerium untersagten Veranstaltung der fünf veireinigten Berliner Hochshulen am 28 Juni 1929*, Berlin, G. Stilke.

Delteil, Joseph, 1926. *Les Poilus*, Paris, Grasset, repr. 1986.

Dobson, Sean, 2001. *Authority and upheaval in Leipzig 1910–1920: the story of a relationship*. New York, Columbia University Press.

Doise, Jean and Vaïsse, Maurice, 1989. *Diplomatie et outil militaire, (1871–1991)*, Paris, Impr. Nationale, 1992.

Dombrowski, Nicole Ann (ed.), 1999. *Women and war in the twentieth century: enlisted with or without consent*, New York/London, Garland.

Douglas, Allen, 2002. *War, memory, and the politics of Humor. The Canard enchaîné and World War I*, Berkeley, University of California Press.

Downs, Laura Lee, 1995. *Manufacturing inequality: gender division in the French and British metalworking industries 1914–1939*, Ithaca, Cornell University Press [French trans. *L'inégalité à la chaîne: la division sexuelle du travail dans l'industrie métallurgique en France et en Angleterre, 1914–1939*, Paris, A. Michel, 2001].

Drachkovitch, Milorad, 1953. *Les Socialistes français et le problème de la guerre 1870–1914*, Geneva, Droz.

Droz, Jacques, 1973. *Les Causes de la Première Guerre mondiale, essai d'historiographie*, Paris, Seuil.

Droz, Jacques (ed.), 1974. *Histoire générale du socialisme*, vol. II: *De 1875 à 1918*, Paris, PUF.

Ducasse, André, 1932. *La Guerre racontée par les combattants. Anthologie des écrivains du front*, Paris, Flammarion, 2 vols.

Ducasse, André, Meyer, Jacques, and Perreux, Gabriel, 1959. *Vie et mort des français 1914–1918*, presented by Maurice Genevoix, Paris, Hachette.

Dülffer, Jost and Holl, Karl (eds.), 1986. *Bereit zum Krieg: Kriegsmentalität im wilhelminischen Deutschland 1890–1914; Beiträge zur historischen Friedensforschung*, Göttingen, Vandenhoeck and Ruprecht.

Duménil, Anne, 2002. *Le Soldat allemand de la Grande Guerre: institution militaire et expérience du combat*, thesis, Université de Picardie Jules-Verne.

Duroselle, Jean-Baptiste, 1960. *De Wilson à Roosevelt. Politique extérieure des Etats-Unis*, Paris, A. Colin.

1970. *L'Europe de 1815 à nos jours, vie politique et relations internationales*, Paris, PUF [series 'Nouvelle Clio'].

1972. *La France et les Français: 1914–1920*, Paris, Ed. Richelieu.

1989. *La Grande Guerre, Les grands dossiers de 'l'Illustration'*, Paris, le Livre de Paris, 2 vols.

1994. *La Grande Guerre des Français. L'incompréhensible*, Paris, Libr. académique Perrin [repr.: 1998, 2003].

Eckart, Wolfgang U. and Gradmann, Christoph (eds.), 1996. *Die Medizin und der Erste Weltkrieg*, Pfaffenweiler, Centaurus Verlag.

Ecole française de Rome, 1987. *Les Internationales et le problème de la guerre au XXe siècle*, actes du colloque organisé à Rome, 22–24 novembre 1984, Rome, Ecole française de Rome and Milan, Universita di Milano.

Eksteins, Modris, 1989. *Rites of spring: the Great War and the birth of the modern age*, Boston, Houghton Mifflin.

Erdmann, Karl-Dietrich (ed.), 1972. *Kurt Riezler. Tagebücher, Aufsätze, Dokumente*, Göttingen, Vandenhoeck.

Evans, Robert J. W. and Pogge von Strandmann, Hartmut (eds.), 1988. *The coming of the First World War*, Oxford, Clarendon Press.

Falls, Cyril, 1930. *War books, a critical guide*, London, P. Davies.

Farcy, Jean-Claude, 1995. *Les Camps de concentration français de la Première Guerre mondiale (1914–1920)*, Paris, Anthropos/Economica.

Farrar, Marjorie Milbank, 1974. *Conflict and compromise. The strategy, politics and diplomacy of the French blockade, 1914–1918*, La Haye, Martin Nijhoff.

Fay, Sidney B., 1929. *The origins of the World War*, New York, Macmillan, 2 vols.

Fayolle, Maréchal Marie-Emile, 1964. *Carnets secrets de la Grande Guerre*, presented and annotated by Henry Contamine, Paris, Plon.

Feis, Herbert, 1930. *Europe, the world's banker, 1870–1914; an account of European foreign investment and the connection of world finance with diplomacy before the war*, London, Oxford University Press.

Feldman, Gerald D., 1966. *Army, industry and labor in Germany 1914–1918*, Providence and Oxford, Berg, 1992 (new edn) [1st edn, Princeton, Princeton University Press].

1993. *The great disorder: politics, economics and society in the German inflation, 1914–1924*, New York, Oxford University Press.

Feldman, Gerald D. and Homburg, Heidrun, 1977. *Industrie und Inflation: Studien und Dokumente zur Politik der deutschen Unternehmer, 1916–1923*, Hamburg, Hoffman and Campe.

Ferguson, Niall, 1999. *The pity of war*, New York, Basic Books.

Ferrel, Robert H., 1985. *Woodrow Wilson and World War I, 1917–1921*, New York, Harper and Row.

Ferro, Marc, 1967. *La Révolution de 1917*, vol. I: *La chute du tsarisme et les origines d'octobre*, Paris, Aubier-Montaigne.

1969. *La Grande Guerre 1914–1918*, Paris, Gallimard.

1976. *La Révolution de 1917*, vol. II: *Octobre, naissance d'une société*, Paris, Aubier-Montaigne.

1980. *L'Occident devant la révolution soviétique: l'histoire et ses mythes*, Brussels, Ed. Complexe.

Field, Frank, 1991. *British and French writers of the First World War*, Cambridge, Cambridge University Press.

Fischer, Fritz, 1961. *Griff nach der Weltmacht. Die Kriegszielepolitik des kaiserlichen Deutschland, 1914–1918*, Düsseldorf, Droste [English trans., *Germany's war aims in the First World* War, London, Chatto and Windus, 1967; French trans., *Les Buts de guerre de l'Allemagne impériale 1914–1918*, Paris, Ed. de Trévise, 1970].

1969. *Krieg der Illusionen: die deutsche Politik von 1911 bis 1914*, Düsseldorf, Droste [English trans. *War of illusions: German policies from 1911 to 1914*, trans. Marian Jackson, Chatto and Windus, 1975].

Flood, P. J., 1990. *France 1914–18, public opinion and the war effort*, London and Basingstoke, Macmillan.

Foch, Maréchal Ferdinand, 1931. *Mémoires pour servir à l'histoire de la guerre de 1914–1918*, Paris, Plon, 2 vols.

Fontaine, Arthur, 1924. *L'Industrie française pendant la guerre*, Paris, PUF [Publication of the Carnegie Endowment for International Peace].

Fontana, Jacques, 1973. *Attitude et sentiments du clergé et des catholiques français devant et durant la guerre de 1914–1918*, Lille, Service de reproduction des thèses.

    1990. *Les Catholiques français pendant la Grande Guerre*, Paris, Ed. du Cerf.

Frédéric, Madeleine and Lefèvre, Patrick (eds.), 2000. *Sur les traces de Norton Cru*, Actes du Colloque international du 18–19 novembre 1999, Brussels, Musée royal de l'Armée, Centre d'histoire militaire, Travaux, no. 32.

French, David, 1982. *British economy and strategic planning, 1905–1915*, London, Allen and Unwin.

    1986. *British strategy and war aims, 1914–1916*, London, Allen and Unwin.

    1995. *The strategy of the Lloyd George coalition, 1916–1918*, Oxford, Clarendon Press.

Fridenson, Patrick, 1972. *Histoire des usines Renault. 1. Naissance de la grande entreprise 1898/1939*, Paris, Seuil.

Fridenson, Patrick (ed.), 1977. *14–18, L'autre front*, Paris, Les Éditions ouvrières [English trans. with additions: *The French home front, 1914–1918*, Providence, Berg, 1992].

Fuller, John G., 1990. *Troop morale and popular culture in the British and Dominion armies 1914–1918*, Oxford, Clarendon Press.

Fussell, Paul, 1975. *The Great War and modern memory*, New York, Oxford University Press.

Gaffney, Angela, 1998. *Aftermath. Remembering the Great War in Wales*, Cardiff, University of Wales Press.

Gallieni, Général Joseph, 1926. *Mémoires*, Paris, Payot.

Gambarotto, Laurent, 1996. *Foi et Patrie. La prédication du protestantisme français pendant la Première Guerre mondiale*, Geneva, Labor et Fides.

Gambiez, Général F. and Suire, Colonel M., 1968–71. *Histoire de la Première Guerre mondiale*, Paris, Fayard, 2 vols.

Gammage, Bill, 1974. *The broken years, Australian soldiers in the Great War*, Canberra, Australian National University Press.

Gatrell, Peter, 1999. *A whole empire walking. Refugees in Russia during World War I*, Bloomington, Indiana University Press.

Geiss, Imanuel (ed.), 1963. *Julikrise und Kriegsausbruch 1914: eine Dokumentansammlung*, Hanover, Verlag für Literatur und Zeitgeschehen.

Georges, Bernard and Tintant, Denise, 1962. *Léon Jouhaux. Cinquante ans de syndicalisme*. Tome I, *Des origines à 1921*, Paris, PUF.

Gérin, René and Poincaré, Raymond, 1930. *Les responsabilités de la guerre: quatorze questions de René Gérin; Quatorze réponses par Raymond Poincaré*, Paris, Payot.

Gibelli, Antonio, 1991. *L'officina della guerra. La Grande Guerra e le transformazioni del mondo mentale*, Turin, Bollati Boringhieri.

    1998. *La Grande Guerra degli Italiani*, Milan, Sansoni.

Gide, Charles and Daudé-Bancel, Achille, 1926. *De la lutte contre la cherté par les organisations privées*, Paris, PUF [Publication of the Endowment for International Peace].

Gignoux, Claude-Joseph, 1926. *Bourges pendant la guerre*, Paris, PUF [Publication of the Carnegie Endowment for International Peace].

Gilbert, Martin, 1970. *First World War Atlas*, London, Weidenfeld & Nicolson.

Girault, René, 1973. *Emprunts russes et investissements français en Russie, 1887–1914. Recherches sur l'investissement international*, Paris, Publ. de la Sorbonne/A. Colin.

Godfrey, John F., 1987. *Capitalism at war. Industrial policy and bureaucracy in France, 1914–1918*, Leamington Spa, Berg.

Gras, Yves, 1990. *Castelnau ou l'art de commander, 1851–1944*, Paris, Denoël.

Grayzel, Susan R., 1999. *Women's identities at war: gender, motherhood, and politics in Britain and France during the First World War*, Chapel Hill, University of North Carolina Press.

Grebler, Leo and Winkler, Wilhelm, 1940. *The cost of the world war to Germany and to Austria–Hungary*, New Haven, Yale University Press [Publication of the Carnegie Endowment for International Peace].

Gregory, Adrian, 1994. *The silence of memory. Armistice Day, 1919–1946*, Oxford, Berg.

Grieves, Keith, 1988. *The politics of manpower, 1914–18*, Manchester, Manchester University Press.

Griffith, Paddy, 1994. *Battle tactics on the Western Front. The British army's art of attack, 1916–1918*, New Haven, Yale University Press.

Guichard, Louis, 1929. *Histoire du blocus naval (1914–1918)*, Paris, Payot.

Guinn, Paul, 1965. *British strategy and politics, 1914–1918*, Oxford, Clarendon Press.

Gullace, Nicoletta F., 2002. *Men, women, and the renegotiation of British citizenship during the Great War*, New York and Basingstoke, Palgrave-Macmillan.

Haber, Ludwig Fritz, 1986. *The poisonous cloud: chemical warfare in the First World War*, Oxford, Oxford University Press.

Haimson, Leopold (ed.), 1974. *The Mensheviks: from the revolution of 1917 to the Second World War*, Chicago, University of Chicago Press.

Haimson, Leopold and Sapelli, Giulio (eds.), 1992. *Strikes, social conflict and the First World War: an international perspective*, Milan, Feltrinelli.

Haimson, Leopold and Tilly, Charles (eds.), 1989. *Strikes, war and revolutions in an international perspective*, Cambridge, Cambridge University Press and Paris, Ed. de la Maison de Science de l'Homme.

Halévy, Elie, 1930. *The world crisis of 1914–1918, an interpretation*, Oxford, Clarendon Press, reprinted in French in *L'ère des tyrannies*, Paris, Gallimard, 1990 [1st edn 1938].

Halpern, P. G., 1994. *A naval history of World War I*, Newport, Naval Institute Press.

Hanna, Martha, 1996. *The mobilization of intellect. French scholars and writers during the Great War*, Cambridge, Mass., Harvard University Press.

Hanotaux, Gabriel, 1915–23. *Histoire illustrée de la guerre de 1914*, Paris, Gounouilhou, 16 vols.

    1920. *Circuit des champs de bataille de France: histoire et itinéraires de la grande guerre*, Paris, L'édition française illustrée.

    1922. *La Bataille de la Marne*, Paris, Plon-Nourrit.

Hardach, Gerd, 1973. *The First World War 1914–1918*, London, Penguin, 1977 [1st edn Munich, Deutscher Taschenbuch Verlag].

Hardier, Thierry and Jagielski, Jean-François, 2001. *Combattre et mourir pendant la Grande Guerre (1914–1925)*, Paris, Imago.

Hartcup, Guy, 1988. *The war of invention. Scientific developments, 1914–18*, London, Brassey's.

Haupt, Georges, 1965. *Le Congrès manqué. L'Internationale à la veille de la première guerre mondiale*, Paris, Maspero.

Headon, David, Warden, James and Gammage, Bill (eds.), 1994. *Crown or country: the traditions of Australian republicanism*, St. Leonards, Allen and Unwin.

Healy, Maureen, 2003. *Vienna and the fall of the Habsburg Empire*, Cambridge, Cambridge University Press.

Herriot, Edouard, 1924. *Lyon pendant la guerre*, Paris, PUF [Publ. of the Carnegie Endowment for International Peace].

Herwig, Holger H., 1997. *The First World War. Germany and Austria 1914–1918*, London, Arnold.

Higonnet, Margaret R., 2001. *Nurses at the front. Writing the wounds of the Great War*, Boston, Northeastern University Press.

Higonnet, Margaret, Jenson, Jane, Michel, Sonya and Weitz, Margaret Collins (eds.), 1987. *Behind the lines: gender and the two world wars*, New Haven, Yale University Press.

Hindenburg, General Feld Marschall Paul von, 1920. *Aus meinem Leben*, Leipzig, S. Hirzel [Eng. trans. *Out of my life*, London/New York, Cassel & Co., 1920; Fr. trans. by Louis Koeltz, Paris, Ch. Lavauzelle, 1921].

Hinton, James, 1973. *The first shop stewards' movement*, London, Allen and Unwin.

Hirschfeld, Gerhard, Krumeich, Gerd, Langewiesche, Dieter and Ullmann, Hans-Peter (eds.), 1997. *Kriegserfahrungen. Studien zur Sozial- und Mentalitätsgeschichte des Ersten Weltrkriegs*, Essen, Klartext.

Hirschfeld, Gerhard, Krumeich, Gerd and Renz, Irina (eds.), 1993. *Keiner fühlt sich hier mehr als Mensch. Erlebnis und Wirkung des Ersten Weltkriegs*, Essen, Klartext.

Holquist, Peter, 2002. *Making war, forging revolution: Russia's continuum of crisis 1914–1921*, Cambridge, Mass., Harvard University Press.

Holtfrericht, Carl-Ludwig, 1986. *The German inflation 1914–1923; causes and effects in international perspective*, New York, W. de Gruyter.

Horn, Daniel, 1969. *The German naval mutinies of World War I*, New Brunswick, N.J., Rutgers University Press.

Horn, Martin, 2002. *Britain, France and the financing of the First World War*, Montreal, McGill-Queen's University Press.

Horne, John, 1991. *Labour at war: France and Britain 1914–1918*, Oxford, Clarendon Press.

Horne, John (ed.), 1997. *State, society, and mobilization in Europe during the First World War*, Cambridge, Cambridge University Press.

Horne, John and Kramer, Alan, 2001. *German atrocities, 1914: a history of denial*, New Haven, Yale University Press.

Hough, Richard, 1983. *The Great War at Sea 1914–1918*, Oxford, Oxford University Press.

Housman, Laurence (ed.), 1930. *War letters of fallen Englishmen*, London, V. Gollancz [rcpr. Philadelphia, Pine Street Books, 2002].

Howard, Sir Michael, 2002. *The First World War*, Oxford, Oxford University Press.

Huber, Michel, 1931. *La Population de la France pendant la guerre*, Paris, PUF [Publication of the Carnegie Endowment for International Peace].

Hudemann, Rainer and Walter, François (ed.), 1997. *Villes et guerres mondiales en Europe au XXe siècle*, Paris, l'Harmattan.

Hurwitz, Samuel J., 1949. *State intervention in Great Britain, a study of economic control and social response, 1914–1919*, New York, Columbia University Press.

Huss, Marie-Monique, 2000. *Histoires de famille: cartes postales et culture de guerre*, Paris, Noêsis [publ. à l'occasion de l'exposition présentée à l'Historial de la Grande Guerre, Péronne, 16 juin–1er octobre 2000].

Hynes, Samuel, 1992. *A war imagined. The First World War and English culture*, London, Pimlico.

1997. *The soldiers' tale. Bearing witness to modern war*, New York, A. Lane.

Inglis, Kenneth S., 1998. *Sacred places. War memorials in the Australian landscape*, Melbourne, Melbourne University Press.

Ingram, Norman, 1991. *The politics of dissent. Pacifism in France 1919–1939*, Oxford, Clarendon Press.

Isaac, Jules, 1921. *Histoire de la Grande Guerre*, supplement to Malet, A. and Grillet, P., *XIXe siècle. Histoire contemporaine (1815–1920)*, classes de philosophie et de mathématiques, Paris, Hachette.

1922. *Joffre et Lanrezac. Etude critique des témoignages sur le rôle de la 5e armée (août 1914)*, Paris, E. Chiron, Publication de la Société de l'histoire de la guerre.

1933. *Un Débat historique, le problème des origines de la guerre*, Paris, Rieder.

1938. *L'Enseignement de l'histoire contemporaine et les manuels scolaires allemands. A propos d'une tentative d'accord franco-allemand*, conférence au Congrès international de l'Enseignement primaire, le 28 juillet 1937, Paris, A. Costes.

Isnenghi, Mario, 1970. *Il Mito della grande guerra: da Marinetti a Malaparte*, Bari, Laterza.

1982. *Operai e contadini nella Grande Guerra*, Bologna, L. Cappelli.

1989. *Le guerre degli italiani: parole, imagini, ricordi, 1848–1945*, Milan, Mondadori.

Isnenghi, Mario and Rochat, Giorgio, 2000. *Storia d'Italia nel secolo ventesimo. Parte prima, L'Italia liberale*, vol. II, *La grande guerra: 1914–1918*, Scandicci, La nuova Italia.

Jacobzone, Alain, 1988. *En Anjou, loin du front*, La Botellerie-Vauchrétien, ed. Ivan Davy.

Jahn, Hubertus F., 1995. *Patriotic culture in Russia during World War I*, Ithaca, Cornell University Press.

Jahr, Christoph, 1998. *Gewönliche Soldaten. Desertion und Deserteure im deutschen und britischen Heer 1914–1918*, Göttingen, Vandenhoeck and Ruprecht.

Joffre, Maréchal Joseph, 1932. *Mémoires*, Paris, Plon, 2 vols.

Joll, James, 1968. *1914. The unspoken assumptions*, London, Weidenfeld and Nicolson.

1984. *The origins of the First World War*, London, Longman.

Kantorowicz, Hermann, 1967. *Gutachten zur Kriegsschuldfrage 1914*, Frankfurt, Europäische Verlagsanstalt.

Kaspi, André, 1978. *Le temps des américains 1917–1918*, Paris, Publ. de la Sorbonne.

Kautsky, Karl, 1919. *Wie der Weltkrieg entstand*, Berlin, P. Cassirer.

Keegan, John, 1976. *The face of battle*, London, Jonathan Cape.

1998. *The First World War*, London, Hutchinson.

Keene, Jennifer D., 2001. *Doughboys, the Great War and the remaking of America*, Baltimore, Johns Hopkins University Press.

Kehr, Eckart, 1965. *Der Primat der Innenpolitik. Gesammelte Aufsätze zur preussisch-deutschen Sozialgeschichte im 19 und 20 Jahrhundert*, Berlin, De Gruyter [English translation of selected essays, Berkeley, University of California Press, 1977].

Keiger, John F. V., 1983. *France and the origins of the First World War*, Basingstoke/London, Macmillan.

Kennedy, David M., 1980. *Over here. The First World War and American society*, New York, Oxford University Press.

Kennedy, Paul (ed.), 1979. *The war plans of the Great Powers, 1880–1914*, London/Boston, G. Allen and Unwin.

Keynes, John Maynard, 1919. *The economic consequences of the peace*, London, Macmillan.

King, Alex, 1998. *Memorials of the Great War in Britain*, Oxford, Berg.

King, Jere C., 1951. *Generals and politicians. Conflicts between France's high command, parliament and government, 1914–1918*, Berkeley, University of California Press.

Kitchen, Martin, 1976. *The silent dictatorship: the politics of German high command under Hindenburg and Ludendorff, 1916–1918*, London, Croom Helm.

Knoch, Peter (ed.), 1989. *Kriegsalltag: Die Rekonstruktion des Kriegsalltags als Aufgabe der historischen Forschung und der Friedenserziehung*, Stuttgart, Metzler.

Kocka, Jürgen, 1973. *Facing total war. German society 1914–1918*, Cambridge, Mass., Harvard University Press, 1984 [1st edn Göttingen, Vandenhoeck and Ruprecht].

Koeltz, Louis, 1919. *L'Aveu de la défaite allemande; Les origines de l'armistice: documents officiels allemands publiés par ordre du Cabinet des Ministres d'Empire*, Paris, la Renaissance du Livre.

1928. *La Bataille de France (21 mars–5 avril 1918)*, Paris, Payot.

1930. *Les Documents allemands sur la bataille de la Marne, Général Feldmaréchal von Bulow*, Paris, Payot.

1966. *La Guerre de 1914–1918; vol. I: Les Opérations militaires*, Paris, Sirey.

Koenker, Diane and Rosenberg, William, 1989. *Strikes and revolution in Russia in 1917*, Princeton, Princeton University Press.

Koistinen, Paul A., 1997. *Mobilizing for modern war. The political economy of American warfare*, Lawrence, University of Kansas Press.

Kolko, Gabriel, 1994. *Century of war. Politics, conflicts and society since 1914*, New York, The New Press.

Kriegel, Annie, 1964. *Aux origines du parti communiste français (1914–1918)*, Paris/La Haye, Mouton, 2 vols.

Kriegel, Annie and Becker, Jean-Jacques, 1964. *1914, la guerre et le mouvement ouvrier français*, Paris, A. Colin.

Krumeich, Gerd, 1981. *Armaments and politics in France on the eve of the First World War*, London, Berg, 1984 [1st edn, Wiesbaden, Franz Teiner Verlag].

Krumeich, Gerd (ed.), 2001. *Versailles 1919: Ziele-Wirkung-Wahrnehmung*, Essen, Klartext Verlag.

Kuisel, Richard F., 1981. *Capitalism and the state in modern France*, Cambridge, Cambridge University Press.

La Gorce, Paul-Marie de (ed.), 1991. *La Première Guerre mondiale*, Paris, Flammarion, 2 vols.

Labanca, Nicola, Procacci, Giovanna and Tomassini, Luigi, 1997. *Caporetto: Esercito state e societa*. Milano, Giunti.

Landau, Philippe-E., 1999. *Les Juifs de France et la Grande Guerre: un patriotisme républicain 1914–1941*, Paris, CNRS-Editions.

Lansing, Robert, 1935. *War memoirs of Robert Lansing, Secretary of State*, Indianapolis/New York, Bobbs Merrill Company.

Lasswell, Harold D., 1927. *Propaganda technique in the world war*, New York, A. A. Knopf.

Le Naour, Jean-Yves, 2002a. *Le Soldat inconnu vivant*, Paris, Hachette.

 2002b. *Misères et tourments de la chair durant la Grande Guerre: les moeurs sexuelles des Français, 1914–1918*, Paris, Le grand livre du mois.

Leed, Eric J., 1979. *No man's land. Combat & identity in World War I*, London, Cambridge University Press.

Leese, Peter 2002. *Shell shock, traumatic neurosis and the British soldiers of the First World War*, New York, Palgrave/Macmillan.

Lepick, Olivier, 1998. *La grande guerre chimique: 1914–1918*, Paris, PUF.

Lerner, Paul Frederick, 2003. *Hysterical men. War, psychiatry and the politics of trauma in Germany, 1890–1930*, Ithaca, Cornell University Press.

Lhéritier, Michel and Chautemps, Camille, 1926. *Tours et la guerre, étude économique et sociale*, Paris, PUF [Publication of the Carnegie Endowment for International Peace].

Liddell Hart, Basil, 1930. *The real war, 1914–1918*, London, Faber & Faber.

 1934. *A history of the World War, 1914–1918*, London, Faber & Faber.

Liddle, Peter, Bourne, John and Whitehead, Ian (eds.), 2000. *The Great World War 1914–1945*, London, Harper and Collins, 2 vols.

Lindemann, Thomas, 2001. *Les Doctrines darwiniennes et la guerre de 1914*, Paris, Economica.

Lipp, Anne, 2003. *Meinungslenkung im Krieg. Kriegserfahrungen deutscher Soldaten und ihre Deutung 1914–1918*, Göttingen, Vandenhoeck and Ruprecht.

Liulevicius, Vejas Gabriel, 2000. *War land on the Eastern Front: culture, national identity and German occupation in World War I*, Cambridge, Cambridge University Press.

Liversey, Anthony, 1994. *Atlas de la Première Guerre mondiale, 1914–1918*, Paris, Autrement.

Livre noir, 1921. *Un livre noir: diplomatie d'avant-guerre d'après les documents des archives russes: novembre 1910–juillet 1914*, Paris: Librairie du travail, s.d. [1921–3], 2 vols.

Lloyd, David W., 1998. *Battlefield tourism, pilgrimage and the commemoration of Great War in Britain, Australia and Canada, 1919–1939*, Providence/Oxford, Berg.

Lohr, Eric, 2003. *Nationalizing the Russian empire: the campaign against enemy aliens during World War I*, Cambridge, Mass., Harvard University Press.

Luckau, Alma M., 1941. *The German delegation at the Paris Peace Conference*, New York, Columbia University Press.

Luxemburg, Rosa, 1922. *La Révolution russe*, trans. and presented by Gilbert Badia, Pantin, Le Temps des cerises, 2000 [1st edn, Frankfurt, Verlag Gesellschaft und Erziehung G.m.b.H.].

McAuley, Mary, 1991. *Bread and justice. State and society in Petrograd 1917–1921*, Oxford, Clarendon.

Macdonald, Lyn, 1978. *They called it Passchendaele: the story of the Third Battle of Ypres and the men who fought it*, London, Joseph.

1988. *1914–1918: voices and images of the Great War*, London, Joseph.

1993. *1915, the death of innocence*, London, Headline.

1998. *To the last man: spring 1918*, London, Viking.

McDonough, Frank, 1997. *The origins of the First and Second World Wars*, Cambridge, Cambridge University Press.

McKibbin, David, 2001. *War and revolution in Leipzig 1914–1918: the German Independent Socialist Party in the Revolution of 1918*, New York, Peter Lang.

McKibbin, Ross, 1974. *The evolution of the Labour Party 1910–1924*, Oxford, Oxford University Press.

Macmillan, Margaret, 2001. *Peacemakers 1919; six months that changed the world*, London, John Murray.

McPhail, Helen, 2001. *The long silence: civilian life under German occupation of Northern France, 1914–1918*, London, I. B. Tauris.

Maier, Charles S., 1975. *Recasting bourgeois Europe: stabilization in France, Germany, and Italy in the decade after World War I*, Princeton, Princeton University Press.

Malet, Albert and Isaac, Jules, 1930. *Histoire contemporaine depuis le milieu du XIXe siècle*, Paris, Hachette.

Mangin, Général Charles, 1920. *Comment finit la guerre*, Paris, Plon.

Mantoux, Etienne, 1946. *La paix calomniée ou les conséquences économiques de M. Keynes*, Paris, L'Harmattan, 2002 [1st edn Paris, Gallimard].

Marder, Arthur, 1961–70. *From the Dreadnought to Scapa Flow. The Royal Navy in the Fisher Era, 1904–1919*, London, Oxford University Press, 5 vols.

Marder, Arthur (ed.), 1952–9. *Fear God and Dread nought. The correspondence of Admiral of the Fleet Lord Fisher of Kilverstone*, London, Jonathan Cape, 3 vols.

Marrus, Michael R., 1985. *The unwanted: European refugees in the 20th century*, New York, Oxford University Press [French trans. *Les Exclus, les réfugiés européens au XXe siècle*, Paris, Calmann-Levy, 1986].

Marwick, Arthur, 1964. *The deluge: British society and the First World War*, London, Penguin Books.

1977. *Women at war: 1914–1918*, s.l., Fontana Paper Backs.

Masson, Paul, 1926. *Marseille pendant la guerre*, Paris, PUF [Publication of the Carnegie Endowment for International Peace].

Maurin, Jules, 1982. *Armée – Guerre – Sociétés: soldats languedociens (1889–1919)*, Paris, Publ. de la Sorbonne.

Maurin, Jules and Jauffret, Jean-Charles (eds.), 2002. *La Grande Guerre 1914–1918, 80 ans d'historiographie et de représentations*, Colloque international, Montpellier, 20–21 novembre 1998, Montpellier, Université de Montpellier III.

Mayer, Arno J., 1959. *Political origins of the new diplomacy, 1917–1918*, New Haven, Yale University Press.

1967. *Politics and diplomacy of peacemaking, containment and counterrevolution at Versailles, 1918–1919*, New York, Knopf.

Meerwarth, Rudolf, Günther, Adolf and Zimmermann, Waldemar, 1932. *Die Einwirkung des Krieges auf Bevölkerungsbewegung, Einkommen und Lebenshaltung in Deutschland*, Stuttgart/Berlin, Deutsche Verlagsanstalt.

Meigs, Mark, 1997. *Optimism at Armageddon: voices of American participants in the First World War*, Basingstoke, Macmillan.

Melograni, Piero, 1969. *Storia politica della grande Guerra 1915–1918*, Bari, G. Laterza.

Meyer, Jacques, 1966. *La vie quotidienne des soldats pendant la Grande Guerre*, Paris, Hachette.

Meynier, Gilbert, 1981. *L'Algérie révélée: la guerre de 1914–1918 et le premier quart du XX° siècle*, Geneva and Paris, Droz.

Micale, Mark and Lerner, Paul Frederick (eds.), 2001. *Traumatic pasts. History, psychiatry, and trauma in the modern age, 1870–1930*, Cambridge, Cambridge University Press.

Michalka, Wolfgang (ed.), 1994. *Der Erste Weltkrieg: Wirkung, Wahrnehmung, Analyse*, Munich, Piper Verlag.

Michel, Bernard, 1991. *La chute de l'Empire austro-hongrois: 1916–1918*, Paris, R. Laffont.

Michel, Marc, 1982. *L'Appel à l'Afrique:contributions et réactions à l'effort de guerre en A. O. F., 1914–1918*, Paris, Publ. de la Sorbonne.

Middlebrook, Martin, 1971. *The first day on the Somme, 1 July 1916*, London, A. Lane.

Mignon, Médecin-Général inspecteur Albert, 1926–7. *Le Service de Santé pendant la guerre 1914–1918*, Paris, Masson, 4 vols.

Miller, Susanne, 1974. *Burgfrieden und Klassenkampf: die Deutschesocialdemocratie im Ersten Weltkrieg*, Düsseldorf, Droste.

Millman, Brock, 2000. *Managing domestic dissent in First World War Britain*, London, F. Cass.

2001. *Pessimism and British policy in First War Britain 1916–1918*, London, F. Cass.

Milward, Alan S., 1984. *The economic effects of the two world wars on Britain*, London, Macmillan.

Miquel, Pierre, 1972. *La Paix de Versailles et l'opinion publique française*, Paris, Flammarion.

1983. *La Grande Guerre*, Paris, Fayard.

1995. *Mourir à Verdun*, Paris, Tallandier.

2000. *Les Poilus: la France sacrifiée*, Paris, Plon.

Mitchell, Allan, 1965. *Revolution in Bavaria, 1918–1919; the Eisner regime and the Soviet Republic*, Princeton, Princeton University Press.

Moeller, Robert G., 1986. *German peasants and agrarian politics, 1914–1924: the Rhineland and Westphalia*, Chapel Hill, University of North Carolina Press.

Mombauer, Annika, 2002. *The origins of the First World War: controversies and consensus*, London/New York, Longman.

Mommsen, Wolfgang, 1995. *Imperial Germany 1867–1918: Politics, Culture and Society in an Authoritarian State*, London, Arnold.

(ed.), 1990. *Der autoritäre Nationalstaat:Verfassung, Gesellschaft und Kultur des deutschen Kaiserreiches*, Frankfurt am Main, Fischer.

(ed.), 1996. *Kultur und Krieg. Die Rolle der Intellektuellen, Künstler und Schiftsteller im Ersten Weltkrieg*, Munich, Oldenbourg.

Moore, Barrington jr., 1978. *Injustice. The social basis of obedience and revolt*, London, Macmillan.

Mordacq, Henri, 1929. *Le Commandement unique: comment il fut réalisé*, Paris, Tallandier.

Morelli, Aldo and Tomassini, Luigi, 1976. *Socialismo e classe operaia a Pistoia durante la prima Guerra mondiale*, Milan, Feltrinelli.

Morhardt, Mathias, 1924. *Les Preuves, le crime de droit commun, le crime diplomatique*, Paris, Librairie du travail.

Mosse, George L., 1990. *Fallen soldiers: reshaping the memory of the world wars*, New York, Oxford University Press [French trans. *De la Grande Guerre au totalitarisme. La brutalisation des sociétés européennes*, Paris, Hachette, 1999, preface by Stéphane Audoin-Rouzeau].

Moutet, Aimée, 1997. *Les Logiques de l'entreprise: La rationalisation dans l'industrie française de l'entre-deux-guerres*, Paris, Ecole des Hautes Etudes en Sciences Sociales.

Moyer, Laurence V., 1995. *Victory must be ours. Germany in the Great War 1914–1918*, London, Leo Cooper.

Natter, Wolfgang G., 1999. *Literature at war 1914–1940: representing the 'time of greatness' in Germany*, New Haven, Yale University Press.

Nef, John Ulric, 1949. *La Route de la guerre totale: essai sur les relations entre la guerre et le progrès humain*, Paris, A. Colin [Cahiers de la Fondation nationale des sciences politiques, 11].

1950. *War and human progress; an essay on the rise of industrial civilization*, Cambridge, Mass., Harvard University Press [French trans. *La guerre et le progrès humain*, Paris, Alsatia, 1954].

Nettl, John Peter, 1966. *Rosa Luxemburg*, London, Oxford University Press.

Nicolson, Sir Harold G., 1933. *Peacemaking, 1919*, London, Constable.

Nicot, Jean, 1998. *Les Poilus ont la parole: dans les tranchées, lettres du front, 1917–1918*, Paris, Le Grand livre du mois.

Nobécourt, R. G., 1965. *Les Fantassins du Chemin des Dames*, Paris, R. Laffont.

Nolan, Mary, 1981. *Social democracy and society: working-class radicalism in Düsseldorf, 1890–1920*, Cambridge, Cambridge University Press.

Nolte, Ernst, 1987. *Der Europäische Bürgerkrieg 1917–1945: Nationalsozialismus und Bolshewismus*, Frankfurt am Main, Propyläen [French trans., *La Guerre civile européenne 1917–1945: national-socialisme et bolchévisme*, Paris, Ed. des Syrtes, 2000].

Nouailhat, Yves-Henri, 1977. *La France et les Etats-Unis, août 1914 – avril 1917*, Lille, Service de reproduction des thèses, 2 vols.

Offenstadt, Nicolas, 1999. *Les Fusillés de la Grande Guerre et la mémoire collective (1914–1999)*, Paris, Odile Jacob.

Offer, Avner, 1989. *The First World War, an agrarian interpretation*, Oxford, Clarendon Press.

Oualid, William and Picquenard, Charles, 1928. *Salaires et tarifs; conventions collectives et grèves; la politique du ministère de l'Armement et du ministère du Travail*, Paris, PUF [Publication of the Carnegie Endowment for International Peace].

Panichas, George Andrew (ed.), 1968. *Promise of greatness. The war of 1914–1918*, New York, John Day Co.

Pedersen, Susan, 1995. *Family, dependence, and the origins of the welfare state: Britain and France, 1914–1945*, Cambridge, Cambridge University Press.

Pedroncini, Guy, 1967. *Les Mutineries de 1917*, Paris, PUF/Publ. de la Sorbonne.

Pedroncini, Guy, 1968. *1917, Les Mutineries de l'armée française*, Paris, Julliard [series 'Archives'].

1969. *Les Négociations secrètes pendant la Grande Guerre*, Paris, Flammarion.

1971. *Le haut Commandement, la conduite de la guerre, mai 1917 – novembre 1918*, Lille, service de reproduction des thèses de l'Université, 3 vols.

1974. *Pétain, général en chef, 1917–1918*, Paris, PUF/Publ. de la Sorbonne [abridged version of Pedroncini, 1971].

1989. *Pétain*, vol. I: *Le Soldat et la gloire: 1856–1918*, Paris, Perrin.

Pedroncini, Guy (ed.), 1997. *Histoire militaire de la France*, sous la dir. d'André Corvisier, vol. III, *De 1871 à 1940*, Paris, PUF.

Percin, Général Alexandre, 1921. *Le Massacre de notre infanterie, 1914–1918*, Paris, A. Michel.

Péricard, Jacques, 1933. *Verdun, histoire des combats qui se sont livrés de 1914 à 1918 sur les deux rives de la Meuse*, Paris, Librairie de France.

Perreux, Gabriel, 1966. *La Vie quotidienne des civils en France pendant la grande guerre*, Paris, Hachette.

Peschaud, Marcel, 1926. *Politique et fonctionnement des transports par chemin de fer pendant la guerre*, Paris, PUF [Publication of the Carnegie Endowment for International Peace].

Peukert, Detlev J., 1987. *Die Weimarer Republik: Krisenjahre der klassischen Moderne*, Frankfurt, Suhrkampf [French trans. *La République de Weimar: années de crise de la modernité*, Paris, Aubier, 1995; English trans. *Weimar Republic: the crisis of classical modernity*, London, Allen Lane, 1991].

Picard, Roger, 1928. *Le Mouvement syndical pendant la guerre*, Paris, PUF [Publication of the Carnegie Endowment for International Peace].

Pingaud, Albert, 1938. *Histoire diplomatique de la France pendant la Grande Guerre*, vols. I and II, *Les Alliances et les interventions*, Paris, Alsatia, 1938, vol. III, *Les Neutralités et les tentatives de paix*, Paris, Alsatia, 1940.

Pöhlmann, Markus, 2002. *Kriegsgeschichte und Geschichtspolitik: Der Erste Weltkrieg. Die amtliche deutsche Militärgeschichtsschreibung, 1914–1956*, Paderborn, F. Schöningh.

Poidevin, Raymond, 1969. *Les Relations économiques et financières entre la France et l'Allemagne de 1898 à 1914*, Paris, A. Colin.

1975. *Les Origines de la Première guerre mondiale*, Paris, PUF.

Poincaré, Raymond, 1921. *Les Origines de la guerre: conférences prononcées à la 'Société des conférences'*, Paris, Plon-Nourrit.

Pourcher, Yves, 1994. *Les Jours de guerre. La vie des Français au jour le jour entre 1914 et 1918*, Paris, Plon.

Prior, Robin, 1983. *Churchill's 'world crisis' as history*, London, Croom Helm.

1996. *Passchendaele: the untold story*, New Haven, Yale University Press.

1999. *The First World War*, London, Cassell.

Prior, Robin and Wilson, Trevor, 1992. *Command on the Western Front: the military career of Sir Henry Rawlinson, 1914–18*, Oxford, Basil Blackwell.

Procacci, Giovanna, 1993. *Soldati e prigionieri italiani nella Grande Guerra*, Rome, Ed. Riuniti.

1999. *Dalla rassegnazione alla rivolta: mentalità e comportamenti popolari nella grande guerra*, Rome, Bulzoni.

Procacci, Giovanna (ed.), 1983. *Stato e classe operaia in Italia durante la prima guerra mondiale*, Milan, F. Angeli.

Prochasson, Christophe, 1993. *Les Intellectuels, le socialisme et la guerre, 1910–1938*, Paris, Le Seuil.

Prochasson, Christophe and Rasmussen, Anne, 1996. *Au nom de la patrie: les intellectuels et la première guerre mondiale (1910–1919)*, Paris, La Découverte.

Prochasson, Christophe and Rasmussen, Anne (eds.), 2004. *Vrai et faux dans la Grande Guerre*, Paris, La Découverte.

Prost, Antoine, 1977a. *Les Anciens combattants et la société française, 1914–1939*, Paris, Presses de la FNSP, 3 vols.

1977b. *Les Anciens combattants, 1914–1940*, Paris, Gallimard-Julliard [series 'Archives' trans. *In the wake of war, 'les Anciens Combattants' and French society 1914–1939*, Oxford, Berg, 1992].

Rachamimov, Alon, 2002. *POWs and the Great War: captivity on the Eastern Front*, Oxford, Berg.

Reader, William Joseph, 1970. *Imperial Chemical Industries. A history.* vol. I. *The forerunners 1870–1926*, London, Oxford University Press.

Rearick, Charles, 1997. *The French in love and war. Popular culture in the era of world wars*, New Haven, Yale University Press.

Reichsarchiv von der Kriegsgeschichtlichen Forschungsanstalt, des Heeres, 1925–65. *Der Weltkrieg 1914 bis 1918*, Berlin, E. S. Mittler & Sohn, 14 vols.

Reimann, Aribert, 2000. *Der Grosse Krieg der Sprachen: Untersuchungen zur historischen Semantik in Deutschland und England zur Zeit des Ersten Weltkriegs*, Essen, Klartext Verlag.

Renouvin, Pierre 1925a. *Les formes du gouvernement de guerre*, Paris, PUF [Publication of the Carnegie Endowment for International Peace].

1925b. *Les origines immédiates de la guerre (28 juin–4 août 1914)*, Paris, A. Costes, 2nd edn 1927.

1934. *La crise européenne et la grande guerre (1914–1918)*, Paris, Félix Alcan [series 'Peuples et civilisations', ed. by L. Halphen and P. Sagnac, vol. XIX]. Revised editions: 1939, 1948, 1962, and 1969.

1955–7. *Histoire des relations internationales*, vol. VI: *Le XIXᵉ siècle, II. De 1871 à 1914: l'apogée de l'Europe*. Vol. VII: *Les crises du XXᵉ siècle. I. De 1914 à 1929*, Paris, Hachette.

1965. *La Première guerre mondiale*, Paris, PUF [series 'Que sais-je?'].

1968. *L'Armistice de Rethondes, 11 novembre 1918*, Paris, Gallimard [series 'Trente journées qui ont fait la France'].

Renouvin, Pierre, Préclin, Edmond and Hardy, Georges, 1939. *L'Epoque contemporaine. 2. La paix armée et la Grande Guerre 1871–1919*, Paris, PUF [series 'Clio']. Repr.: 1947, 1960.

Reynolds, Francis J., Churchill, Allen L. and Miller, Francis Trevelyan (eds.), 1916–20. *The story of the Great War. History of the European war from official sources*, New York, P. F. Collier and Sons, 8 vols.

Ribeill, Georges, 1988. *Les cheminots en grève 1914–1920. Les métamorphoses d'une corporation*, Paris, CERTES-ENPC.

Richter, Donald, 1992. *Chemical soldiers. British gas warfare in World War I*, Lawrence, Kansas, University Press of Kansas.

Riegel, Léon, 1978. *Guerre et littérature. Le bouleversement des consciences dans la littérature romanesque inspirée par la Grand Guerre (littératures française, anglo-saxonne et allemande), 1910–1930*, Paris, Klincksieck.

Ricuncau, Maurice, 1972. *Guerre et révolution dans le roman français, 1919–1939*, Genève, Slatkine, 2000 [1st edn Lille, Service de reproduction des thèses].

Ritter, Gerhard, 1948. *Dämonnie der Macht. Europa und die deutsche Frage*, Munich, Leibnitz.

1954–68. *Staatskunst und Kriegshandwerk: das Problem des 'Militarismus' in Deutschland*, Munich, R. Oldenbourg, 4 vols. [English trans., *The sword and the scepter; the problem of militarism in Germany*, Coral Gables (Fla.), University of Miami Press, 1969–73].

Rivé, Philippe (ed.), 1991. Secrétariat d'Etat aux Anciens combattants et victimes de guerre, Mission permanente aux commémorations et à l'information historique, *Monuments aux morts de la Première Guerre mondiale*, Paris, La Documentation française.

Robert, Jean-Louis, 1980. *La Scission syndicale de 1921. Essai de reconnaissance des formes*, Paris, Publ. de la Sorbonne.

1989. 'Ouvriers et mouvement ouvrier parisiens pendant la grande guerre et l'immédiat après-guerre. Histoire et anthropologie', Thèse d'Etat Paris, 9 vols.

1995. *Les Ouvriers, la Patrie et la Révolution. Paris 1914–1919*, Besançon, Les annales littéraires de l'Université de Besançon no. 592, Série historique.

Roberts, Mary Louise, 1994. *Civilization without sexes: reconstructing gender in postwar France, 1917–1927*, Chicago, University of Chicago Press.

Roshwald, Aviel and Stites, Richard (eds.), 1999. *European culture in the Great War. The arts, entertainment and propaganda 1914–1918*, Cambridge, Cambridge University Press.

Rosmer, Alfred, 1936. *Le Mouvement ouvrier pendant la guerre*, tome I, *De l'Union sacrée à Zimmerwald*, Paris, Libr. du travail.

1959. *Le Mouvement ouvrier pendant la première guerre mondiale*, vol. II, *De Zimmerwald à la Révolution russe*, Paris-La Haye, Mouton.

Rothwell, Victor H., 1971. *British war aims and peace diplomacy, 1914–1918*, Oxford, Clarendon Press.

Rousseau, Frédéric, 1999. *La Guerre censurée: une histoire des combattants européens de 14–18*, Paris, Seuil.

2003. *Le Procès des témoins de la grande guerre. L'affaire Norton Cru*, Paris, Seuil.

Rozenblit, Marsha L., 2001. *Reconstructing a national identity. The Jews of Habsburg Austria during World War I*, New York, Oxford University Press.

Rürup, Reinhard, 1968. *Probleme der Revolution in Deutschland 1918/19*, Wiesbaden, F. Steiner.

Salewski, Michael, 1979. *Tirpitz: Aufstieg, Macht, Scheitern*, Göttingen, Musterschmidt.

Schaeffer, Werner, 1940. *Guerre contre les femmes et les enfants; blocus décrété par l'Angleterre pour affamer l'Allemagne, 1914–1920*, Brussels, Maison internationale d'édition.

Schaffer, Ronald, 1991. *America in the Great War. The rise of the war welfare state*, New York, Oxford University Press.

Schivelbusch, Wolfgang, 2003. *The culture of defeat. On national trauma, mourning and recovery*, New York, Metropolitan Books.

Schmitt, Bernadotte E., 1930. *The coming of the war*, New York, Scribner's, 2 vols. [French trans. *Comment vint la guerre (1914)*, Paris, A. Costes, 1932].

Scott, W.-R. and Cunnison, J., 1924. *The industries of the Clyde Valley during the war*, New Haven, Yale University Press [Publication of the Carnegie Endowment for International Peace].

Sellier, Henri, Bruggeman, André and Poëte, Marcel, 1926. *Paris pendant la guerre*, Paris, PUF.

Shaper, Bertus Willem, 1959. *Albert Thomas: trente ans de réformisme social*, Assen, Van Gorcum.

Sharp, Alan, 1991. *The Versailles settlement. Peacemaking in Paris, 1919*, Basingstoke, Macmillan.

Sheffield, Gary and Till, Geoffrey (eds.), 2003. *The challenges of High Command: the British experience*, Basingstoke, Palgrave Macmillan.

Shepherd, Ben, 2000. *A war of nerves*, London, Jonathan Cape.

Sherman, Daniel J., 1999. *The construction of memory in interwar France*, Chicago, The University of Chicago Press.

Shotwell, James T., 1924. *Economic and social history of the World War. Outline of plan. European series*, Washington, Carnegie Endowment for International Peace.

Showalter, Elaine, 1985. *The female malady: women, madness and English culture*, New York, Pantheon Books.

Silver, Kenneth E., 1989. *Esprit de corps. The art of the Parisian avant-garde and the First World War 1914–1925*, London, Thames and Hudson [French trans. *Vers le retour à l'ordre: l'avant-garde parisienne et la première Guerre mondiale*, Paris, Flammarion, 1991].

Simkins, Peter, 1988. *Kitchener's army: the raising of the new armies, 1914–1916*, Manchester, Manchester University Press.

Siney, Marion C., 1957. *The Allied blockade of Germany, 1914–1916*, Ann Arbor, University of Michigan Press.

Smith, Leonard V., 1994. *Between mutiny and obedience. The case of the French Fifth Infantry Division during World War I*, Princeton, Princeton University Press.

Smith, Leonard V., Audoin-Rouzeau, Stéphane and Becker, Annette, 2003. *France and the Great War, 1914–1918*, Cambridge, Cambridge University Press.

Société politique d'études critiques et documentaires sur la guerre, 1926. *Les savants américains devant le problème des origines de la guerre*, Paris, Libr. du Travail.

Sombart, Werner, 1932. *L'apogée du capitalisme*, Paris, Payot, 2 vols.

Soulez, Philippe (ed.), 1988. *Les philosophes et la guerre de 14*, Saint-Denis, Presses universitaires de Vincennes.

Soutou, Georges-Henri, 1989. *L'Or et le sang. Les buts de guerre économiques de la Première Guerre Mondiale*, Paris, Fayard.

Spriano, Paolo, 1964. *L'Occupation des usines: Italie, septembre 1920*, Claix, La Pensée sauvage, 1978 [1st edn Turin, G. Einaudi].

Steinberg, Jonathan, 1965. *Yesterday's deterrent; Tirpitz and the birth of the German battle fleet*, London, Macdonald.

Steiner, Zara, 1977. *Britain and the origins of the First World War*, New York, St Martin's Press.

Stevenson, David, 1982. *French war aims against Germany 1914–1919*, Oxford, Clarendon Press.

1991. *The First World War and international politics*, Oxford, Clarendon Press.

Stone, Norman, 1975. *The Eastern front, 1914–1917*, New York, Scribner.

Strachan, Hew, 2000. *The First World War. Vol. I: To arms*, Oxford, Oxford University Press.

Strachan, Hew (ed.), 1998. *The Oxford illustrated history of the First World War*, New York, Oxford University Press.

Sturmthal, Adolf 1951. *The tragedy of European labor 1918–1939*, New York, Columbia University Press.

Tardieu, André, 1921. *La Paix*, preface by Georges Clemenceau, Paris, Payot.

Taylor, Alan John Percivale, 1964. *The First World War, an illustrated history*, London, Hamilton.

1965. *English history 1914–1945*, vol. XV of *The Oxford history of England*, Oxford, Clarendon Press.

1969. *War by timetable. How the First World War began*, New York, American Heritage [French trans. *La Guerre des plans: 1914, les dernières heures de l'ancien monde*, Lausanne, ed. Rencontre, 1971].

Temperley, Harold W., 1920–4. *A history of the peace conference of Paris*, London, H. Frowde and Hodder & Stoughton, 6 vols.

Terraine, John, 1960. *Mons: the retreat to victory*, London, B. T. Batsford.

1963. *Douglas Haig, the educated soldier*, London, Hutchinson [French trans. *Douglas Haig, soldat de métier*, Paris, Presses de la Cité, 1964].

1965. *Ordeal of victory*, Philadelphia; New York, Lippincott. [French trans. *C'est arrivé en 14*, Paris, Presses de la cité, 1965].

1970. *Impacts of war 1914 & 1918*, London, Hutchinson.

1977. *The road to Passchendaele: the Flanders offensive of 1917: a study in inevitability*, London, L. Cooper.

Thébaud, Françoise, 1986. *La Femme au temps de la guerre de 14*, Paris, Stock.

Theweleit, Klaus, 1977–8. *Männerphantasien*. Vol. I: *Frauen, Fluten, Körper, Geschichte;* vol. II: *Männerkörper, zur Psychoanalyse des weissen Terrors*, Frankfurt am Main, Verlag Roter Stern [English trans., *Male fantasies*, Minneapolis, University of Minnesota Press, *c*.1987–*c*.1989].

Thobie, Jacques, 1973. *Intérêts et impérialisme français dans l'Empire ottoman, 1895–1914*, Paris, Publ. de la Sorbonne, 1977 [1st edn Lille, Service de reproduction des thèses].

Tippett, Maria, 1984. *Art at the service of war. Canada, art and the Great War*, Toronto, University of Toronto Press.

Tomassini, Luigi, 1997. *Lavoro e Guerra. La mobilizatione industriale italiana 1915–1918*, Naples, Edizioni scientifische italiane.

Travers, Timothy, 1987. *The killing ground. The British army, the Western Front and the emergence of modern warfare*, London, Allen & Unwin.

1992. *How the war was won. Command and technology in the British army on the Western Front 1917–1918*, London, Routledge.

Trevisan, Carine, 2001. *Les fables du deuil. La Grande Guerre: mort et écriture*, Paris, PUF.

Truchy, Henri, 1926. *Les finances de la guerre de la France*, Paris, PUF [Publication of the Carnegie Endowment for International Peace].

Ullrich, Volker, 1982. *Kriegsalltag: Hamburg im ersten Weltkrieg*, Köln, Prometh.

Unruh, Karl, 1986. *Langemark, Legende and Wirklichkeit*, Koblenz, Bernard & Graefe.

Vance, Jonathan F., 1997. *Death so noble. Memory, meaning and the First World War*, Vancouver, UBC Press.

Verhey, Jeffrey, 2000. *The spirit of 1914: militarism, myth and mobilization in Germany*, Cambridge, Cambridge University Press.

Vincent, Charles Paul, *The politics of hunger: the Allied blockade of Germany, 1915–1919*, Athens, Ohio University Press.

Vondung, Klaus (ed.), 1980. *Kriegserlebnis: der Erste Weltkrieg in der literarischen Gestaltung Symbolischen Deutung der Nationen*, Göttingen, Vandenhoeck and Ruprecht.

Waites, Bernard, 1987. *A class society at war, England 1914–18*, Leamington Spa, Berg.

Wall, Richard and Winter, Jay (eds.), 1988. *The upheaval of war. Family, work and welfare in Europe 1914–1918*, Cambridge, Cambridge University Press.

Watkins, Glenn, 2003. *Proof through the night: music and the Great War*, Berkeley, University of California Press.

Wegerer, Alfred von, 1928. *Die Widerlegung der Versailler Kriegsschuldthese*, Berlin, R. Hobbing [English trans. *A refutation of the Versailles war guilt thesis*, New York and London, A. A. Knopf, 1930].

1939. *Der Ausbruch des Weltkrieges 1914*, Hamburg, Hanseatische Verlagsanstalt, 2 vols.

Weill, Claudie and Badia, Gilbert (eds.), 1986. *Rosa Luxemburg aujourd'hui*, colloquium held in Paris on 30–31 May 1983, Saint-Denis, Presses universitaires de Vincennes.

Werth, German, 1979. *Verdun: die Schlacht und der Mythos*, Bergisch Gladbach, G. Lübbe.

Wildman, Allan, 1980. *The end of the Russian Imperial Army*, vol. I: *The old army and the soldiers' revolt (March–April 1917)*, vol. II: *The road to Soviet power and peace*, Princeton, Princeton University Press.

Wilkinson, Alan, 1978. *The Church of England and the First World War*, London, SPCK.

Williamson, Samuel R., 1991. *Austria–Hungary and the origins of the First World War*, New York, St Martin's Press.

Wilson, Keith (ed.), 1996. *Forging the collective memory: government and international historians through two World Wars*, Providence, Berghahn books.

Wilson, Trevor, 1986. *The myriad faces of war. Britain and the Great War 1914–1918*, Cambridge, Polity Press.

Winter, Denis, 1978. *Death's men: soldiers of the Great War*, London, Allen Lane.

1991. *Haig's command: a reassessment*, London, Viking.

1994. *25 April 1915: the inevitable tragedy*, St Lucia, University of Queensland Press.

Winter, Jay M., 1974. *Socialism and the challenge of war. Ideas and politics in Britain 1912–18*, London, Routledge & Kegan Paul.

1986. *The Great War and the British people*, Cambridge (Mass.), Harvard University Press.

1988. *The experience of World War I*, London, Macmillan.

1995. *Sites of memory, sites of mourning. The Great War in European cultural history*, Cambridge, Cambridge University Press.

Winter, Jay and Baggett, Blaine, 1996. *The Great War and the shaping of the twentieth century*, New York, Penguin studio [French trans. *14–18: le grand bouleversement*, Paris, Presses de la Cité, 1997].

Winter, Jay, Habeck, Mary, and Geoffrey, Parker (eds.), 1999. *The Great War and the twentieth century*, New Haven, Yale University Press.

Winter, Jay and Robert, Jean-Louis, 1997. *Capital cities at war, London, Paris, Berlin 1914–1919*, Cambridge, Cambridge University Press.

Witkop, Philipp (ed.), 1928. *Kriegsbriefe gefallener Studenten. In Verbindung mit den Deutschen Unterrichts-Ministerien*, München, Georg Müller [English trans. of some of these letters, *German students' war letters*, London, Methuen, 1929, republished, Philadelphia, Pine Street Books, 2002].

Wohl, Robert, 1980. *The generation of 1914*, London, Weidenfeld & Nicolson.

Woodward, David, 1983. *Lloyd George and the generals*, London, Associated University Presses.

Woollacott, Angela, 1995. *On her their lives depend. Munition workers in the Great War*, Berkeley, University of California Press.

Woronoff, Denis, 2001. *François de Wendel*, Paris, Presses de Sciences Po.

Wrigley, Chris J., 1976. *David Lloyd George and the British labour movement: peace and war*, Hassocks, Harvester.

Zeman, L. A. B., 1963. *The break up of the Habsburg empire, 1914–1918*, Oxford, Oxford University Press.

Ziemann, Benjamin, 1997. *Front und Heimat: ländliche Kriegserfahrungen im südlichen Bayern 1914–1923*, Essen, Klartext.

Index

This index is both thematic and nominal. We include here the names of persons referred to in the text, the titles of journals, and the names of authors whose works are cited, with the date of each publication in parentheses.

14-18, Aujourd'hui, Today, Heute 164, 191
1914, Les Psychoses de guerre? (1979) 53, 58
Abbal, Odon (2001) 102
Acton, Lord 31
Afflerbach, Holger (1994) 68
Agadir 6, 53
agriculture 165–6
Agulhon, Maurice 22
Albert, King of Belgium 177
Albertini, Luigi 57; (1942–3) 42
Aldington, Richard 86
Algeria, War of 3, 19, 73, 98, 178
All quiet on the Western Front (1930) 86, 176, 189
Alltagsgeschichte 27
Amalgamated Society of Engineers 143, 144
American Historical Review 16, 17
American Legion 173
Andreski, Stanislav (1954) 157
Angell, Norman 53, 110, 116
Annales E.S.C. 12, 45, 88, 134, 172
Appuhn, Charles 36; (1926) 36
Armaments, Ministry of (French) 128, 145
Aron, Raymond 44, 194–5, 200, 204
Artaud, Denise (1978) 45
Ashworth, Tony (1980) 30, 92–3, 94
Asquith, Herbert H. 67, 74, 78, 79, 157
Association Nationale du Souvenir de la Bataille de Verdun 180
Association Républicaine des anciens combattants (ARAC) 175
atrocities, German in 1914 30, 102–3, 107, 155, 171
Attenborough, Richard 189
Attlee, Clement 207

Auban, David 125
Audoin-Rouzeau, Stéphane 25, 98, 105, 162–4, 172, 180, 184, 213; (1986) 98, 99, 104; (1993) 28, 164; (1995a) 28; (1995b) 164; (2001) 29, 164
Audoin-Rouzeau, Stéphane (ed.) (1998) 100
Audoin-Rouzeau, Stéphane and Becker, Annette (2000) 104, 105, 163, 164, 171, 172
Audoin-Rouzeau, Stéphane *et al.* (eds.) (2002) 29, 102
Augé-Laribé, Michel (1925) 112
Auschwitz, Great War as prelude to 181
Australian and New Zealand Army Corps (ANZAC) 62, 95, 178
Australian War Memorial (Canberra) 179, 186, 204

Babington, Anthony (1983) 185
Baconnier, Gérard, Minet, André and Soler, Louis (1985) 178
Badia, Gilbert (1964) 133–4; (1967) 133–4; (1975) 133, 134
Bainville, Jacques (1920) 41
Balfour, Lord 121
Bane, Suda Lorena and Lutz, Ralph Haswell (eds.) (1942) 114
baraques Vilgrain 154
Barbusse, Henri 14, 84, 85, 175, 189
Bardet, Jean Pierre and Dupâquier, Jacques (1998) 160
Bariéty, Jacques (1977) 45
Barker, Pat 189
Barnes, Harry Elmer 39; (1926) 39, 42
Barnett, Corelli 20, 65, 80; (1963) 65, 66, 67
Barral, Pierre 165

Barrès, Maurice 86
Barthas, Louis 99, 178
Bartov, Omer (ed.) (2000) 180; (2002) 103
Bauer, Colonel Max 69, 117
Bean, Charles 62, 180; (1934) 62
Becker, Annette 32, 105, 183, 184; (1988) 183; (1994) 28, 101, 164, 168; (1998) 102
Becker, Jean-Jacques 25, 32, 107, 131, 134, 135, 159, 162, 170, 213; (1973) 22, 135; (1977) 22, 90, 159; (1996) 194
Becker, Jean-Jacques and Audoin-Rouzeau, Stéphane (eds.) (1990) 25
Becker, Jean-Jacques, in collaboration with Annette Becker (1988) 76, 134
Becker, Jean-Jacques et al. (eds.) (1994) 25, 57, 163
Beckett, Ian F. W. (2001) 73
Beckett, Ian F. W. and Simpson, Keith (eds.) (1985), Winter's article in 160
Bédarida, François 32
Bell, Archibald C. (1961) 114; (1943) 114
Benès, Edvard 54
Benjamin, René 85
Berghahn, Volker (1971) 47, 71, 116
Bergson, Henri 170
Bernard, Léon (1929) 155
Bernard, Philippe (1975) 23
Bernhardi, Friedrich von 54
Berr, Henri 57
Bessel, Richard (1993) 63
Bethmann-Hollweg, Theobald von 30, 38, 47, 67, 68, 72, 119
Beveridge, William H. 8, 154; (1928) 154; (1939) 114
Béziers 91
Bianchi, Bruna (2001) 186
Bibliothèque de Documentation Internationale Contemporaine (BDIC) 1, 9, 31, 179, 186, 204
Bibliothèque Nationale de France (BNF) 17, 18
Bidou, Henri 12; (1936) 12
Bidou, Henri, Gauvain, André and Seignobos, Charles (1922) 11, 84
Bieber, Hans Joachim (1981) 117
Binneveld, Hans (1998) 185
Birdsall, Paul (1941) 41
Blackadder 190
Bloch, Camille 9, 36; (1925) 11, 111; (1933) 36

Bloch, Marc 12, 172
Blockade, Allied, of Germany 114, 115, 119
Boasson, Marc 86
Bock, Fabienne (2002) 76
Boemeke, Manfred (ed.) (1998) 51
Bogart, Ernest L. (1919) 113
Bond, Brian (ed.) (1991) 75
Bond, Brian and Cave, Nigel (eds.) (1999) 80
Bonnefous, Georges (1957) 69
Bordeaux, Carnegie history of 112
Bouillon, Jacques and Petzold, Michel (1999) 183
Bourges, Carnegie history of 112, 154
Bourget, Jean-Marie (1932) 11, 12, 32
Bourke, Joanna (1996) 100; (1999) 29, 103
Boutefeu, Roger (1966) 19, 88
Bowley, Arthur L. (1921) 128
Braudel, Fernand 23
Braunthal, Julius (1961–3) 128
Brémond, Henri 107
Brest-Litovsk, Treaty of (1918) 49
Brett, Patrice 125
British Broadcasting Corporation (BBC) 20, 26, 72, 80
British Legion 173
British Museum (Library) (BM/BL) 17, 18
Britten, Benjamin 188; War Requiem 188
Bröckling, Ulrich (1997) 101
Brusilov offensive (1916) 66
brutalization 29, 105, 180, 181, 187
Bryder, Linda (1988) 160
Buitenhuis, Peter (1987) 156
Bülow, Bernhard von 57
Burgess, Keith 144
Burk, Kathleen (ed.) (1982) 120; (1985) 120

Cabanes, Bruno 107
Calvados 22
Cambridge University Press 199
Canadian War Memorial (Ottawa) 204
Canard enchaîné, Le 98
Canini, Gérard 99
Canini, Gérard (ed.) (1988) 99; (1989) 99, 107
Capdevilla, Luc and Voldman, Danièle (2002) 169
Capitaine Conan 189
Caporetto, Battle of (1917) 95; Italian mutiny after 95, 139
Carlier, Claude and Pedroncini Guy (eds.) (1997) 91

Carmaux 22
Carnegie Endowment For International
  Peace, Series on the Economic and
  Social History of the War 4, 8, 11,
  110–13, 115, 123, 128, 159, 176, 199
'Carnet B' 131, 134–5
Caron, François (1973) 121
Carrel, Alexis 120
Cazals, Rémy 99
Ceadel, Martin (1980) 202
Cecil, Hugh and Liddle, Peter (eds.)
  (1996) 101
Céline (Louis-Ferdinand Destouches) 176
Chaline, Nadine-Josette (ed.) (1993) 168
Charle, Christophe (2001) 54, 89, 171,
  194
Chartier, Roger 106
Chemin des dames offensive (1917) 66,
  67, 74, 77, 97, 189
Chemnitz 147
Chevalier, Gabriel 86
Chickering, Roger (1998) 68
Chickering, Roger and Förster, Stig (eds.)
  (2000) 103
Churchill, Sir Winston 55, 71, 79, 207;
  (1933–4) 174, 175
Civil War, American, as precedent for
  Great War 84, 109
Clark, John Bates 110, 113
Clausewitz, Carl von 25
Clemenceau, Georges 41, 52, 67, 103,
  164; (1930) 174
Clémentel, Etienne 8, 112, 118; (1931)
  112
Cochin, Denys et al.(1926) 114
Cohen, Yves (2001) 121, 143
Cole, George Douglas Howard 132, 136;
  (1923a) 128; (1923b) 128; (1923c)
  128; (1965) 132
Collinet, Paul and Stahl, Paul (1928) 12
colonial troops 91
Columbia University 110
Committee of Action (French) 138
Communist party (Chinese) 52
Communist party (French) 126, 131,
  134–6, 158
Confédération Générale du Travail (CGT)
  128, 130, 131, 134, 135, 138, 144, 149
Connelly, Mark (2002) 184
Contamine, Henry (1970) 81
Corbin, Alain 106
Corriera della sera 57
Craiglockhart Hospital, Edinburgh 185
Craonne, war memorial at 105
Crapouillot, Le 98

Creveld, Martin van (1985) 76
Crocq, Louis (1999) 186
Croix de Feu 90
Cru, Jean Norton 27, 32, 106, 176, 199;
  (1929) 14, 87, 176
Cruttwell, C. R. M. F. (1934) 10, 63

Dagen, Philippe (1996) 184
Dallas, Gloden and Gill, Douglas (1985)
  94
Daniel, Ute (1997) 166, 213
Darrow, Margaret H. (2000) 167
Daviet, Jean-Pierre (1988) 121
Davis, Belinda J. (2000) 158
de Gaulle, Charles 19, 32, 80, 207
Deist, Wilhelm 95, 161; (1970) 161
Delaporte, Sophie (1996) 103
Delbrück, Hans von 38, 57; (1929) 38
Delvert, Charles 177
Désert, Gabriel 22
Diaghilev, Serge 183
dilution of skilled labour 143, 144
Dix, Otto 177, 187
Dobson, Sean (2001) 140, 141
Doise, Jean and Vaïsse, Maurice (1989) 81
Dolchstosslegende (stab-in-the-back legend)
  63, 74, 161
Domansky, Elisabeth 138
Dorgelès, Roland 14, 84, 85
Douaumont, ossuary of 173
Douglas, Allen (2002) 98
Downs, Laura Lee (1995) 142, 166
Drachkovitch, Milorad (1953) 132
Dresden 147, 202
Droz, Jacques 24; (1973) 24, 57; (1974)
  132, 133
Dubesset, Mathilde 141
Ducasse, André 87; (1932) 14, 86
Ducasse, André, Meyer, Jacques and
  Perreux, Gabriel (1959) 18–19, 88, 179
Dufy, Raoul 177
Dugain, Marc 189
Duhamel, Georges 85, 177
Dülffer, Jost and Holl, Karl (eds.) (1986)
  53
Dumoulin, Georges 149, 151
Dumoulin, Olivier 12
Durassié, Georges 86
Duroselle, Jean-Baptiste 45; (1994) 1, 29,
  30, 88
Düsseldorf 141, 164

Ebert, Friedrich 146, 147, 148
Eckart, Wolfgang U. and Gradmann,
  Christoph (eds.) (1996) 186

Ecole Libre des Sciences Politiques 129
Ecole normale supérieure 18
Eden, Anthony 207
Einaudi, Luigi 113
Eisenhower, Dwight David 109
Eksteins, Modris (1990) 176, 183
entente Cordiale (1904) 37
Erdmann, Karl-Dietrich (ed.) (1972) 48
Etaples, riot at, in 1917 94

Falkenhayn, Erich von 67, 73, 74
Falls, Cyril (1930) 63, 87
Farcy, Jean-Claude (1995) 102
Farrar, Marjorie Milbank (1974) 119
Faulk, Sebastian 189
Fay, Sidney B. (1929) 14, 42
Febvre, Lucien 12, 52, 172, 201
Feis, Herbert (1930) 113
Feldman, Gerald (1966) 69, 116, 117,
    123, 124; (1993) 51, 122
Feldman, Gerald and Homburg, Heidrun
    (1977) 121, 122
Fellowes, Harry 188
Ferguson, Niall (2000) 51, 122–3, 124
Ferro, Marc 20, 21, 28, 32, 72, 133, 134;
    (1969) 23
Field, Frank (1991) 196
Fischer, Fritz 40, 46–8, 51, 68, 71, 116,
    197; (1961) 40, 46–8, 68, 116; (1969)
    68, 71
Fisher, Admiral John (Jackie), first Baron
    Fisher of Kilverstone 70, 71
Fleury (village) 180
Flood, P. J. (1990) 172
Foch, General Ferdinand 77, 78
Fondation Nationale des Sciences
    Politiques 9, 203
Fontaine, Arthur 8, 112; (1924) 112
Fontana, Jacques (1990) 168
Ford, Ford Madox (1924–6) 85
Foucault, Michel 205
Franz-Ferdinand, Archduke, assassination
    of 6, 37
French, David 79; (1982) 79; (1986) 55;
    (1995) 142, 145
Fridenson, Patrick 213; (1977) 145, 150,
    158; (1972) 121, 142
Frontiers, Battle of the (1914) 73
Fuller, John G. (1990) 93, 94, 163
Fussell, Paul (1975) 27, 29, 181, 182, 196

Gaffney, Angela (1998) 183
Gallipoli 189
Gallipoli, invasion of (1915) 62, 71, 79,
    175, 178, 180

Gallieni, Joseph 73
Gambarotto, Laurent (1996) 168
Gambiez, General F. and Suire, Colonel
    M. (1968–71) 81
Gammage, Bill (1974) 95, 180
Gance, Abel 189
Garcia, Patrick 213
Geiss, Imanuel (1963) 46
gender, and war 166–8
Genevoix, Maurice 18, 19, 85, 177
genocide 27, 29, 171, 205, 209; Armenian
    171, 205; Jewish 27, 29, 205, 209
Georges, Bernard and Tintant, Denise
    (1962) 132
Gérin, René and Poincaré, Raymond
    (1930) 39
Gibelli, Antonio (1991) 186
Gide, Charles 8, 112
Gide, Charles and Daudé-Bancel, Achille
    (1926) 112
Gignoux, Claude-Joseph (1926) 12, 112
Girault, René (1973) 45
Godfrey, John (1987) 118
Goodbye to all that 196
Grande Illusion, La 189
Graves, Robert 86, 196
Grayzel, Susan R. (1999) 166
Grebler, Leo and Winkler, Wilhelm (1940)
    113
Gregory, Adrian (1994) 184
Grey, Sir Edward 25, 39, 124
Grieves, Keith (1988) 118
Griffith, Paddy (1994) 75
Groener, General Wilhelm 69, 146, 148
Guerres Mondiales et Conflits Contemporains
    9
Guichard, Louis (1929) 114
Guinn, Paul (1965) 67, 79
Guizot, François 26

Haber, Fritz 120
Haber, L. F. (1986) 120
Haig, Sir Douglas 64, 67, 74, 75, 76, 78,
    79, 80
Haimson, Leopold 139, 140, 141, 193
Haimson, Leopold and Sapelli, Giulio
    (eds.) (1992) 139, 141, 193
Haimson, Leopold and Tilly, Charles
    (eds.) (1989) 139, 193
Halévy, Elie (1930) 12, 48, 129–30, 209
Halpern, P. G. (1994) 71
Halphen, Louis 10
Hanna, Martha (1996) 170
Hanotaux, Gabriel 7, 61, 177; (1915–23)
    62; (1920) 61, 177

Hardach, Gerd (1973) 118, 122
Hardier, Thierry and Jagielski,
    Jean-François (2001) 104
Harrison, Royden 150
Hartcup, Guy (1988) 120
Hatry, Gilbert 145
Haupt, Georges (1965) 130, 133
Hauser, Henri 8, 112
Healy, Maureen (2003) 161
Heckscher, Eli F. 113
Hélias, Pierre-Jakez 166
Henderson, Arthur 136
Hentsch, Lt-Col. Richard 76
Herriot, Edouard (1924) 154
Herwig, Holger H. (1997) 161
Higonnet, Margaret R. (2001) 167
Higonnet, Margaret R. et al. (eds.) (1987)
    167
Hindenburg, General Paul von 63, 73,
    117, 161
Hinton, James (1973) 143, 144
Hiroshima 202
Hirschfeld, Gerhard, Krumeich, Gerd,
    Langewiesche, Dieter, and Ullmann,
    Hans-Peter (eds.) (1997) 164
Hirschfeld, Gerhard, Krumeich, Gerd, and
    Renz, Irina (eds.) (1993) 164
Historial de la grande guerre, Péronne
    28–9, 98, 163, 164, 187, 203
Historisches Zeitschrift 15
Hitler, Adolf 47, 48, 63, 156, 161, 175,
    179, 197, 207
Hobsbawm, Eric J. 22
Hoffman, Colonel Max 73
Holocaust see genocide
Holtfrericht, Carl-Ludwig (1986) 122
Horn, Daniel (1969) 72, 95
Horne, John (1991) 22, 138
Horne, John and Kramer, Alan (2001) 30,
    102, 171
Huber, Michel (1931) 11, 12, 155
Hubert, Emile 146
Hughes, Ted 190
Huss, Marie-Monique (2002) 28, 33
Hynes, Samuel (1992) 29, 182

Imagerie d'Epinal 177
Imperial Chemical Industries 121
Imperial (Commonwealth) War Graves
    Commission 184, 188
Imperial War Museum 80, 91, 103, 179,
    184, 186, 187, 188, 204
inflation, wartime 109, 117, 118, 122
Inglis, Kenneth (1998) 183
Ingram, Norman (1991) 202

Institut de France 10
Institut d'histoire du temps présent 29, 98
International Labour Office 112
Invalides, Les 186
Irish uprising (1916) 157
Isaac, Jules 10, 13, 31, 32, 36, 83, 87,
    176–7; (1921) 9, 82; (1933) 40
Isnenghi, Mario (1982) 141; (1970) 180
Isnenghi, Mario and Rochat, Giorgio
    (2000) 95

J'Accuse (1919 and 1937) 189
Jacobzone, Alain (1988) 172
Jahn, Hubertus F. (1995) 170
Japrisot, Sébastien 189
Jaurès, Jean 131, 195
Jeanneney, Jean-Noël 89
Jellicoe, Admiral Sir John 64, 65, 66
Jena, Battle of 197
Joffre, General Joseph 73
Joll, James 25, 52–3, 54, 195; (1968) 52,
    54; (1984) 44, 53
Jospin, Lionel 105
Jouhaux, Léon 131–2
Journey's End 86, 196
Julliard, Jacques 130
July crisis (1914) 37–40
Jünger, Ernst 85, 175, 187
Jutland, Battle of (1916) 66, 70–1

Kaspi, André 58; (1978) 45
Kautsky, Karl 35; (1919) 35
Keegan, John 27, 92, 93, 194; (1976) 27,
    92; (1998) 194
Kehr, Eckart (1965) 48, 57, 116
Kennedy, Paul (ed.) (1979) 43
Keynes, John M. 8, 51, 116, 123; (1919)
    41, 113
King, Alex (1998) 183
King, Jere C. (1951) 69
King and Country 189
Kitchen, Martin (1976) 68
Kitchener, Lord Horatio H. 93
Klee, Paul 177
Kocka, Jürgen (1973) 22, 141, 159, 170,
    213
Koeltz, Louis 81
Kohl, Helmut 173
Koselleck, Reinhard 173, 184
Kramer, Alan 30, 102
Kriegel, Annie 21; (1964) 22, 133,
    134–6, 140
Kriegel, Annie and Becker, Jean-Jacques
    (1964) 134
Kriegsschuldfrage 34–6, 40, 46, 57

Krumeich, Gerd 57, 196; (1981) 53; (2001) 52
Kubrick, Stanley 189
Kuisel, Richard F. (1981) 122

Labanca, Nicola, Procacci, Giovanna and Tomassini, Luigi (1997) 139
Labour and the new social order 136, 144
Labour party (British) 136, 137, 157
La Gorce, Paul Marie de (1991) 30
Landau, Philippe-E. (1999) 168
Langemarck, Battle of (1914) 178
Langevin, Paul 120
Langlois, Charles Victor 10, 31
Lanrezac, General Charles 73
Lasswell, Harold (1927) 156
Lavisse, Ernest 11, 84
League of Nations 11, 111, 207
'learning curve' in British military history of the war 59, 75, 76, 79, 80
Leed, Eric J. (1979) 100, 185
Leese, Peter (2002) 185
Leipzig 140, 141
Lemercier, Eugène-E. 177
Le Naour, Jean-Yves (2002a) 169; (2002b) 103
Lepick, Olivier (1998) 120
Lequin, Yves 22
Lerner, Paul Frederick (2003) 185
Lheritier, Michel and Chautemps, Camille (1926) 12
Liberal party (British) 136, 137, 157
Liddell Hart, Sir Basil 15, 20, 63, 64
Liddle, Peter, Bourne, John and Whitehead, Ian (eds.) (2000) 81
Liebknecht, Karl 133, 147
Life and nothing but 189
Lindemann, Thomas (2001) 54
Lipp, Anne (2003) 101
Liulevicius, Vejas (2000) 169, 171
Lloyd, David W. (1998) 184
Lloyd George, David 52, 67, 74, 78, 79, 118, 157, 174
London School of Economics 25, 52, 54
Losey, Joseph 189
Luckau, Alma M. (1941) 41
Ludendorff, General Erich 64, 65, 68, 73, 74, 76, 117, 174
Luxemburg, Rosa 133–4, 147
Lyautey, General Louis 67
Lyon, Carnegie history of 112, 154

Maastricht, Treaty of (1992) 187, 204
McAuley, Mary (1991) 161
Macdonald, Lyn 94

McKibbin, Ross (1974) 137, 157
Macmillan, Margaret (2001) 51–2, 193
McPhail, Helen (2001) 102
Maier, Charles (1975) 122, 195
Malet, Albert 9, 31
Malet, Albert and Isaac, Jules (1930) 31, 177
Malherbe, Henry 85, 107
Malvy, Louis 131, 134, 135, 138
Mangin, General Charles 11, 96
Mantoux, Etienne (1946) 41
Mantoux, Paul 57
Marder, Arthur 70–1
Marne, Battle of the (1914) 7, 19, 23, 76
Marseille, Carnegie history of 112, 154
Marshall Plan 118
Marwick, Arthur 157
Marx, Karl 26
Marxism, influence on historiography 21–3, 24, 26, 27, 30, 45, 46, 115, 128, 132, 158, 162, 207, 209
Masaryk, Thomas 54
Masson, Paul (1926) 12
Masson, Paul-Maurice 177
Maurin, Jules (1982) 90–1, 108
Maurin, Jules and Jauffret, Jean-Charles (eds.) (2002) 5, 57
May 1968 151
Mayer, Arno (1959) 24, 48; (1967) 24, 48, 49
Meerwarth, Rudolf, Günther, Adolf and Zimmermann, Waldemar (1932) 155
Melchior, Carl 123
Mémorial de Verdun 180
Mende 91, 108
Mendelssohn-Bartholdy, Albrecht 57
Meyer, Jacques 18, 86, 88, 177; (1966) 18, 88
Meynier, Gilbert (1981) 91
Micale, Mark and Lerner, Paul Frederick (eds.) (2001) 185
'Michael offensive' (1918) 162
Michalka, Wolfgang (1994) 72
Michel, Marc (1982) 91
Michelin (Guides) 85, 177
Middlebrook, Martin (1971) 88
Milestone, Lewis 189
'military–industrial complex' 109
Miller, Susanna (1974) 134
Millman, Brock (2001) 55
Mills, C. Wright 116
Miquel, Pierre (1972) 45; (1983) 81
Mitchell, Allan (1965) 158
Mitterrand, François 173

Moeller, Robert G. (1986) 165
Moltke, General Helmuth von 65, 67, 74, 76
Mombauer, Annika (2002) 42, 57
Mommsen, Wolfgang J. 53, 68
Monatte, Pierre 131
Monde, Le 163
Monnet, Jean 118, 207
Montgelas, Count Max 57
Moore, Barrington (1978) 146–7, 153, 158
Morhardt, Mathias 57; (1924) 36, 39
Mosse, George 183; (1990) 28, 29, 56, 163, 180
Mottram, R. H. (1926–8) 85
Moureux, Charles 120
Moutet, Aimée (1997) 121
Moyer, Laurence V. (1995) 30
Mrs Dalloway 189
Mucchielli, Laurent 12
Munitions, Ministry of (British) 111, 118
Museums (War) 28, 91, 103, 163, 180
Mussolini, Benito 207
mutinies, French 10, 11, 12, 24, 30, 65, 89, 96–7; British 94; German naval mutinies 72, 95; Italian 95; shell shock as a form of mutiny 185

Nanterre (University of Paris – X) 25
Nash, Paul 177
Natter, Wolfgang G. (1999) 178
naval war 69–72
Nettl, John Peter (1966) 134
Nevinson, C. E. W. 177
Nicolson, Sir Harold G. (1933) 41
Nivelle, General Robert 66, 67, 74, 76
Nobécourt, R. G. (1965) 19, 88
Nolan, Mary (1981) 141, 158
Nolte, Ernst 209
Nouailhat, Yves-Henri (1977) 45

Offenstadt, Nicolas (1999) 105
Offer, Avner (1989) 118, 123
Oh! What a lovely war! 189
Orwell, George 164
Oualid, William and Picquenard, Charles (1928) 12, 128
Owen, Wilfred 178, 185

pacifism, pacifists 57, 146, 148, 201–2
Painlevé, Paul 67; (1923) 60
Paléologue, Maurice 39, 40
Pals' battalions 93
Panichas, George Andrew (ed.) (1968) 88

Parade's end 85
Paris 112, 146, 154; Carnegie history of 146, 154
Passchendaele, Battle of (1917) 79, 94, 186, 190, 202
Pathé Film Company 20
Paths of Glory 189
Patriotic Auxiliary Service Law (1916) 117, 138
Pedersen, Susan (1995) 167
Pedroncini, Guy 24, 65, 76, 77, 78, 80, 89, 96
Pedronicini, Guy (ed.) (1997) 80
Péricard, Jacques (1933) 14, 83, 86–7
Péricat, Raymond 148
Perreux, Gabriel (1966) 18, 88, 159
Perrin, Jean 120
Perrot, Michèle 22
Peschaud, Marcel (1926) 12
Pétain, General Philippe 10, 64, 65, 67, 74, 76, 77–8, 89, 207
Peugeot factories, Taylorism in 143
Pézard, André 177
Picard, Roger (1928) 11, 12, 128
Pingaud, Albert (1938) 43
Pirenne, Henri 113
Pöhlmann, Markus (2002) 63
Poidevin, Raymond (1969) 45, 46, 53
Poincaré, Raymond 35, 36, 53, 67, 174; (1921) 39
Popovics, Alexander 111
Popular, Front (French) 22, 201
population 11, 12, 159–61, 162, 168, 208
Pourcher, Yves (1994) 159
Presses Universitaires de France 199
Prior, Robin (1983) 191
Prior, Robin and Wilson, Trevor (1992) 75, 79; (1996) 75, 79; (1999) 75, 79
prisoners of war 102, 108
Procacci, Giovanna (1983) 150; (1999) 147
Prochasson, Christophe and Rasmussen, Anne (1996) 170
profiteers, wartime indictment of 147–8, 149
propaganda 155–6
Prost, Antoine 22, 32, 107, 183, 191; (1977a) 22, 181, 183; (1977b) 22
Prudential Assurance Company 160
Public Broadcasting Service (US) 26

Rachamimov, Alon (2002) 102, 108
Rathenau, Walter 117
Reader, William Joseph (1970) 121

Rearick, Charles (1997) 170
Rebérioux, Madeleine 133
Regeneration 189
Reichsbanner 173
Reid, Alastair 144
Reimann, Aribert (2000) 101
Remarque, Erich Maria 86, 176, 189
Renault, Louis 121, 142
Renoir, Jean 189
Renouvin, Pierre 9–11, 12, 13, 14, 20, 23,
    40, 42, 43, 45, 57, 83, 84, 87, 88, 89,
    107, 200, 212; (1925a) 9–11; (1925b)
    9–11, 13, 14; (1934) 9–11, 13, 43, 84,
    87, 200; (1939) 9–11; (1955–7) 43
Renouvin, Pierre, Préclin, Edmond and
    Hardy, Georges (1939) 10, 83
Revolution, German (1918–19) 133, 146,
    179
Revue d'histoire de la Guerre Mondiale 7, 9,
    11
Revue de synthèse historique 57
Revue historique 1, 7, 9, 11, 15, 16, 31
Ribeill, Georges (1988) 146
Richter, Donald (1992) 120
Ricoeur, Paul 198
Riegel, Léon (1978) 86
Rieuneau Maurice (1972) 86
Riley, Denise 167
Rist, Charles 8, 112
Ritter, Gerhard 42, 47–8, 67–8;
    (1954–68) 67–8
Rivé, Philippe (ed.) (1991) 183
Rivers, W. H. R. 185
Robert, Jean-Louis 30, 140, 145, 148,
    149, 165; (1980) 140; (1989) 30, 148,
    149, 165; (1995) 145, 148, 149
Roberts, Mary-Louise (1994) 166
Robertson, Sir William 67, 74
Roshwald, Aviel and Stites, Richard (eds.)
    (1999) 170
Rosmer, Alfred (1936) 22, 131–2; (1959)
    131–2
Rouaud, Jean 189
Rouault, Georges 177
Roudebush, Marc 191
Rouen, Carnegie history of 112, 154
Rousseau Frédéric (1999) 101, 103, 105;
    (2003) 106
Royal Institute of International Affairs
    203
Rozenblit, Marsha (2001) 169
Rürup, Reinhard (1968) 134, 146

Sagnac, Philippe 10
St Petersburg 140, 141

Salewski, Michael (1979) 71
Salonika front 69
Samsonov, General Alexandre V. 74
Sandhurst, Royal Military Academy
    92
Sarajevo 6
Sarrail, General Maurice 69
Sassoon, Siegfried 86, 185
Schaeffer, Werner (1940) 115
Scheer, Admiral Reinhard 72
Scheidemann, Philipp 147
Schlieffen plan 76
Schmitt, Bernadotte E. (1930) 14, 42
Scott, Jim 96, 108
Scott, Joan W. 166, 172
Scott, W. R. and Cunnison, J. (1924)
    128
Second World War 52, 103, 124, 178,
    202, 207
Seignobos, Charles 9, 11, 31
Sellier, Henri, Bruggeman, André and
    Poëte, Marcel (1926) 154
Sen, Amartya 161
Shaper, B. W. (1959) 138
Sharp, Alan (1991) 51
Sheffield, Gary and Till, Geoffrey (eds.)
    (2003) 80
shell shock 101, 184–6
Shepherd, Ben (2000) 185
Sherriff, R. C. 86
shop stewards 144–5
Shotwell, James T. 8, 110, 152, 176;
    (1924) 8
Showalter, Elaine (1985) 185
Silver, Kenneth E. (1989) 184
Simkins, Peter 75, 80; (1988) 93
Siney, Marion C. (1957) 119
Smith, Leonard V. 30, 96–7; (1994) 30,
    96–7
Smuts, Jan Christiaan 52
Soboul, Albert 32
Socialist International (2nd) 22, 25, 130,
    131, 132, 133
Société politique d'études critiques et
    documentaires sur la guerre (1926) 36
Somme, Battle of the (1916) 23, 55, 61,
    77, 79, 88, 117, 163, 190
Sorbonne 9, 36, 45
Soulez, Philippe (ed.) (1988) 170
Soutou, Georges-Henri (1989) 50, 119,
    124
Spriano, Paolo (1964) 139
Stahlhelm 173, 175
Steinberg, Jonathan (1969) 71
Stendhal, on Waterloo 83

Stevenson, David (1982) vii, 50; (1991) 51
Stinnes–Legien accord (1918) 138
Stone, Norman (1975) 66
Strachan, Hew 31, 73; (1998) 73, 194; (2000) 73, 80
Stravinsky, Igor 183
strikes 10, 11, 135, 139, 140, 148, 149, 193; Britain 139, 193; France 10, 11, 135, 148, 149; Germany 139, 193; Italy 139; Russia 140, 193
Stumpf, Seaman Richard 95
Sturmthall, Adolf (1951) 128
Stuttgart 164

Tannenberg, Battle of (1914) 73, 74
Tardieu, André (1921) 41
Tavernier, Bertrand 189
Tawney, R. H. 136
Taylor, A. J. P. 21, 44, 196; (1964) 21, 196; (1965) 21
Taylorism 142
Terraine, John 20, 75, 80; (1963) 65, 78
Thébaud, Françoise (1986) 141, 166
Theweleit, Klaus (1977–8) 166, 180
Thimme, Friedrich von 36
Third International (Communist) 131, 140
'Thirty Years War of twentieth century', Great War seen as part of 6, 29, 181, 206, 207
Thobie, Jacques (1973) 45
Thom, Deborah 141
Thomas, Albert 128, 138, 145
Thompson, Edward P. 22, 143
Tippett, Maria (1984) 183
Tirpitz, Admiral Alfred von 71, 72
Tolliday, Steven 151
Tours, Carnegie history of 112, 154; Congress of (1920) 135–6
trade unions and trade unionism 11, 12, 22, 30, 128, 131, 132, 137, 144, 145, 146, 149
Travers, Timothy (1987) 75; (1992) 75
Treitschke, Heinrich von 53–4
Trempé, Rolande 22
trench journals 98, 99, 101, 104
Trevisan, Carine (2001) 29, 170
Tübingen 164
Tuffrau, Paul 100
Turner, Victor 100

Unknown Soldier, burial of 173
Unruh, Karl (1986) 178
Urbain, Georges 120

USPD (Independent Social Democratic Party) 35, 134

Valéry, Paul 84
Vance, Jonathan F. (1997) 183
Vatican, peace initiative (1915) 50
Verdun 23, 25, 73, 87, 173, 181, 183, 186, 190, 202; Battle of (1916) 23, 73, 202; Memorial 180, 186
Verhey, Jeffrey (2000) 170
Versailles, Treaty of 8, 35, 41, 49, 51–2, 56, 113, 115, 119, 123, 124, 200; Article 231 8, 35, 41
veterans' organizations 175, 183
Vietnam war 3, 73, 103, 156, 181, 184
Vincent, Catherine 141
Vincent, Charles Paul (1985) 119
Viviani, René 37
Vondung, Klaus (1980) 54

wages 12, 145, 149
Waites, Bernard (1987) 22, 143, 148, 158, 159
Wall, Richard and Winter, Jay (eds.) (1988) 119, 150, 167
'war culture' 105, 164, 165, 171, 184
War Emergency Workers' National Committee (WEWNC) 136, 137, 138, 150
war enthusiasm in 1914, myth of 90, 170
war memorials 28, 181, 183–4
Watkins, Glenn (2003) 184
Webb, Sidney and Beatrice 136
Weber, Max 57, 162, 197
Wegerer, Alfred von 35, 197; (1928) 35; (1939) 35
Weimar Republic 128
Weir, Peter 189
Weizmann, Chaim 120
White, Hayden 106
Wildman, Allan (1980) 95
Wilhelm II 14, 38, 67, 146
Wilkinson, Alan (1978) 168
Williamson, Samuel R. (1991) 54
Wilson, Keith (1996) 57
Wilson, Woodrow 41, 49, 52, 67
Winter, Denis (1978) 95; (1991) 80
Winter, Jay 22, 25, 26, 57, 80, 119, 123, 124, 160, 168, 170, 182–3; (1974) 22; (1986) 160, 168; (1988) 26, 124; (1995) 170, 182–3
Winter, Jay and Baggett, Blaine (1996) 26, 28, 185
Winter, Jay and Robert, Jean-Louis (1997) 161, 165, 193

Witkop, Philipp (1928) 178
Wohl, Robert (1980) 170
women's work in wartime 141,
    142
Woodward, David (1983) 75
Woolf, Virginia 189
Woollacott, Angela 141
Wrigley, Chris (1976) 118, 137

Yale University Press 199
Ypres, Third battle of (1917) *see*
    Passchendaele
Yugoslavia, war crimes in former 153

Ziemann, Benjamin (1997) 165
Zietlin, Jonathan 151
Zimmerwald conference (1915) 132

Studies in the Social and Cultural History of Modern Warfare

Titles in the series:

1 *Sites of Memory, Sites of Mourning: The Great War in European Cultural History*
Jay Winter

2 *Capital Cities at War: Paris, London, Berlin 1914–1919*
Jay Winter and Jean-Louis Robert

3 *State, Society and Mobilization in Europe during the First World War*
Edited by John Horne

4 *A Time of Silence: Civil War and the Culture of Repression in Franco's Spain, 1936–1945*
Michael Richards

5 *War and Remembrance in the Twentieth Century*
Edited by Jay Winter and Emmanuel Sivan

6 *European Culture in the Great War: The Arts, Entertainment and Propaganda, 1914–1918*
Edited by Aviel Roshwald and Richard Stites

7 *The Labour of Loss: Mourning, Memory and Wartime Bereavement in Australia*
Joy Damousi

8 *The Legacy of Nazi Occupation: Patriotic Memory and National Recovery in Western Europe, 1945–1965*
Pieter Lagrou

9 *War Land on the Eastern Front: Culture, National Identity and German Occupation in World War I*
Vejas Gabriel Liulevicius

10 *The Spirit of 1914: Militarism, Myth and Mobilization in Germany*
Jeffrey Verhey

11 *German Anglophobia and the Great War, 1914–1918*
Matthew Stibbe

12 *Life between Memory and Hope: The Survivors of the Holocaust in Occupied Germany*
Zeev W. Mankowitz

13 *Commemorating the Irish Civil War: History and Memory, 1923–2000*
Anne Dolan

14 *Jews and Gender in Liberation France*
Karen H. Adler

15 *America and the Armenian Genocide of 1915*
Edited by Jay Winter

16 *Fighting Different Wars: Experience, Memory, and the First World War in Britain*
    Janet S. K. Watson

17 *Vienna and the Fall of the Habsburg Empire: Total War and Everyday Life in
    World War I*
    Maureen Healy

18 *The Moral Disarmament of France: Education, Pacifism, and
    Patriotism, 1914–1940*
    Mona L. Siegel

19 *National Cleansing: Retribution against Nazi Collaborators in
    Post-War Czechoslovakia*
    Benjamin Frommer

20 *China and the Great War: China's Pursuit of a New National Identity
    and Internationalization*
    Xu Guoqi

21 *The Great War in History: Debates and Controversies, 1914 to the Present*
    Jay Winter and Antoine Prost